Ives Studies is a collection of essays on the life and music of American composer Charles Ives (1874–1954). In it, leading scholars address significant issues in Ives scholarship, including the hotly debated chronology of his work, the nature of his compositional philosophy and style, and his place in music history. The essays take their place in a rapidly growing Ives literature that is finally starting to understand and demythologize a most complex man, and that has brought new enlightenment to a stunningly original body of music.

IVES STUDIES

Ives Studies

EDITED BY PHILIP LAMBERT

City University of New York

PUBLISHED BY THE PRESS SYNDICATE OF THE UNIVERSITY OF CAMBRIDGE
The Pitt Building, Trumpington Street, Cambridge CB2 1RP, United Kingdom

CAMBRIDGE UNIVERSITY PRESS
The Edinburgh Building, Cambridge CB2 2RU, United Kingdom
40 West 20th Street, New York, NY 10011–4211, USA
10 Stamford Road, Oakleigh, Melbourne 3166, Australia

First published 1997

Printed in the United Kingdom at the University Press, Cambridge

Typeset in Adobe Minion 10.25/14 pt, in QuarkXpress™ [SE]

A catalogue record for this book is available from the British Library

Library of Congress cataloguing in publication data

Ives studies / edited by Philip Lambert.
p.   cm.
Includes bibliographical references.
ISBN 0 521 58277 6
1. Ives, Charles, 1874–1954 – Criticism and interpretation.
I. Lambert, Philip, 1958–   .
ML410.I94I98   1998
780′.92–dc21   97–7588 CIP MN
ISBN 0 521 58277 6 hardback

Contents

Preface

These essays appear at a time of heightened interest in the life and music of Charles Ives (1874–1954). As J. Peter Burkholder observes in his concluding chapter, the twenty or so years since the Ives centennial have seen an unprecedented proliferation of Ivesian performances, recordings, books, festivals, and critical editions. The essays here both contribute to and comment on Ives's evolving popularity and reputation.

The first four chapters engage prominent themes of recent revisionist scholarship: Ives's debt to his European musical ancestors, the nature of his working methods, and the chronology of his work. Robert P. Morgan explains how Ives's response to the issues and problems confronting the first generation of post-tonal composers was unique and extraordinary, yet at the same time firmly rooted in the musical heritage he shared with his European contemporaries. Morgan views Ives's gifts and debts through the lens of one of the composer's greatest songs, "The Things Our Fathers Loved." Geoffrey Block addresses issues that have long troubled performers and scholars: whether there is a definitive version of the *Concord Sonata*, and what the complicated state of the source materials for that work reveals about Ives's compositional practices. Block's answers, like H. Wiley Hitchcock's in the subsequent chapter, portray a composer who knew what he wanted but whose ideas often lost definition in the swirl of a business man–composer's complicated life. Hitchcock's essay concerns the new edition he is producing of Ives's songs and the ambiguities and problems Ives left for an editor to resolve. The historic problems Gayle Sherwood addresses are those of chronology. Using proven, verifiable methods of handwriting and paper study, Sherwood for the first time provides reliable datings for Ives's choral music, and suggests wide ramifications of her results.

The three essays in the next group establish contexts for Ives's life and work that sometimes complement, sometimes question the ideas of the previous four. Wolfgang Rathert discusses Ives's use of vague or incomplete musical ideas to create an ambiguous, indefinable sense of musical "potentiality." For Rathert this trait reflects a uniquely American sensibility, thereby distinguishing Ives from the more formalistic Europeans. Judith Tick also sees Ives primarily in a more local context, finding in his political beliefs a reflection of popular trends in American politics of the time. Tick finds evidence of Ives's political sympathies both in his substantial writings on the subject and in his music. Stuart Feder then offers a third intra-cultural perspective, in exploring the profound impact of Henry David Thoreau on Ives's music and thought. Feder sees in Thoreau a psychological substitute for the most important figure in the composer's life, his father.

The next two chapters concern what is arguably the most significant musical event in the recent Ives surge, the first performance and recording of the incomplete *Universe Symphony*. In his essay Larry Austin describes the symphony's extant source materials, the problems inherent in any attempt to complete the work, and the choices he made in order to produce the first performable version of the work, which was premiered in 1994. My essay then complements Austin's by considering the symphony's overall conception, situating the work within a long tradition of artistic explorations of cosmic themes.

Finally, J. Peter Burkholder offers a perspective on the entirety of the Ives phenomenon. He provides historical context, identifies scholarly trends, and summarizes the state of knowledge about the composer and his music.

Several of the essays address what is perhaps the most widely publicized and controversial issue in recent Ives scholarship, the chronology of his work. The discussion and debate began in earnest in 1987, when Maynard Solomon questioned the veracity of Ives's datings and suggested that Ives had intentionally distorted the chronological record to claim undeserved historical priority for various compositional modernisms. Morgan, Block, and Hitchcock all have something to say on the subject, and Sherwood offers logically grounded solutions intended to resolve the matter as far as the choral music is concerned. These essays, together with Burkholder's comments on the issues and their general impact on Ives scholarship, help show the way toward irrefutable answers to Solomon's questions, an accurate chronology of Ives's entire *œuvre*, and a new strengthening of his rightfully claimed historical position.

Philip Lambert
City University of New York

Bibliographical notes:

The following works are cited in abbreviated form at every appearance:

Charles Ives, *Essays Before a Sonata, The Majority, and Other Writings*, ed. Howard Boatwright (New York: Norton, 1970). [*Essays*]

Charles Ives, *Memos*, ed. John Kirkpatrick (New York: Norton, 1972). [*Memos*]

John Kirkpatrick, *A Temporary Mimeographed Catalogue of the Music Manuscripts and Related Materials of Charles Edward Ives 1874–1954* (New Haven: Library of the Yale School of Music, 1960). [*JKCat*]

References to specific manuscripts catalogued in the latter take the form of microfilm frame numbers, preceded by the letter "f" (e.g., "f1846").

Tradition, revision, and chronology

1 "The Things Our Fathers Loved": Charles Ives and the European tradition

ROBERT P. MORGAN

I

That Ives's historical position remains a matter of controversy is not surprising, for he forms a unique figure in twentieth-century music: a major composer who remained an amateur throughout his mature creative life, writing music primarily for his own amusement and gratification, cultivating a style that seemed – at least for most listeners – utterly dissociated from the musical mainstream of his day. Ives was in truth a quintessential outsider, an American maverick who followed his own idiosyncratic path in pursuit of private artistic goals, with little apparent regard for the demands of the world around him. In a period noted for its musical insurgency, not one among his contemporaries to have achieved comparable fame or importance even remotely matched him in this regard.[1]

Ives is both praised and blamed for his obstinate independence. Some see him as a musical charlatan, even a sort of madman – an interesting figure, but ultimately dismissible for his lack of professionalism and a fatal

This essay was originally presented in February 1988 in a considerably shorter version at the International Symposium "Charles Ives und die amerikanische Musiktradition bis zur Gegenwart" in Cologne; and it was published in that form as "Charles Ives und die europäische Tradition" in the conference *Bericht, Kölner Beiträge zur Musikforschung* 164, ed. Klaus Wolfgang Niemöller (Regensburg: Bosse, 1990), 17–36.

[1] One might think of Webern or Satie, composers also affected by considerable personal isolation, as possible rivals. Yet Webern was at least occasionally performed during his creative years, when his music attracted considerable – if largely negative – attention; and he was professionally active as a conductor and teacher. As for Satie, he achieved notable veneration in his later, post-Schola Cantorum years, especially among the young (above all Jean Cocteau); and the premieres of his works came to be greeted as major events.

3

isolation from the larger musical-cultural environment.[2] Others worship him as a musical saint – an innocent who created an entirely personal, imaginary musical realm where he could cultivate a private vision free from all external constraints. (Ives reminds us of the close ties linking our notions of the idiot and the savant.)

Yet both of these views ignore an essential aspect of Ives: despite his extraordinary originality, he was deeply grounded in his own particular historical moment and inescapably confronted with its larger musical and cultural issues. Properly viewed (and heard), Ives's music reflects the musical turmoil of the years immediately following the turn of the century as accurately as that of any composer of his generation – indeed, perhaps more so. This is most apparent in his peculiar attitude toward musical conventions inherited from the eighteenth and nineteenth centuries, conventions associated with functional harmonic tonality and the musical forms with which it was joined.[3]

Consideration of Ives's music reveals that at a remarkably early moment he came to view traditional tonality as a "historical" language – that is, as having become in some basic sense consigned to the past. This is not to say that he viewed the language of tonality as invalid, or obsolete; rather, he grasped, with what now seems remarkable foresightedness, that it could no longer function as Western music's mother tongue, and thus no longer continue to evolve according to seemingly natural – since largely unconscious – processes of historical transformation. One recognizes this, for example, in Ives's belief that there no longer existed any reason to be stylistically "up-to-date." Indeed, for Ives the traditional notion of historical evolution itself seems to have become dated, a thing of the past. Thus his continued use of such old-fashioned markers as pure diatonicism, unal-

---

[2] See, for example, Kurt Stone's negative assessment in "Ives's Fourth Symphony: a review," *The Musical Quarterly* 52/1 (1966): 1–16. Even Elliott Carter, who as a young man knew Ives well and whose music reflects similar interests in complex rhythmic and textural combinations, at times speaks disparagingly of him in his essays and reviews. See the many references to Ives in *The Writings of Elliott Carter*, ed. Else Stone and Kurt Stone (Bloomington: Indiana University Press, 1977), especially the extended 1939 review of the *Concord Sonata* written for *Modern Music* (pp. 48–51).

[3] To be sure, the idea that Ives was an American innocent, free of European influences, has by now been thoroughly discounted. See, for example, J. Peter Burkholder, *Charles Ives: The Ideas Behind the Music* (New Haven: Yale University Press, 1985), passim (especially 63–66).

tered triads, and undisguised tonal functions. And thus also his realization that there was no longer any necessity for seeking absolute stylistic or structural consistency.

Though he still frequently employs the language of traditional tonality, Ives no longer uses it as a natural, "living" language but as an essentially artificial one. He does not so much use it, in fact, as appropriate and manipulate it, exploiting it for his own particular purposes without regard for how anomalous (or non-tonal) the result may be. For Ives the language of common-practice Western music, having passed into history, had been neutralized. Though the remnants of common-practice music are still everywhere evident in his work, their meaning has been fundamentally transformed. They are treated as available material, as elements to be refashioned at will without consideration for their origins or previous implications. For Ives, then, musical modernism consisted not so much in discarding previous compositional modes as in rethinking them within a new, more variable and more contingent framework. He fashioned his own compositional voice largely by rehearing the voices of his musical past.

It is, I believe, Ives's willed conception of tonality as a historically terminated and, to that extent, no longer living language that accounts for the peculiar aura of his music. (From this perspective, for example, the quotations appear as surface manifestations of a more fundamental condition.) Of course many other historically conscious composers of Ives's generation also felt that the conventions of traditional tonality could no longer be maintained as a lingua franca. What set Ives apart, however, was how drastically he drew the consequences.

Of the major European figures of the time, perhaps the one who comes closest to Ives is Mahler. Although the external features of the two composers – the sound and manner of their music – are quite different, they share many attributes. Both employ tonal procedures as part of an uninhibited stylistic mix; both frequently write music of almost painful simplicity, even banality, only to combine it simultaneously and successively with music of the utmost complexity; and both employ quite ordinary attributes of common-practice tonality while subjecting them to distortion, fragmentation, and concealment.[4]

---

[4] These relationships are explored in more detail in Robert P. Morgan, "Ives and Mahler: mutual responses at the end of an era," *19th-Century Music* 2/1 (1978): 72–81.

There is one aspect of Ives's music, however, that distinguishes him emphatically from Mahler: he often goes beyond the conventions of common-practice music entirely. Unlike Mahler, all of whose works end for example with a relatively well-established tonal focus, Ives frequently becomes in some definite sense "atonal." Here one might turn to Schoenberg as a possible European counterpart; for he too, at approximately the same time as Ives, concluded that the increasing strains placed on traditional tonality had reached a point where attempts at preservation were impractical and ill-advised. For Schoenberg, however, the consequences were radically different. Deeply convinced of the historical inevitability of the evolution of music toward greater complexity and differentiation, he saw the abandonment of tonality as a necessary precondition for its progress toward a subsequent, more developed stage.

Here one notes a profound difference with Ives, who, uncommitted to such a quasi-Darwinian conception of historical development, saw no reason why the historicization of tonality should necessarily entail its rejection, or why it should be tied to the emergence of a new and distinct common practice to which twentieth-century music should conform. Ives seems rather to have concluded that the end of tonality, or rather its transformation into a phenomenon of the past, marked a more fundamental historical divide, and implicated a more profound aesthetic reorientation, than would be entailed by the mere passage from one stylistic stage into the next.

It was Ives's remarkable realization – the more so for having been intuitive and unconscious – that on the other side of this divide all musical styles and techniques had become in principle equally valid. One recognizes this, for example, in Ives's relationship to atonality. Though it becomes available to him, it is not adopted as a matter of historical principle. Having grasped that the notion of technical-stylistic consistency was itself revealed as historically conditioned, Ives saw no need – or means – to formulate a new musical language distinct from tonality. Even his most extreme non-tonal moments are not purged of distinct tonal references and associations – of triads, octave doublings, or even functional harmonic progressions. The "ruins" of tonality, to use Walter Benjamin's striking metaphor, continue to be heard, sounding through the layers of accumulated sonic debris. For Ives, then, there is no essential difference

6

between tonality and atonality, and thus no reason to keep them separate, or to renounce one in favor of the other.

In a famous statement from his article "Some 'quarter-tone' impressions," written well after the fact (1923), Ives made this point explicitly:

> Why tonality as such should be thrown out for good, I can't see. Why it should be always present, I can't see. It depends, it seems to me, a good deal – as clothes depend on the thermometer – on what one is trying to do, and on the state of mind, the time of day or other accidents of life.[5]

The passage indicates that Ives, more than Mahler or Schoenberg, grasped the full implications of his historical moment, responding in a way that subsequent history has shown to be prophetic. He saw that with the demise of tonality, with its reemergence as a historical category, all musical decision had in some sense been rendered arbitrary. Every imaginable sonic material was suddenly placed at the disposal of the composer, who was forced to assume the full burden of choice. Such formerly valid distinctions as those separating new music from old music, popular music from concert music, even music from noise, could no longer be assumed. Each composer had to determine what music should be; and the range of choices, even within the first fifteen years of the century (encompassing both Stravinsky's primitivistic neotonality and Schoenberg's atonality, Satie's detached and ironic simplicity and Russolo's Futurist art of noises), exposed the extraordinary degree to which "everything had changed."

II

Ives's song "The Things Our Fathers Loved," completed in 1917 but based on a sketch dating back to c.1905, offers an ideal vehicle for considering the composer's new manner of handling traditional musical materials (Example 1.1).[6] Although brief, it is especially suitable because of its text,

---

[5] *Essays*, 117. Henry and Sidney Cowell make a similar point, though in a more restricted context, with reference to *The Unanswered Question* in *Charles Ives and His Music* (New York: Oxford University Press, 1955), 176: "One of Ives's most spectacular achievements is the invention of a form which logically uses consonance and dissonance in a single piece."

[6] The song is included in the *114 Songs* (no.43) collected and distributed by Ives in 1922. Information concerning provenance is found in *JKCat*, 43, 201.

Example 1.1 Ives: "The Things Our Fathers Loved"

The Things Our Fathers Loved
(and the greatest of these was Liberty)

Example 1.1 (*cont.*)

Example 1.1 (*cont.*)

which is itself concerned with music of the past, and its heavy reliance upon traditional musical associations, evoked in part by actual quotation. My comments will be directed especially toward formal, tonal, and motivic matters, as it is above all these that reveal Ives's radical reshaping of inherited conventions. As with Mahler, traditional elements are constantly present, though ultimately dissolved so that new configurations can be fashioned out of their remains; and, as with Schoenberg, the compositional procedures lead to a final negation of tonal focus, though here the music remains in some essential sense unmistakably tonal. Yet the final result is unquestionably Ives, as far removed in expressive effect from either Schoenberg or Mahler as imaginable.

"The Things Our Fathers Loved" is based on a text written by Ives himself, and the overall structure and character of the music is intimately tied to the form and content of the words. The music's asymmetrical two-part structure – A, mm. 1–14; B, mm. 15–22 – mirrors that of the poem, whose first part consists mostly of a series of isolated images, evoking the musical memories of childhood, primarily couched in incomplete sentences, while the second offers a single, complete declarative statement that comments upon the meaning of those images:

Part I
1 I think there must be a place in the soul
2 all made of tunes, of tunes of long ago;

3 I hear the organ on the Main Street corner,
4 Aunt Sarah humming Gospels;
5 Summer evenings,
6 The village cornet band, playing in the square.
7 The town's Red, White and Blue,
8 all Red, White and Blue

Part II
9 Now! Hear the songs!
10 I know not what are the words
11 But they sing in my soul
12 of the things our Fathers loved.

Since lines 1 and 2 are to some degree both textually and musically distinct from the remainder of the first part, they have been separated from lines 3–8. They set the stage, as it were, associating the "things" of Ives's title with tunes located in the interior world of memory ("a place in the soul") and in the chronological world of the distant past ("of long ago"). Lines 3–8 then bring a series of audio-visual vignettes evoking musical memories from childhood: an organ grinder (line 3), Aunt Sarah singing hymns (line 4), summer evenings (line 5), and a village band (lines 6–8). In the second part Ives speaks in his own voice, as it were, as poet/composer, who comments on the significance these images have for him. The disconnected phrases of the first part, held together like the fragments of a collage, give way to a single continuous thought, its parts joined into a unified syntactical whole.

Ives realizes this text musically with a two-part structure that consists of a relatively open-ended first section and a more conclusive second one, a variation on the standard antecedent–consequent formal type, or the so-called musical period. Yet he shapes this period entirely according to the specific features of his text, fusing words and music in an integrated conception.

Example 1.2 Quoted passage from "Dixie's Land"

I   wish I   was in de land ob cot - ton

Example 1.3 Quoted passage from "My Old Kentucky Home"

The sun shines bright   in the   old Ken-tuck-y home

The music of the antecedent thus mirrors the abrupt juxtapositions of the text, producing a series of relatively brief, fragmented phrases, each itself a sort of small-scale antecedent. The first phrase (mm. 1–5) has a clearly defined opening gesture and more tenuous conclusion, consistent with the first two lines of text, which, like a rising curtain, serve to reveal the conceptual space – the realm of time and memory – where the "action" of the poem will unfold.

In light of what follows, it is notable that the vocal line of this opening segment is constructed entirely from quotations, from the opening of "Dixie's Land" (Example 1.2, where the quoted part is bracketed), a well-known Confederate song (m. 1.4 to m. 3.1), and from "My Old Kentucky Home" (Example 1.3), Stephen Foster's equally well-known minstrel tune (mm. 3.2–4.2, partially repeated with rhythmic "corrections" in 4.4–5.3).[7] These quotations are virtually unrecognizable, however, as a result of major distortions in rhythm (throughout), tempo ("Dixie" would normally be much faster), and pitch (most noticeably the last two notes of "My Old Kentucky Home," whose original D and C are raised chromatically to D♯ and C♯ – an alteration explaining Ives's otherwise eccentric switch from flats to sharps here). The second tune's quotation, moreover, begins in mid-phrase and off the beat, joined to the preceding "Dixie's Land" quote

---

[7] Numbers with decimals are used to indicate specific beats: e.g., 2.1 indicates the first beat of the second measure, 3.3 the third beat of the third measure, etc.

Example 1.4 Quoted passage from "On the Banks of the Wabash"

Oh, the moon-light's fair to - night a - long the Wa - bash

Example 1.5 Quoted passage from *Nettleton*

Let thy king - dom bless-ed Sa - vior

so that its beginning sounds like that tune's sequence rather than a different song.

A significant feature of this first phrase is the lack of a well-defined ending. Whereas the first portion (mm. 2–3) moves energetically forward, from I to IV, suggesting a balancing two-measure continuation in mm. 4–5 (perhaps progressing from ii to a half cadence on V in m. 5), the last measure brings only a varied repeat of m. 4, the music seeming to have lost its way, slipping into uncertainty as if overwhelmed by the stream of musical memories about to ensue.

What follows first are two considerably shorter phrases (mm. 6–7 and 8–9), both of which also sound like antecedents: that is, they do not so much continue what precedes them as establish new beginnings. The resulting formal fragmentation, the musical equivalent of the text's isolated images, is strengthened by each phrase's quotation in the voice of a different melody, easily recognizable in its new context. The two phrases are thus set off not only by their varied musical characters but by their distinct sources, each appropriate for the text it accompanies: the late nineteenth-century popular tune "On the Banks of the Wabash" (Example 1.4) in mm. 6–7 and the traditional hymn *Nettleton* (Example 1.5) in mm. 8–9.

These two phrases are followed by an even more fragmentary phrase, the single-measure gesture that accompanies "Summer evenings" (m. 10). The briefness of this unit is consistent with the musical-textual

13

development to this point, which has brought increasingly shorter phrases along with greater formal fragmentation. At m. 10 there is neither a definite beginning nor ending, but only a transitional – or parenthetical – interjection, holding the music in momentary suspension before the final and most extended musical image of the first half: the village band of mm. 11–14. Though the final chord of m. 10 is ultimately treated as a dominant seventh of F, its tenuousness is underlined by the $\frac{4}{2}$ position ("incorrectly" resolved so that the B♭ bass moves to F, anticipating the subdominant–tonic bass motion of the subsequent band music) and by the bass's approach to this B♭ through half-step deflection from the previous A chord (recalling the "deceptive" bass motion from F to F♯ in mm. 3–4).[8]

The final segment of the first part also employs a quotation, this time in the accompaniment, again providing an appropriate musical equivalent for the text: the opening two phrases of the chorus of the popular Civil War march tune "The Battle Cry of Freedom" (Example 1.6, quoted mm. 11–14). This segment is different from the previous ones in that here the voice, itself composed largely of fragments from the verse of the same song, attempts to produce a definite conclusion in the third measure (m. 13); but its ending is contradicted by the accompaniment, which is still in mid-phrase – and mid-quotation – in m. 13 and which alters the quoted tune when it continues into m. 14 so that instead of reaching a half cadence

---

[8] Following a presentation of an earlier version of this paper at Harvard University in 1990, David Kopp, then a graduate student at Brandeis and now my colleague on the music faculty at Yale, remarked that the top voice of the piano in m. 10 could be heard as a rhythmically altered quotation of the top line of the *Tristan* Prelude (as it moves to the Prelude's first deceptive cadence, mm. 16–17), transposed down a major second. David Lewin, also present, wrote me shortly afterwards noting that the bass could also be viewed as *Tristan*-derived, but transposed up a perfect fourth rather than down by major second. Indeed, it could be argued that the entire harmonic progression of m. 10, as well as the bass motion, evokes *Tristan*, with Ives's V^7 of D to V^4_2 of F offering a sort of doubly deceptive move carrying the music *back* to its previous tonic rather than – as in the Wagner – away from it. Although in listening to the song I now inevitably hear the *Tristan* reference, I am not quite sure what to make of it. It can be understood of course as a reference to "art music," associated with the song's only textual reminiscence that does not explicitly evoke some form of vernacular music; but it also has a decidedly erotic tinge (how could it otherwise, given its source?), especially in conjunction with the text's "Summer evenings," so evocative of the world of *Tristan*.

Example 1.6 Quoted passage from "The Battle Cry of Freedom"

The Un - ion for-ev-er, Hur - rah boys, hur-rah!

Down with the Trai-tor, Up with the star; While we ral - ly round the flag

as in the original it modulates toward G, the key of the second part of the song. The voice, as if realizing its failure to close in m. 13, repeats "Red, White and Blue" in m. 14 before giving way to the transition, doubling the piano's top voice.

To summarize: the first half of the song consists almost entirely of quotations and produces a series of seemingly unrelated antecedents, none of which manages to reach a proper conclusion or to find a satisfactory continuation. Each ends in uncertainty, on an unresolved harmony. The undecided, suspended quality is especially evident at the end of the first, second, and third phrases (mm. 5, 7, and 9), where static harmony and repeated syncopated figures in the accompaniment leave the music rocking gently in a state of hazy, dream-like equilibrium, echoes of the falling fourth from the second phrase reverberating in the third (cf. mm. 7 and 9). The brief fourth phrase (m. 10) is barely underway before it too breaks off in hesitation; while the fifth and last, after beginning assertively, ultimately deflects toward the second half.

The second section supplies the long-awaited consequent. If the first part offers only beginnings, the second is, or attempts to be, all ending: a two-staged cadence whose first half begins by prolonging V (mm. 15–17) before closing deceptively on ii (rather than vi) in m. 18, and whose second half begins by moving through I in m. 19 (still combined with dominant suggestions in the upper voices) to vi in m. 20 before closing even more deceptively (and now against all expectations) on a dissonant, non-tonic chord. Except for this unexpected ending, however, the consequent is distinguished by a strongly unified overall structure, its two

Example 1.7 Chorus of "Sweet By-and-By"

subphrases (mm. 15–18 and 19–22) forming a complementary pair linked by clear correspondences in both voice and accompaniment. Its phrases do not sound isolated but are joined in a larger process. The abrupt shifts of memory that characterized the first half have disappeared, replaced by a continuous statement couched "in the present" (underscored by the emphatic "Now!" opening the second part). And although the second half is, like the first, also characterized by quotation, there is only one principal quote running throughout the section, comprehending the entire voice part and derived from a single, complete, and almost entirely unaltered source: the refrain of the gospel tune "Sweet By-and-By" (Example 1.7).

Leaving aside for the moment the fact that things go awry at the song's end, what we have is a fascinating reformulation of a traditional musical period: an opening section whose inconclusiveness is intensified by *several* opening gestures (a series of antecedents without consequents), and a closing section whose conclusiveness is supported by its overall goal-directed continuity. The latter is given an added sense of urgency by the faster tempo and more active accompaniment. These differences are complemented by significant tonal ones: the first section focuses on F major, but does so only gradually and intermittently in what is, taken as a whole, a relatively unstable segment; while the second is firmly anchored in G major (at least until the final cadence).

Since what I refer to as the antecedent takes up considerably more time than the consequent, whereas traditionally the two units would be equal in length, or the consequent would be longer, a word on the song's proportions is in order. Even if one ignores tempo, the differences are pronounced: fourteen measures for the first section, eight for the second.[9] What should be stressed, however, is that Ives's distortion of "classical" antecedent–consequent balances is, rather than a defect, the necessary consequence of his rethinking of the formal prototype. The generally slow, hesitant, and unfocused quality of the first part takes time, while the assertive determination of the second presses quickly toward its goal. One can nevertheless speak logically of two balancing "halves" of the song, mm. 1–14 and 15–22, set off by tonal focus (F major vs. G major), degree of tonal solidity (unstable vs. stable), formal structure (fragmented vs. continuous), motivic content, textural layout, tempo, and surface rhythm, even if when mathematically measured the two are quite unequal.

Despite these marked sectional contrasts, "The Things Our Fathers Loved" forms a unified whole; and it is instructive to examine how Ives achieves a degree of reconciliation between the two parts. The unusual overall tonal organization is one factor. The first section's underlying F major orientation is subtly and elusively defined to preserve the fragmentary quality of the individual subphrases. Thus the references to F are intermittent, and they emerge only gradually, taking on increasing definition as the section unfolds. F major first appears in m. 3, apparently as a IV chord subordinate to the opening C major. It is subsequently suggested (but only that) following the chromatic deflections of mm. 4–5, when the accompaniment of mm. 6–7 moves toward F, but in conjunction with a melody quoting a tune in G major ("On the Banks of the Wabash"). In m. 8, F major is unambiguously expressed for the first time in both melody and accompaniment, only to drift off again in m. 9, where the G suggestions of m. 7 are echoed (the voice's G–D, mm. 8.4–9.4, accompanied by an arpeggiated G minor triad in the top voice of the piano, the G preceded by a leading-tone F♯, and a G minor chord outlined in the two upper voices of the piano), and in the parenthetical, tonally less focused divergence of m. 10. Finally, the closing march segment (mm. 11–13) provides a more comprehensive, extended, and coordinated F major segment, though it too

---

[9] If more detailed distinctions are taken into consideration, however, interesting correspondences do emerge: five introductory measures, followed by eight measures of antecedent (mm. 6–13), one of transition (m. 14), and eight more of consequent (mm. 15–22).

gives way when the piano alters "The Battle Cry of Freedom" in m. 14, skewing things toward G major and the second half.

The gradual tendency toward stabilization of F major throughout the first half forms part of a larger process of tonal clarification that culminates in the more consistently maintained G major of the second, linking the song's two parts. In conjunction with various motivic factors (considered below), it helps project an overall, forward-directed character: the second half, rather than simply being set off from the first, seems to fulfill the tendency toward tonal and formal stabilization initiated there. An important contributing factor concerns tempo, the shift to a quicker pace – along with a more animated surface rhythm – at the march music in m. 11, followed by "in a gradually excited way" and *più accelerando* in mm. 13–14, providing a seamless transition to the faster tempo of the second half.

As has already been mentioned, the opening phrase of "On the Banks of the Wabash," heard in mm. 6–7, is quoted in G major, not F major. Although the stability of G is significantly weakened by the accompaniment, which pulls the music toward F, this anticipation of the key of the second part has important ramifications. Ives takes one of this phrase's most prominent features, the falling G–D with which it ends, as the basis for a network of motivic associations that both links the individual phrases of the first half and connects them to the second. The D–G motive appears first in the piano, as the top voice of the tonally ambiguous accompaniment in m. 6, and the voice picks it up in m. 7 and again, echo-like, in m. 9 (with upbeat). (The association linking mm. 7 and 9 is expressly created by Ives, as both G–Ds require alteration of the quoted melody, the only change in either tune.) The motive is further echoed in the piano in m. 9.1–2 and, transposed to D–A, throughout the rest of measure; and it also appears inverted in the voice in m. 12.[10]

This G–D motive thus appears six times within the last nine measures of the first half (mm. 6–14), providing an important binding force. It is prepared by the emergence of the fourth as a prominent interval during the song's first subphrase: in the filled-in C–F motion of the voice in mm. 2–3

---

[10] Given these important anticipations of G in the first half, it is notable that the piano's top voice in m. 10 quotes *Tristan* transposed down a major second (see footnote 8), thereby repositioning the melodic arrival on g^2 rather than a^2, as in the Prelude.

(accompanied by a sequence of the entire accompaniment of m. 2 a fourth higher in m. 3), the sequence of this filled-in C–F a fourth higher in mm. 3–4, and by the voice's enharmonically spelled B♭–E♭ (D♯) that immediately follows in m. 4 (repeated in m. 5). Thus a system of rising fourths (C–F–B♭–E♭) unfolds during this more expansive, opening unit (reflected in the offbeat tolling fourths and sevenths of the accompaniment, mm. 4–5), followed by the fixed G–D fourths in the more fragmentary remainder of the section.

That the G–D motive appears so prominently in the increasingly clarified F major context of the first section as a form of "dissonance" to the prevailing key, and is especially prevalent at the ends of subphrases (mm. 7, 9, and 12), contributes significantly to the somewhat blurred, hesitant, and reflexive character of this section. It also serves as a link to the second part, where – no longer dissonant – it supplies the principal intervallic frame for the entire vocal part (and, by implication, the accompaniment as well). Consistent with the altered musical atmosphere of this part, however, the two pitches no longer function motivically but take on a more structural role, controlling the melodic motion of the voice part throughout: d^2 to g^1 in mm. 15–18 and again in mm. 19–20; g^1 to d^1 in mm. 20–21; and d^1 back to (presumably) g^1 in the closing phrase, mm. 21–22. (The avoidance of this final g^1 will concern us later.)

Through these G–D connections Ives welds together the two sections in a remarkably original and convincing manner, at once preserving the distinctiveness of each part (the first remains not only more fragmented but tonally less focused and in a distantly related key) and linking them through a shared, yet differently realized, pitch correspondence.

Other, more obvious, unifying factors are also at work. The consistently developed accompanimental figures play a cohesive role in the first part, at least up to "The Battle Cry of Freedom" quotation in m. 11 (and even here, for Ives has laid the groundwork for the conventional left-hand march accompaniment in the gently rocking fourths of m. 9). There are also numerous surface motivic associations: e.g., the anticipation of the head motive of "On the Banks of the Wabash" (m. 6.1–2) in the varied repetition of the m. 4 melodic line in m. 5.1–2, and the more distant anticipation of the march's dotted stepwise rising third figure (piano, m. 11.1–2) in the voice and piano, mm. 4.4–5.1. The latter is also related to the almost ubiquitous, though constantly varied, recurrences of the voice's opening descending stepwise third motive in mm. 1.4–2.1 (the triadic upbeat of the original "Dixie's Land" melody being expressly altered to form this motive).[11] On a slightly larger scale, the voice also outlines a b^1–g^1 stepwise descent on the principal beats of mm. 6–7, and, on a still larger one, transposed to a^1–f^1, from mm. 7.4 to 8.4 to 11.1 (repeated in mm. 11.2–13.4). Notable too is the close diastematic connection between the voice's quotations from *Nettleton*, mm. 7.4–9.1, and "The Battle Cry of Freedom," mm. 10.4–12.3.

Of the motivic connections between the two sections, the most immediately evident involves the opening of the march music, mm. 10.4–11.3 in the piano, which reverberates in the accompaniment throughout all but the final two measures of the second part. It is first heard in mm. 15.2–16.1, transferred to the top register, as part of the chromatically altered dominant seventh harmonic complex on D that controls so much of this section. It offers here a hint of tonal uncertainty, even of "bitonality" (C major – despite the F♯s – in confrontation with G major), that recalls the more elusive tonal quality of the first half, as well as distinct references to the whole-tone configurations initiated by the piano's voice imitations in mm. 2.2–3 and 3.2–3. The sense of recall is further enhanced by the static, non-developmental manner in which the motive is treated, almost as if it were independent of the principal musical events. The more paraphrastic nature of the first section has not entirely disappeared.

By way of summary, Example 1.8 offers a sketch of the more important cohesive factors, both tonal and motivic, for the song as a whole. As there are too many motivic associations to include all, those with particularly important ties to the larger tonal structure have been favored, grouped where possible by appropriate slurs, beams, and – for the G–D motives – brackets. The graph contains as well a number of quasi-Schenkerian configurations, most notably the four descending third-spans in the top line, all associated with the voice part, two descending to G major tonics and

---

[11] Other instances of these falling thirds include: the voice in m. 3.1–3 (the sequence of the opening motive), in mm. 7.4–8.1 (the upbeat to *Nettleton*), and in m. 13.3–4; and the piano in m. 2.2–3, in m. 3.2–3 (the former's sequence), and in m. 3.3–4 (the former's overlapping extension, slightly elaborated). The motive also appears in inverted form in the voice in mm. 2.3–4, 3.3–4, 4.4–5.1, 11.1–2, 13.1–2, and 14.1–2; and in the piano in mm. 4.4–5.1, 11.1–2, 12.1–2, and 13.1–2. There are in addition recurrences in the voice part in almost every measure of the second half.

Example 1.8 Graph of tonal structure of "The Things Our Fathers Loved"

two to F major, the first of the latter undergoing what Schenker calls an "interruption." Because of the altered nature of the overall tonal framework, these spans obviously have a somewhat different meaning than they would in Schenker. Indeed, in general the graph may seem to suggest a structural neatness and consistency that are at odds with Ives's piece. Yet these spans, along with other graphically presented tonal configurations, offer an additional indication of that critical compositional feature we have stressed throughout: the use of processes derived from traditional tonal music, transformed – here as elsewhere – by the composer's more fragmented, multidimensional hierarchies (above all the F major–G major dichotomies). Particularly suggestive is the interrupted third-span (a procedure associated with traditional antecedent–consequent phrases) at m. 9, during the F major music of mm. 8–13, here intensified by the insertion of the parenthetical music of m. 10 before the descent's reinitiation and completion.

Two versions of the ending are given in Example 1.8, the first altered to show the fulfillment of the tonal implications of the second half (and of the quoted tune), the second reflecting Ives's actual conclusion. In addition, a long-range (non-Schenkerian) line encompassing virtually the entire song is traced in the voice part, from c^1 in m. 2 to $c\#^2$ in mm. 4–5 (embellished by $d\#^2$ and followed by an extensive move into inner voices in mm. 6–13), to the climactic d^2 in m. 15 that opens the second half.[12] d^2 then persists almost to the close, eventually transferred to the lower (original) octave (m. 21.1) before disappearing completely into the wayward close of the (actual) ending.

I have saved for last Ives's most mysterious means of achieving unity: the unexpected, yet seemingly inevitable, deflection of the final cadence in the last two bars. After the vi chord in m. 20, one expects a move to the dominant followed by resolution to the tonic, joined with voice motion from d^1 to g^1. (This is of course just what happens in the quoted tune: see Example 1.7, for which the reader will have no trouble supplying the omitted harmonization.) Instead, Ives lets the bass slip downward by half step, E–D$\#$, then essentially freezes the harmonic motion, at the same time altering the last two melodic notes upward by half step, from a^1–g^1 to $a\#^1$–$g\#^1$. The music is thus left hanging in mid-air, recalling the more tonally suspended quality of the first half, an association strengthened by the sudden absence of virtuosic figurations and a return to the simple, more chordal gestures and slower tempo of the opening.

Paradoxically, Ives achieves a more encompassing unity by subverting the obvious tonal implications of the second section, negating its promised conclusion. By reestablishing something of the musical atmosphere of the song's opening, he forges an alternative unity, undermining precisely that gesture that would have secured a traditional one: the final cadence. Given the complexities and ambiguities of the work, such a traditional close would represent a musical and psychological breach, destroy-

---

12 The graph does not indicate the continuing alternation of $c\#^2$ with c^2 between m. 5 and m. 13: $c\#^2$ (m. 5), c^2 (m. 8, voice), $c\#^2$ (m. 10, voice), and c^2 (mm. 10.4–13, piano).

Example 1.9 Correspondences between end of first phrase and end of song

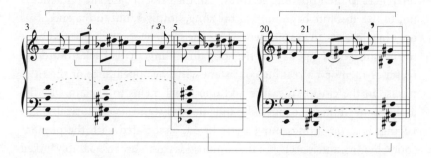

ing the song's peculiar ambivalence. Consider the matter of tonality. Although we have seen that Ives forms strong associations between the traditionally distant keys of the two halves, F major and G major, their full reconciliation would compromise the tenuousness of the whole. The pretense of a traditional cadential haven, achieved as if by miraculous wave of magic wand, would be both aesthetically flawed and historically anachronistic. Ives dismantles the conventions of traditional tonality in order to reassemble them in a new and more ambivalent way. The song ends "atonally" – but only in the sense of standing "beyond tonality." It does not negate the elements of tonality, but neutralizes them, making them more responsive to a post-tonal mentality.

This final phrase requires further comment, for it not only evokes the music of the first half in the general ways mentioned but contains a specific reference to an earlier passage: the "Old Kentucky Home" quotation in mm. 3.1–4.3 (and thus also its partial echo in mm. 4.4–5.4). That is, Ives alters the final phrase of "Sweet By-and-By" (mm. 20.4–22.1) not only to avoid a tonic close but also to recall this earlier moment. The melodic association is supported by an analogous bass motion by half step, the downwards E–D♯ of mm. 20–21 mirroring the upwards F–F♯ of mm. 3–4; and the chromatic alteration of the last two melodic notes, A♯–G♯ in mm. 21–22, mirrors the similar D♯–C♯ alterations in m. 4 and m. 5. In addition, the final chords of the two passages are identical in pitch content: both are "dominant ninths," in different transpositions and inversions, the first (m. 5) on E♭ in root position, the second (mm. 21.4–22) on G♯ in second inversion – a relationship retaining E♭ as bass note for both chords (respelled as D♯ when it returns). These connections are sketched in Example 1.9.

23

It is a characteristic of Ives's compositions that they often end with references to their opening gestures.[13] In the present case, the reference is not to the absolute beginning of the song, however, but to the end of its opening phrase – to the moment where the sequence of memories is about to rush in. This suggests that the song, in ending, drifts back toward the realm of memory, a reading consistent with the appearance of the title-phrase in the closing measure and one which helps to explain why the ambivalent ending is so musically and poetically (and also historically) satisfying. For the "things our fathers loved," associated with the popular songs, hymns, and marches of the composer's youth, are inseparably linked in Ives's mind to the conventions of traditional tonality. And as his music so poignantly expresses, these must now be consigned to the past – to the realm of memory, where they can maintain an only fragmentary existence, the remnants of an irrevocably lost world. That is why the close does not (cannot) confirm either of the two principal keys, but instead evokes a previous moment of tonal uncertainty. In the end it is the tonally tangential that is endorsed, not the essential – or "structural."

To my ear, Ives's song sounds as if it is striving to put the shreds of tonality back together again (especially in the second half, with its rush toward a G major cadence); but ultimately it is unable to do so. It can deal with them only as scraps, as momentary evocations strung together according to the fleeting analogies and unconscious associations of time remembered.[14] The "things" evoked by the title can no longer be rendered whole;

[13] For a more general discussion of this characteristic see Robert P. Morgan, "Spatial form in Ives," in *An Ives Celebration: Papers and Panels of the Charles Ives Centennial Festival-Conference*, ed. H. Wiley Hitchcock and Vivian Perlis (Urbana: University of Illinois Press, 1977), 145–58.

[14] After the publication of the original German version of this article, Stuart Feder sent me a copy of his very insightful study of the same song, written some years earlier, "The nostalgia of Charles Ives, an essay in affects and music," *The Annual of Psychoanalysis* 10 (1981): 301–32. Though Dr. Feder offers a rather different reading of the form of the song, his comments on the way the music evokes the past through distorted recollections of older music are extremely illuminating for my reading as well as his. Feder, a practicing psychoanalyst, is especially concerned with the way the music communicates "a sense of the distinctive amalgamation of memory and affect which we call nostalgia." I should also mention a more recent study, appearing in Larry Starr's *A Union of Diversities* (New York: Schirmer Books, 1992), 57–67, though it strikes me as much less successful than Feder's. To begin with, I do not agree that "the piece clearly

24

there can be no final cadence. But that, paradoxically, is how Ives achieves what his subtitle refers to as "the greatest of these."

III

One thinks of Ives – and rightly so – as a quintessentially American figure; and it would be difficult to imagine a more typically home-grown product than this song, so steeped in Americana both textually and musically. Yet "The Things Our Fathers Loved" also offers a profound response to – even a commentary upon – the crisis in European music evident at the time of its conception. It confronts the same tonal and formal issues as did the most searching European compositions of its day, and in a manner that, while strikingly original, is also entirely convincing (and not only on its own terms, but those transmitted by the Western musical tradition itself). It is closely tied to both the Old World and the New, and acquires greater depth when heard within their combined frames of reference.

Recently Ives's originality, even his veracity, has been called into question by the suggestion that he consciously misdated works in order to make them appear to have been written earlier than they were.[15] Although I do not wish (nor am I competent) to comment upon Ives's datings as such, I do

presents a sequence of varying styles" (p. 58) – which, significantly, Starr does not identify. Nor do I think the five sections Starr refers to as "transitions" (except for m. 14) have anything to do with what we normally mean by this term in referring to musical form. (The designation of mm. 18–20 as a transition, or "quasi-transition," is particularly puzzling.) I will pass over in stunned silence Starr's notion that mm. 1–20 "strongly suggest an overall harmonic plan of very traditional cast, centering upon the tonality of C major" (p. 65). But his failure to discuss, or even identify, any of the quotations seems truly perplexing, since Starr himself emphasizes their general expressive importance. (If he recognized "Sweet By-and-By," for example, he would presumably not refer to the voice's G–F♯ in m. 20 as a "half-step displacement," since these notes continue the quotation of the original tune, unaltered.)

[15] See Maynard Solomon, "Charles Ives: some questions of veracity," *Journal of the American Musicological Society* 40/3 (1987): 443–70, along with the replies by J. Peter Burkholder, "Charles Ives and his fathers: a response to Maynard Solomon," *Newsletter of the Institute for Studies in American Music* 18/1 (1988): 8–11; and Philip Lambert, "Communication," *Journal of the American Musicological Society* 42/1 (1989): 204–09. Also valuable in this connection is the revised Ives chronology that Gayle Sherwood has begun to develop in her "Questions and veracities: reassessing the chronology of Ives's choral works," *The Musical Quarterly* 78/3 (1994): 429–47.

want to reflect on the subject of his originality in this context. It seems to me that "The Things Our Fathers Loved," superficially considered so remarkably traditional in caste (as are many of the composer's works), clearly reveals that Ives's true importance does not lie in specific "modernist" techniques – in dissonance treatment, textural layerings, tone rows, serialized rhythms, and the like. Although the question of whether or not Ives anticipated his European contemporaries in these matters is no doubt of considerable historical interest, it is not one upon which his achievement depends. What is most original in Ives, to put it in his own terms, is the substance, not the manner, of his music: the multivalent, eclectic mixing of various technical and expressive modes, drawn together into an encompassing whole. Not one of Ives's contemporaries, European or otherwise, wrote music remotely resembling his in this respect; and his work would remain just as daring, as radical and visionary, if it were revealed that all of it had been completed after 1920 (or even 1930 or 1940, for that matter).

This is confirmed by even so brief a work as "The Things Our Fathers Loved." It projects a quality quite unlike that associated with any other composer of the first half of the twentieth century. There is not one note or gesture that evokes Schoenberg or his followers, for example, nor one that recalls Stravinsky, Bartók, or anyone else active at the time. Yet Ives's song interacts with the music of these Europeans in definite, if mysterious and perhaps ultimately inexplicable ways. Although unmistakably Ives's own, "The Things Our Fathers Loved" was not formed out of thin air. It manipulates the conventions of the European past, and in doing so leans so heavily upon them. Its roots are deeply anchored.

2 Remembrance of dissonances past: the two published editions of Ives's *Concord Sonata*

GEOFFREY BLOCK

In 1920 and 1921 Ives published and distributed, at his own expense, his first *magnum opus*, the Second Piano Sonata ("Concord, Mass., 1840–1860"), accompanied by a lengthy and wide-ranging volume of philosophical program notes, the *Essays Before a Sonata*.[1] Although Henry Cowell had suggested as early as 1930 that Ives submit his "New England Sonata" for publication in *New Music*,[2] it was not until 1947, more than a quarter century after

I am grateful to J. Peter Burkholder for his detailed and extremely helpful reading of an earlier draft of this essay.

[1] According to Ives's letter to John Kirkpatrick of 11 October 1935, "the sonata was engraved in the fall of 1919." See *Memos*, 202, 331. On 28 May 1920 Ives sketched the following response to Henry F. B. Gilbert's letter of the 26th: ". . . when the *Concord* copies are finished, I'm going to send you one. . . . But you'll be spared this for some time, as it takes longer to correct proofs than I imagined" (*Memos*, 192, n. 13). On all his subsequent lists of works from 1929 to 1950, however, Ives unwaveringly offered 1919 as the publication date, a date contradicted by the inscription on the back flyleaf of the first edition, "C. E. Ives / Redding, / Conn. / 1920" (*Memos*, 150, 163). Ives himself distributed the sonata by early 1921 (see Gilbert's letter of thanks to Ives, 17 February 1921, cited in *Memos*, 192, n. 13). Remarkably, the *Concord Sonata* was the first work Ives had offered to the public in published form since five short compositions were published in 1896 and 1897 during his college years at Yale University. See Geoffrey Block, *Charles Ives: A Bio-Bibliography* (New York: Greenwood Press, 1988), 356–57. For a summary of the complicated genesis of the work prior to 1920 see Block, *Ives: "Concord Sonata"* (Cambridge: Cambridge University Press, 1996), 20–27, 29–30.

[2] "I have been thinking, also, that it is about time for another work of yours to appear in *New Music*. It would be very interesting to have a piano work – a work easier for most people to get at than the orchestra score [the second movement of the Fourth Symphony published in 1929]. What do you think about printing your New England Sonata at the end of the season?" Letter from Henry Cowell to Ives, 28 August 1930, quoted in Rita Mead, *Henry Cowell's New Music 1925–1936: The Society, the Music Editions, and the Recordings* (Ann Arbor MI: UMI Research Press, 1981), 147.

the privately printed first edition and eight years after pianist John Kirkpatrick premiered the work, that the *Concord Sonata* became the first major Ives composition to be published a second time. The eagerly solicited new edition was published by Arrow Music Press under a distinguished board headed by Lehman Engel and Marc Blitzstein.[3] Without Ives's financial backing of this non-profit composers' cooperative, however, the revised *Concord Sonata*, too, might well have gone unpublished.[4]

The catalyst behind a new edition was Kirkpatrick's widely heralded Town Hall premiere of the *Concord Sonata* on 20 January 1939, on the basis of which influential *New York Herald Tribune* critic Lawrence Gilman proclaimed the work "the greatest music composed by an American."[5] Since Ives had already distributed most of the approximately 750 first edition copies by the early 1930s, virtually none were available to the small but growing public interested in acquiring this music.[6] Negotiations for publication soon followed, and the first proofs were ready within a year or two. Several factors conspired against this expeditious activity: 1) prospective editor Kirkpatrick's resistance to Ives's non-pianistic revisions; 2) Ives's various infirmities; 3) Ives's reluctance to complete the finishing touches; and 4) an interruption necessitated by the war from 1944 to 1946.[7] For these reasons the new edition suffered a delay of nearly nine years.

[3] See Lehman Engel, *This Bright Day: An Autobiography* (New York: Macmillan, 1974), 88–89. In 1964 the second edition was acquired by Associated Music Publishers, later a subsidiary of G. Schirmer, Ives's original uncredited publisher. The sonata is currently distributed by Hal Leonard Publishing Corporation.

[4] Ibid., 118. Engel writes: "It was just prior to my first meeting with Ives [1938] that Aaron Copland, Virgil Thomson, Marc Blitzstein, and I had founded the Arrow Music Press. Once I asked Ives, who had made a financial success in the bond firm of Myrich [*sic*] and Ives, if we might publish some of his music, and I explained the terms. He was quite willing for us to do any of his works, left the choice to us, and agreed not only to pay the costs but to give the income to the publishing of young composers' works."

[5] Lawrence Gilman, "Music: a masterpiece of American music heard here for the first time," *New York Herald Tribune*, 21 January 1939, 9.

[6] According to Frank R. Rossiter, Ives "had at least 750 copies of the *Concord Sonata*, and at least 1,500 of *114 Songs*, printed" and "probably most, but not all, of these copies were sent out." Rossiter, *Charles Ives and His America* (New York: Liveright, 1975), 183. Ives's letter to Engel, 25 January 1932 (published in facsimile in Engel, 115), confirms Rossiter's last point: "I'm sorry I have no more complete copies left of the larger book of songs or the printed piano sonata."

[7] See James Sinclair's *catalogue raisonné* of Ives's music (New Haven: Yale University Press, in progress).

Even if Ives had merely wished to correct errors of pitch and rhythm that plagued the first edition, the time was ripe for a second edition that could be purchased commercially. But Ives had an equally compelling artistic reason for wanting to issue a new edition: for more than a decade the first edition had no longer represented his thoughts on the work or the way he played it, especially the "Emerson" movement. In fact, this essay will demonstrate that although Ives continued to make changes until the 1940s, the central features of a future edition and most of its essential details had been determined by 1926, within a few years of the first edition's distribution in 1921.

Revisions by other composers, for example Schumann's in the *Davidsbündlertänze* or Hindemith's in *Das Marienleben*, were prompted by such factors as a composer's disparagement of youthful idealism and innovation, lack of systemization, limitations in technique, or a more competitive response to the commercial marketplace.[8] In contrast, Ives's principal *Concord Sonata* revisions were largely motivated by a wish to *restore* ideas from an earlier work, the *Emerson Overture* of 1907–14 (the never-completed principal source piece for both the "Emerson" movement in the *Concord Sonata* and a separate but related piano work from the early 1920s, the *Four Transcriptions from "Emerson"*). Other second-edition ideas would be drawn from the autograph ink score of the sonata completed in 1919.

Harmony Ives, writing to Lehman Engel on her husband's behalf on 4 July 1939, six months after Kirkpatrick's historic debut, conveys Ives's motivation behind the second edition:

> In the first movement there are a few places in which Mr. Ives thinks more of the original score [either *Emerson Overture*, the autograph ink score of

---

[8] Most pianists elect to perform and record the second edition of *Davidsbündlertänze*, although both editions are published in *Robert Schumann: Werke*, ed. Clara Schumann, Johannes Brahms et al. (Leipzig: Breitkopf und Härtel, 1881–93; repr. New York: Kalmus, 1971). An exception is Charles Rosen, who offers a useful encapsulated comparison in his jacket notes for "The revolutionary masterpieces: Robert Schumann," Nonesuch 79062 (1983). For opposing views on the relative merits of Hindemith's song cycle see Rudolf Stephan, transl. Hans F. Redlich, "Hindemith's *Marienleben*: an assessment of its two versions," *Music Review* 15 (1954): 275–87, and David Neumeyer, *The Music of Paul Hindemith* (New Haven and London: Yale University Press, 1986), 137–67.

1919, or both] should be in and more as he plays it as shown in some of the passages in the Transcriptions [the *Four Transcriptions from "Emerson"* (1921–26)]. In the other movements it is only a matter of correcting details mostly unimportant, and he feels that some of the marginal notes could be left out or at least cut down somewhat.[9]

A significant number of the restorations from the *Emerson Overture* first found their way into the *Four Transcriptions from "Emerson"* noted by Harmony Ives. Since the *Emerson Overture* had been conceived and drafted primarily as an orchestral work, the return to the *Overture* necessitated a thicker piano texture. The denser *Transcriptions* and later the second edition of the sonata consequently "jacked up the level of dissonance," in the words of Elliott Carter's often-quoted observation that is used to question Ives's claims of priority as an avant-garde composer.[10]

This essay will demonstrate that the orchestral nature of the revised "Emerson" in the *Concord Sonata* does not as a rule signify the creation of *new* dissonances (*pace* Carter) but instead marks a return to the earlier dissonances of the *Emerson Overture* and the autograph ink score of the sonata, both of which *preceded* the first edition. Further, the presence of several striking statements of Beethoven's Fifth Symphony motive that appear in the second edition, but not the first, can similarly be traced to sources that pre-date the first edition. The essay will also rebut and suggest an alternative view for two other widespread interpretations of Ives's attitudes and practices: 1) contrary to the permissive relativism of Sondra Rae Clark's detailed comparative study of the *Concord Sonata* sources (including differences between the first and second editions), Ives in fact did have a preferred version of the work, represented by the second edition; and 2) contrary to the image of Ives as a composer whose scores are essentially indeterminate (a subtext of Clark), his music remains faithful to the

---

9 Charles Ives Archive, Yale University, Ives papers, MSS 14, Box 29, Folder no. 4.
10 From the Carter interview in Vivian Perlis, *Charles Ives Remembered: An Oral History* (New Haven and London: Yale University Press, 1974), 138. See also Elliott Carter, "The case of Mr. Ives," *Modern Music* 16/3 (1939): 174, repr. in *The Writings of Elliott Carter: An American Composer Looks at Modern Music*, compiled, edited, and annotated by Else Stone and Kurt Stone (Bloomington: Indiana University Press, 1977), 50.

nineteenth-century tradition of performance options, and his extensive process of revision and flexibility of execution is not different in kind from that of other composers, such as Beethoven or Chopin.[11]

After distributing the first edition in 1921 Ives recast the *Concord Sonata* in new forms. One of these is the *Four Transcriptions from "Emerson,"* especially the first, which combines elements of the abandoned *Emerson Overture* and the *Concord Sonata*'s "Emerson" movement into a new hybrid.[12] *The Celestial Railroad* is more loosely derived from the *Concord Sonata*'s "Hawthorne" movement and the original second movement of the Fourth Symphony and, as persuasively argued by Thomas M. Brodhead, would itself serve as the principal source of a revised second movement of this work.[13] Ives also used seventeen copies of the engraved first edition (R[1]–R[17]) as a workshop for correcting details and exploring new possibilities. These revised copies bring together elements of the *Emerson Overture* in "Emerson," incorporate some material from *The Celestial Railroad* in "Hawthorne," and combine features of both the printed first edition and the future second edition in all the movements of the *Concord Sonata*.

Precise dates for this post-first-edition compositional activity are difficult to determine. In his 1935 letter to Kirkpatrick, Ives recalled drafting the first *"Emerson" Transcription* between 1915 and 1918; various *Celestial Railroad* sketches are extant on pre-1921 papers. Most of the compositional activity for *The Celestial Railroad* seems, however, to have occurred after

---

[11] Sondra Rae Clark, "The evolving *Concord Sonata*: a study of choices and variants in the music of Charles Ives" (Ph.D. dissertation, Stanford University, 1972). See also Clark, "The element of choice in Ives's *Concord Sonata*," *The Musical Quarterly* 60/2 (1974): 167–86.

[12] In the preface to his forthcoming edition of the *Four Transcriptions from "Emerson,"* Thomas M. Brodhead summarizes the correspondence between the *Transcriptions* and "Emerson" (second edition) as follows: No. 1, "all of page 1 through page 2, line 1. But: There is a passage in the transcription (mm. 10–23) taken from the *Overture* that cannot be found in 'Emerson'"; No. 2, "page 6, line 1 through all of page 11"; No. 3, "page 14, line 3, measure 3 through page 16, line 4"; No. 4, "page 17, line 4 through all of page 19." See also Brodhead, "Ives's *Celestial Railroad* and his Fourth Symphony," *American Music* 12/4 (1994), 389–424, especially 411–14. I am indebted to Brodhead for sharing his essay and prefaces to his Ives Society editions of *Four Transcriptions from "Emerson"* and *The Celestial Railroad* prior to their publication by Associated Music Publishers.

[13] Brodhead, "Ives's *Celestial Railroad* and his Fourth Symphony," passim.

1921, in the form of pencil or ink additions on cut-up, pasted, or abbreviated copies. In any event, the *terminus ad quem*, or final date, of *The Celestial Railroad* is probably 1926, one year before the public performance of its close musical relative, the second movement of the Fourth Symphony.[14]

According to Gayle Sherwood, the paper of Ives's ink copy of the *Four Transcriptions from "Emerson"* was not produced until 1925, and the earliest date for the compositionally significant first *"Emerson" Transcription* sketch is most likely 1926.[15] Furthermore, the presumably "functional" address and telephone number for copyist Emil Hanke (46 Cedar St. NY 3663 John) ceased to be functional as of 30 April 1926.[16] Thus although Ives recalled that the second, third, and fourth *Transcriptions* "were made a year or two after the Sonata was printed" all roads seem to converge on 1926 as a likelier date for this work as well.[17]

Although Ives made a number of revisions in the early 1940s, the completion of the *Four Transcriptions from "Emerson"* in 1926 also con-

---

[14] A sketch (f4836) in which Ives enters the business address where he resided from 1914 to 1923 (38 Nassau Street), leads Brodhead to conclude that *The Celestial Railroad* "was created between 1921 and 1923" (ibid., 398). The paper type of f4836, however, 16:SN4 (1917–20), suggests that Ives may have sketched these ideas before the *Concord Sonata*'s first edition.

[15] Gayle Sherwood, "The choral works of Charles Ives: chronology, style and reception" (Ph.D. dissertation, Yale University, 1995). I would like to thank Sherwood for sharing chapter 2 of this dissertation ("Dating methodology and data"), and her essay, "Questions and veracities: reassessing Ives chronology" (*The Musical Quarterly* 78/3 [1994]: 429–47) prior to its publication, and for generously sharing her preliminary findings on the *Concord Sonata* papers and handwriting characteristics.

[16] If 1926 seems a reasonable *terminus ad quem* for both the *Four Transcriptions from "Emerson"* and *The Celestial Railroad*, the revised first edition copy R[7] or Copy "A" (formerly R[3]) also antedates these *Concord Sonata* compositional byproducts by anywhere from one to five years. Of the remaining copies only R[16] or "B," formerly R[14] (with patches in George F. Roberts's hand), and R[17] or "E," formerly R[10] (with references to second edition page proofs), can be dated more precisely: 1940 or later. The "considerably edited" R[4] is the copy that Harmony Ives sent to Lawrence Gilman in 1939 and was later acquired by *New York Times* critic and Ives enthusiast Harold C. Schonberg. R[9] once belonged to Elliott Carter. All R copies are now housed, along with all the other *Concord Sonata* manuscript sources, in the Ives Archive at Yale University.

[17] In light of the revised chronology proposed here Brodhead might perhaps be too accepting of Ives's and Kirkpatrick's 1915–18 dates for the first *"Emerson" Transcription* and 1922–23 for the remaining ones.

cludes the main work on the second edition of the *Concord Sonata*. While it is true from the evidence of the revised first edition copies (R^1–R^{17}) that Ives considered numerous additional changes after 1926, it must be emphasized that in the end Ives chose not to publish his more extensive departures beyond those retained from the *"Emerson" Transcriptions*. Even the revisions derived from the *Transcriptions* extend first edition material beyond a few beats on only one or two occasions. Moreover, Ives's revisions between 1921 and 1926 (or later) do not alter either the structure or the overall dissonance level of the first edition.

Despite the absence of substantive or large-scale structural departures, a comparison of the first and second published editions reveals considerable differences, particularly notes added or subtracted from chords and changes in accidentals. Most of these changes are cited in Clark's system-by-system comparison, although she overlooks four out of the five altered treatments of Beethoven's Fifth Symphony motive in "Emerson."[18] Several revision types can be readily distinguished: 1) restorations of earlier ideas derived from the *Emerson Overture* (c. 1907–14) and the 1919 autograph ink score of the sonata; 2) performance directions, including notational changes and additions that offer more precise ways to depict rhythm, tempo directions, dynamics, accent marks, and hand positions; 3) corrections of first edition errors; and 4) the adoption of musical material (some of which may be new) from revised first edition copy R^{15} (formerly R^{13}) and the seven subsequent sets of second edition proofs.[19] This essay will focus on the first type, addressing the others more generally and briefly.

[18] Clark, "The evolving *Concord Sonata*." For the most thorough comparison of the first and second editions see Wolfgang Rathert, *The Seen and Unseen: Studien zum Werk von Charles Ives*, Berliner musikwissenschaftliche Arbeiten, ed. Carl Dahlhaus and Rudolf Stephan, vol. 38 (Munich and Salzburg: Emil Katzbichler, 1991), 171–82. See also Felix Meyer, *"The Art of Speaking Extravagantly": Eine vergleichende Studie der "Concord Sonata" und der "Essays Before a Sonata" von Charles Ives*, Der schweizerischen musikforschenden Gesellschaft, Series II, vol. 34 (Bern and Stuttgart: Paul Haupt, 1991), 13–16.

[19] Although each type of revision appears in all movements, the restoration of earlier ideas is most concentrated, again not unexpectedly, in "Emerson." Performance directions are most ubiquitous in "Hawthorne," where Ives tries to offer specific advice as well as encouraging words on how to "keep the horse going hard." The third category is useful in determining which *decisions* were made at the last moment, but it is not always possible to determine when Ives is correcting a first edition error and when he is revising a note.

Example 2.1 "Emerson," page 1, system 2
a. second edition
b. first edition

Among the numerous changes between the first and second editions are several that reflect Ives's evolving attitudes about whether to add or highlight, or to obscure or remove, statements of key motives. The revisions that affect the treatment of Ives's central borrowed motive, the opening four notes of Beethoven's Fifth Symphony, are of special structural interest. The largest number of these occur in "Emerson."

After several statements obscured by augmentation or polyphony, the first clearly audible statement of the motive occurs in the left hand at the end of the second system of the first page of "Emerson" (the pitches C#–C#–C#–A# bracketed in Example 2.1a).[20] Although it appears as a minor third, as in the answering statement, F–F–F–D (rather than the opening major third of the symphony, G–G–G–E♭), the resemblance to the Fifth Symphony motive is unmistakable. Since it will remain the clearest rhythmic expression of the motive until the three successive statements on page 3, system 4, its first and only clear rhythmic appearance on page 1 has a notable bearing on how listeners will perceive Beethoven's presence.[21] For

---

[20] For a facsimile of page 1 of the autograph ink score for "Emerson" see Perlis, *Charles Ives Remembered*, 216.

[21] Although Ives clearly presents the major third form of the Fifth Symphony motive one system later (left hand, m. 3), its augmented note values obscure rather than emphasize its rhythmic connection to Beethoven.

this reason the absence of the Fifth Symphony motive in the analogous place in the first edition (shown in Example 2.1b) is compositionally significant. It is equally significant that Ives's decision to assert the Fifth Symphony motive here (as well as his decision to surround the motive in the right hand with a more orchestral and dissonant texture) marks a return to an idea that precedes the first edition.[22]

The version of the Fifth Symphony motive shown in Example 2.1a had previously appeared in Ives's manuscripts on several paper types that Sherwood places with reasonable security between 1907 and 1913. The piano part of an *Emerson Overture* score sketch on f2212 reveals that before Ives introduced one of his distinctive "Emerson" themes, he assigned a bold and dissonant statement of the Fifth Symphony motive to the piano part with a *major* third in rhythmic unison. He then deleted this measure, revised the passage, and cross-referenced the revision with a series of dotted triangles on f2213 in a version that corresponds closely with the second edition of the *Concord Sonata*. These manuscripts demonstrate convincingly that the important decision to state the Fifth Symphony motive forcefully on the second system of "Emerson" was a restoration of an idea that Ives had worked out in his abandoned *Emerson Overture*, probably sometime between 1911 and 1914.[23]

After 1921, on the first edition copy R[7] (formerly R[3]), Ives reminds himself, or a future copyist, to "see slip #2." The closest extant manuscript

---

[22] Brodhead, "Ives's *Celestial Railroad*," 412–14. Figure 8(a–d) of Brodhead's essay offers facsimiles of these passages in the *Emerson Overture* (f2213), the *Concord Sonata* first edition, Emil Hanke's copy of the *Four Transcriptions from "Emerson"* (f4907), and the *Concord Sonata* second edition.

[23] The Fifth Symphony motive also appears on the manuscript of *Study No. 9* (more widely known as *The Anti-Abolitionist Riots*) on paper that can be placed between 1907 and 1913 (f4798 and f4799). In addition to paper types and handwriting evidence, Ives offers a chronological clue: "Harry Kentor comes down and sings whiskey but tenor – Tis the night before Xmas Waverly Pl. 1911." Also on this page Ives followed a borrowing of the important theme that would resurface numerous times in "Emerson" (the same theme as the right hand in Example 2.1) with a more obscure reference to the Fifth Symphony motive in the left hand. Instead of three octave C♯s, Ives states a C♯–D dyad on the second quarter note of the quarter-note triplet, preserved in its dissonant glory in both Henry Cowell's 1949 edition and the forthcoming Charles Ives Society Edition edited by Keith Ward. The *Study No. 9* version returns to, or is perhaps preceded by, the last music in a sketch labeled "Centrifugal cadences 'Emerson Concerto!['],'" i.e., with a C♯–D–C♯ triplet (not in octaves) rather than three C♯s.

relative to this source (now missing) is a page of the *"Emerson"*
Transcription sketches (c. 1926) that opens with a passage that is now
almost as dissonant as the future second edition and that contains for the
first time since the *Emerson Overture* drafts the accented Beethoven motive
(f4870). This version would be retained in the first *"Emerson" Transcription*
and eventually transcribed in the second edition of 1947.[24]

The other notable placement of the Fifth Symphony motive in the
second edition (where none existed in the first edition) occurs at the end of
the second system on page 16 (shown in Example 2.2a). Here, to conclude
one of the most dramatic passages in the sonata, Ives presents a rhythmically modified but clearly recognizable statement of the Fifth Symphony
motive on F (A–A–A–F) as the last idea before the final return of the principal lyric theme on system 3. What makes this understated occurrence of the
Beethoven motto so significant is its uncharacteristic and conspicuous
absence after page 12. In the third *"Emerson" Transcription* (Example 2.2b),
the motive is melodically obscured by the octave displacement of its final F
and, more completely, by Ives's "sometimes better" F♯. In the first edition
(Example 2.2c) Beethoven was completely exiled from this passage.

Since neither the *Emerson Overture* nor the "Emerson" sketches
are extant for this passage, it is not possible to trace it before 1914.
Nevertheless, the autograph ink score of 1919 (f3929) clarifies that, like the
bold statement on page 1, the treatment of the Fifth Symphony motive on
page 16 of the second edition was not a retrospective "jacked up" dissonance added two decades after Ives had ceased being an active composer,
but a restoration of an important compositional idea that he either
rejected or overlooked prior to the publication of the first edition. This
restoration is also compositionally important since Ives returns to F major
melodic statements of the motive twice on the last page of the movement
(page 19, systems 1 and 4), the last time as a fundamental harmony in the
bass.

Other changes in Ives's handling of the Fifth Symphony motive
postdate the 1919 autograph ink score and consequently were not derived
from either the *Emerson Overture* papers or the "Emerson" sketches. One

---

[24] For a facsimile of the first manuscript page of *"Emerson" Transcription No. 1*
(f4873) see Perlis, *Charles Ives Remembered*, 217.

Example 2.2 Excerpts from "Emerson"
a. second edition (page 16, system 2)
b. *"Emerson" Transcription No. 3*, ed. Brodhead (page 13, systems 1–2)
c. first edition (page 15, systems 3–4)

(a)

(b)

(c)

Example 2.3 Comparison of "Emerson" passages
a. second edition (page 6, system 5 through page 7, system 1)
b. first edition (page 6, system 5)

later revision on page 6, system 5 (shown in Example 2.3), uncharacteristically obscures rather than highlights the motive's rhythmic identity. While Ives retains the minor third drop (from B to G♯) in the second edition, the newly added syncopation makes the later presentation of the motive less articulate and forceful. Perhaps after the blatant assertions of the motive on the second system of this page, Ives opted for understatement here. The antecedents of this passage reveal the strong Beethoven presence rather than the subdued motive in the sketches (1915–19) [f3909] and the autograph ink score (1919) [f3923]. The second *"Emerson" Transcription* likewise maintains the identity of the motive. It is therefore noteworthy that Ives indicates the second edition version of the Fifth Symphony motive on R^7 (formerly R^3), the same copy that contains rudimentary planning stages for all four *"Emerson" Transcriptions*. Was Ives consciously trying to make subtle differences between the *"Emerson" Transcriptions* and his Sonata, or should this discrepancy be viewed as an oversight?[25] Either way, the revision in R^7 suggests that the less direct statement of Beethoven was, like most of the changes adapted from the *"Emerson" Transcriptions*, probably conceived by 1926.

The above examples reveal that Ives had conceived two "new" and structurally important statements of the Fifth Symphony motive by 1919. Other treatments of the motive were entered on revised first edition copies and *"Emerson" Transcription* sources almost certainly before 1926. In fact, Ives appears to have made only one revision involving the Fifth Symphony motive after 1926. It occurs on page 4, systems 4 and 5 and is shown in Example 2.4. By removing the tie and lowering the D to D♭ Ives creates a strong statement of the Fifth Symphony motive – albeit with the descending minor third spelled as an augmented second – where none had existed before.[26]

At first glance a chronology of "Hawthorne" revisions is difficult to determine. Although some sketches compatible with Ives's 1911 dating are

---

25 Other examples of subtle differences between "Emerson" and the second
    "Emerson" Transcription occur in the quintuplet and sextuplet figures on page 6,
    system 2, and the G♮ in the figuration on page 10, system 1, m. 2, which subverts
    the whole-tone scale in both the first and second editions. In treating this latter
    figure in the autograph ink score R^7 and *"Emerson" Transcription No. 2*, Ives
    preserves the integrity of the whole-tone scale with a G♭ in every descending
    pattern.
26 Unfortunately, an *Emerson Overture* sketch for this exact moment is not readily
    observable, and this passage does not appear in the *Four Transcriptions from
    "Emerson."* Since the change remains invisible on the extant revised copies, it
    might be a late decision, perhaps from the early 1940s. In addition to making a
    clear statement of Beethoven, Ives also manages to "jack up" the dissonance level
    slightly with the D♭ against a D to match the F♯ against an F♮ that was retained
    from the first edition.

Example 2.4 Comparison of "Emerson" passages
a. second edition (page 4, systems 4–5)
b. first edition (page 4, systems 4–5)

extant, most are missing.[27] Also, in contrast to the complete autograph ink score of "Emerson," the 1919 autograph ink score of "Hawthorne" contains only a discarded draft that corresponds to page 25 of the second edition, a rough autograph draft with three systems of page 34 (systems 1, 2, and 5), a score of page 21 (and the first two beats of page 22), and a continuous score from page 45 to the conclusion of the movement on page 51.

It was previously noted that the *"Emerson" Transcriptions*, which may have grown "away from Emerson in some places," nevertheless served as the foundation for the second edition of "Emerson" twenty years later. *The*

---

[27] In a "memo" from 1933 Ives put the time frame of *Concord Sonata* as "mostly between 1911 and 1915 (when it was finished)" (*Memos*, 79). In a letter to Kirkpatrick two years later, Ives specified a completion date for "Emerson" ("summer of 1912") and a revised date for "The Alcotts" (1915), and confirmed the dates offered in 1933 for "Hawthorne" and "Thoreau," 1911 and 1915 respectively (see *Memos*, 202).

Celestial Railroad, like the *Transcriptions* also completed by 1926, offers another anchor that firmly places many of the second edition revisions of "Hawthorne" in or before 1926. If changes in the second edition of the *Concord Sonata* are found in *The Celestial Railroad,* it is reasonable to conclude that they followed the first edition closely in time, years before their eventual adoption in the sonata's second edition. The only change in the setting of the Fifth Symphony motive in "Hawthorne," for example, was derived from an analogous place in *The Celestial Railroad.*[28]

Keeping in mind Ives's famous admonition to copyist George Price that "all the wrong notes are right," it is frequently difficult to distinguish Ives's second thoughts from corrections. One representative ambiguous example occurs on the final note of "Hawthorne" in the autograph ink score (f3974 and f7814). Here the note is a C♮ (which forms a diminished octave above the C♯ below), but the natural sign is lined out; in the first edition the note is changed to a perfect octave C♯. Did Ives strike the natural sign to create an octave or did he think an accidental was superfluous to achieve his intentions of a diminished octave? Either interpretation is possible. In any event, on R[4] and R[14] (the latter formerly R[12]), the copies he sent to Gilman and Kirkpatrick, respectively, Ives replaced the sharp sign on the first edition engraving with a natural as on the 1919 autograph ink score before its excision.[29]

---

[28] See page 36, system 3, m. 4, of the second edition.

[29] In 1974 Kirkpatrick recalled a conversation with Ives about an unidentified passage at "the end of 'Hawthorne'" that might cast some light on Ives's intentions for this final "octave":

> I remember one time he had given me photostats of the end of "Hawthorne," and I faced him with an octave which showed up in the manuscript between two A-sharps in the course of the counterpoint; but in the first printing of "*Concord,*" there was A♯ against A♮. I showed him this octave of two sharps in his own hand, and he first tried to say, "Well, that doesn't look like a sharp." I told him, "It looks like this other sharp." He finally burst out, "I couldn't possibly have written that. It makes an octave!"

See *An Ives Celebration: Papers and Panels of the Charles Ives Centennial Festival-Conference,* ed. H. Wiley Hitchcock and Vivian Perlis (Urbana: University of Illinois Press, 1977), 68. In any event Kirkpatrick plays the diminished octave on both his 1945 and 1968 recordings (the former released in 1948 on 78 rpm [Columbia MM-749] and re-released on 33 rpm in 1950 [Columbia ML-4250]; the latter appeared on Columbia MS-7192).

The revised first edition copies (R^1–R^{17}) served as a vehicle in which Ives could explore roads not taken. Although he seemed to encourage performers to interpret his score with some freedom, it is probably misguided to interpret such freedom as a form of indeterminism. Despite her acknowledgment of Ives's considerable attention to detail and his zealous strivings to find more successful musical solutions, Clark, in presenting her comprehensive overview of several hundred variants, nevertheless offers a relativist view.[30] For example, from Ives's suggestions to play "Hawthorne" "as fast as possible and not too literally" (second edition performance notes, 73) and his expressed delight in the "pleasure of not finishing" the "Emerson" movement (*Memos*, 80), Clark concludes that "it would be a gross oversimplification to declare the variants to the sonata written prior to the 1947 publication invalid or even superseded by the 1947 version."[31] More probably Ives is advocating freedom for performers to interpret "marks of tempo, expression, etc." in "Hawthorne" according to their personal vision rather than allowing a return to the first edition or the variants on the first edition copies. Such freedom was the birthright of "romantic" *fin-de-siècle* pianists and the literature they favored.

Ives might have looked sympathetically (if somewhat uncomprehendingly) upon future scholars and performers searching through his revised first edition copies and second edition proofs and perusing sketches for the *Emerson Overture* and the *Concord Sonata* autograph ink score for additional variants and alternatives, or creating their own hybrids of the first and second published editions. The fact remains, however, that the composer himself did in fact make some definite choices and that he made most of them within a few years after distributing the first edition. The most radical changes, including three significant deletions and embellishments in R^7 (e.g., a proposed *deletion* of the dissonant and dense climactic passage

---

[30] While aware that "a sort of paradox is seen in the sources in that Ives often devoted so much attention to minute details and then urged the player to ignore the details in favor of projecting the spirit of the whole," Clark in the end views all revisions as equal, with each possessing only "a momentary validity" (Clark, "The evolving *Concord Sonata*," 346).

[31] Prior to the present essay Clark's "pro-choice" arguments had become the prevailing, if not the only, interpretation of Ives's variants among performers and scholars. See especially Clark, "The element of choice in Ives's *Concord Sonata*," 167–86, quotation on 169.

in "Hawthorne" [page 41, system 5 to page 42, system 2] and an optional "flute" part in "Thoreau" [page 62, system 2] in addition to its eventual arrival near the end of the movement), were not adopted. Concerning the use of "shadow" notes, some of which are derived from the 1919 autograph ink score and others from various revised copies, Ives remained indecisive but for the most part favored their inclusion.

While he may have advocated rhythmic flexibility and freedom of tempo, and may have changed his mind on numerous details on the seven sets of proofs he worked on in the 1940s, the compositional record clearly suggests that Ives was not a proto-Cagean composer imagining indeterminate or improvisatory scores, but a Romantic composer in the nineteenth-century tradition of performance options. After he tried a number of variants, before and after the first edition, he settled on a preferred version for the most part within a few years of the first edition. The second edition is his definitive version and the one we should play.

In addition to the compositional features introduced above, Ives's revision process from the first edition to the second contradicts views such as those espoused by William W. Austin that Ives "is unconcerned about performers' ease or gratification" or with making his music idiomatically effective.[32] The strongest evidence of this concern is found in the performance notes, especially those for the second edition.

Ives placed the first edition notes with the musical text. For the second edition all but one of the performance notes were relegated to the back of the score. Upon consideration, however, Ives decided to abandon his original thought that "some of the marginal notes could be left out or at least cut down somewhat."[33] In the end the eight performance notes of the first edition more than quadrupled to thirty-five in the second.

Ives occasionally uses his performance notes to make new philosophical or spiritual points. The vast number of both the retained and the few discarded notes, however, address specific suggestions to help performers either to negotiate all the musical notes or to fudge a little in order to maintain the speed of a passage. An accomplished pianist himself, Ives was acutely aware of the technical problems his sonata might pose, and strove to

[32] William W. Austin, *Music in the 20th Century: From Debussy through Stravinsky* (New York: Norton, 1966), 59.   [33] See note 9.

help other pianists negotiate its considerable difficulties according to their individual limitations.

Despite their utility for the performer – one example is the alternative to the fiendish right-hand chords in "Emerson" (page 9), where the lower notes in the right hand can be omitted to serve speed as well as Ives's request not to arpeggiate the triads – a number of the performance notes that were keyed to the pagination of second edition proofs for "Emerson," "Hawthorne," and "The Alcotts" were unfortunately omitted. The remnants of a number of these notes appear in the form of dangling non-annotated asterisks in the second edition score. A smaller group of performance endnotes lack a corresponding asterisk in this score. One important unpublished note explains the V marks on page 3, systems 2–4, for which Ives wrote (but did not insert) that "the 3 notes in the V mark on this page are played almost but not quite together, (the lowest first) – a kind of quick accent upwards."[34] Without Ives's unpublished note the interpretation of these marks would remain an unanswered question.[35]

Ives's 1943 recordings of "The Alcotts" and two portions of "Emerson" confirm the view espoused here that the future second edition revisions had firmly taken hold in practice as well as in theory some years prior to their published appearance in 1947.[36] In fact, in his recorded "Emerson" excerpts

[34] Clark, "The evolving *Concord Sonata*," 360. Presumably Ives intended a similar rendition of the *Crusader's Hymn* borrowing on the previous page of the first edition (the four-note chords on p. 2, sys. 5). The performance notes are contained in Ives's literary writings in the Ives Archive at Yale University (Series II, A), Box 24, Folders 6 and 7. They are fully transcribed in Clark, "The evolving *Concord Sonata*," 356–75.

[35] One significant category of revision that does not show up in either edition is Ives's frequent suggestion in the unpublished performance notes to use an "assistant pianist." Despite his predilection for this solution to various technical difficulties, he eventually conceded that "most everyone except the composer – rather resented the idea." For this reason "no memoranda or suggestion as to this 'pinch-hitter' was made in the 1st Editions" (or, for that matter, the second) (Clark, "The evolving *Concord Sonata*," 358). See also Clark, "Ives and the assistant soloist," *Clavier* 13/7 (1974): 17–20.

[36] Many of the changes in the revised copies, for example the concluding moments of the sonata, are prefaced with "I play" this note or that. Ives's 1943 *Concord Sonata* excerpts were released on *Charles Ives: The 100th Anniversary* (Columbia M4 32504) in 1974. Ives's first "Emerson" excerpt begins on page 5, system 3 (last three beats) and concludes before the last two beats on page 6 (just prior to

Ives adheres closely to the second edition passages that were derived from the more orchestral and dissonant versions of the second, third, and fourth *"Emerson" Transcriptions.* He also plays the understated but nonetheless important statement of the Fifth Symphony motive prior to the return of the principal lyric theme on page 16 discussed in Example 2.2.[37]

On several occasions in the late 1960s and early 1970s Kirkpatrick, who rigorously followed the first edition at the 1939 premiere but performed mainly the second edition in his 1945 recording, revealed his reservations about Ives's revisions, without acknowledging that the "stepped-up dissonance" could most frequently be attributed to earlier rather than later ideas.[38] He even concludes the jacket notes to his 1968 recording with the comment that "sometimes, those added touches of his are real touches of genius, but sometimes they are his getting in his own way." Thus, in his second recording Kirkpatrick decided to "use some of the old and some of the new in varying degrees" (but mainly the new), and he would continue to mingle old and new versions in future performances.[39]

The contrasting first and second edition treatments of the Fifth Symphony motive explored in the discussion of Examples 2.1 and 2.2 for example inspired consistent responses in both Kirkpatrick's 1945 and 1968 recordings. In interpreting Example 2.1 Kirkpatrick plays the Fifth Symphony motive as mandated in the future second edition (page 1, system 2). Conversely, he follows the first edition in omitting Beethoven from the Example 2.2 passage (page 16, system 2).[40]

Although in later years he espoused a preference for the first version ("I do often find that Ives's first idea was best"), and his recordings incorporate more of the first edition than those of any other pianist including Ives,

---

Example 2.3); the second excerpt begins on page 14, system 2 (last three beats) and ends before the last beat on the first measure of page 18.

[37] Although he observes the second edition closely in his performance of "The Alcotts," Ives nonetheless demonstrates his characteristic flexibility (or ambivalence) regarding the "shadow notes" by playing the first two (both on p. 55, sys. 1), and omitting the two others (p. 55, sys. 3 and p. 56, sys. 2).

[38] See the jacket notes to Kirkpatrick's 1968 recording (Columbia MS-7192), and reminiscences published in Perlis, *Charles Ives Remembered*, 215, and *An Ives Celebration*, 68.   [39] See *An Ives Celebration*, 68.

[40] Kirkpatrick deletes the motive here from his 1968 recording as well. Most of what he plays in the surrounding area in both recordings, however, is derived from the second edition.

the second edition remained the central text for both of Kirkpatrick's recordings.[41] From the late 1970s to the late 1980s, however, Kirkpatrick turned his predilections into concrete action in a new edition that was left unpublished at the time of his death in 1991.[42] Not only was he now operating under the premise that the first edition corresponded more faithfully to Ives's original intentions, Kirkpatrick took on the quixotic task of capturing the way Ives might have played his sonata for Max Smith in 1912.[43]

It is not my intention to minimize the quantity, complexity, and uniqueness of the problems that confront editors and performers in their efforts to determine a reliable scholarly performing edition of the *Concord Sonata*. Nevertheless, it seems possible to conclude that the sonata's considerable editorial problems are no more insurmountable than those posed by other works from the middle ages to the present. Certainly the quandaries posed by the extant *Concord Sonata* manuscripts can be considered comfortably within a long tradition of problematic compositional processes and editorial issues from which few composers are immune. Again it needs to be emphasized that in contrast, for example, to Hindemith's more radically metamorphosed *Das Marienleben* (first version 1922–23; revision 1936–48), Ives did not repudiate his earlier ideas but returned to them. In fact, his notational changes are arguably less prevalent and less consequential than Stravinsky's 1943 rebarrings and other revisions in the "Danse sacrale" from *Le sacre du printemps* (1913).[44]

The image of Ives playing "Thoreau" from illegible sketches in 1912

---

[41] Quotation from *An Ives Celebration*, 73. On the other hand, even as late as his 1968 recording Kirkpatrick would continue to play all the other notes of the *Martyn* passage as in the *first* edition.

[42] In The John Kirkpatrick Papers, compiled by James B. Sinclair (New Haven CT, November 1993), 359–62, Box 74, Folders 712–15.

[43] *Memos*, 186–87. A particularly striking example of Kirkpatrick's returning to a pre-autograph score stage is his insertion of the overtones in thirds above *Martyn* in "Hawthorne" (2nd edn, p. 34, sys. 2 and 3). The "1912" reconstruction was Kirkpatrick's fourth major editorial plan for the *Concord Sonata* since his 1939 premiere. For a summary of these efforts see The John Kirkpatrick Papers, 359.

[44] See Louis Cyr, "Writing *The Rite* right," in *Confronting Stravinsky*, ed. Jann Pasler (Berkeley, Los Angeles, and London: University of California Press, 1985), 157–73.

(*Memos*, 186–87) is not far removed from the recollections of contemporaries who commented on Beethoven's practice of performing from blank piano parts in his early piano concertos, recollections supported by the vacant staves throughout much of the B♭ major and C minor concerto autographs. Like most of Ives's more daring revisions in the first edition copies (R^1–R^{17}), manuscripts for the B♭ piano concerto contain numerous revisions (the autograph exhibits a readily identifiable contrasting gray ink), nearly all of which Beethoven subsequently abandoned prior to publication.[45] And Ives's decision to return to seemingly discarded ideas at a much later stage in the compositional process has its parallels in prominent passages in many other Beethoven works.

Ives was also by no means the first composer to delay completing revisions or to experience intense regret and ambivalence about finishing a work.[46] Just as Ives's copyist George F. Roberts recalled his easily excitable employer's many changes of mind ("he always had something new to put in"),[47] one hundred years earlier contemporaries remarked that Chopin "alters and retouches the same passages endlessly and paces up and down like a madman."[48] In *The Music of Chopin*, Jim Samson writes that "any attempt to prepare a source-chain for a Chopin piece will involve difficulties at almost every stage, due to the multiplicity of sources, including autographs, and the substantial variation among them."[49] Only recently, Chopin scholars were unable to distinguish between Chopin's copies and those of his copyist Julian Fontana. No one who has seen Ives's

---

[45] See Geoffrey Block, "Some gray areas in the evolution of Beethoven's Piano Concerto in B♭ major, Op. 19," in *Beethoven Essays: Studies in Honor of Elliot Forbes*, ed. Lewis Lockwood and Phyllis Benjamin (Cambridge MA: Harvard University Press, 1984), 108–26, and Barry Cooper, *Beethoven and the Creative Process* (Oxford: Clarendon Press, 1990), 283–303.

[46] For some relevant analogies between Ives and Beethoven on this point see Maynard Solomon, "Beethoven's Ninth Symphony: the sense of an ending," *Critical Inquiry* 17/2 (1991): 289–305.

[47] Perlis, *Charles Ives Remembered*, 186.

[48] Josef Filtsch in *Selected Correspondence of Fryderyk Chopin*, ed. Arthur Hedley (London: Heinemann, 1962), 217; quoted in Jim Samson, *The Music of Chopin* (Oxford: Clarendon Press, 1994), 22.

[49] Samson, *The Music of Chopin*, 2. See also Thomas Higgins, "Whose Chopin?", *19th-Century Music* 5/1 (1981): 67–75.

shaky and sometimes indecipherable handwriting could confuse it with the impeccably neat and steady hand of Roberts.

The problems facing the future editor of a *third* edition of Ives's *Concord Sonata* are indeed daunting, but certainly no more so than those that have tormented and intrigued editors and performers of Bach, Handel, Mozart, Beethoven, Schumann, Chopin, Bruckner, Musorgsky, Verdi, and Gershwin, among many others. The work of Kirkpatrick and Clark has already paved the way for the removal of possible errors.[50] Unfortunately, although it represents Ives's considered afterthoughts about the work, the second edition not only presents new errors of rhythm and pitch and omits performance notes, it fails to distinguish from among the various sources in an accessible yet scholarly way that would benefit future performers and musicologists alike. An edition that addresses and resolves these issues would be most welcome. Such an edition should be based on the second edition, which represents Ives's thinking, arrived at (in most instances) as early as 1926 and maintained through the 1947 publication.

And now to recapitulate. Kirkpatrick's 1939 *Concord Sonata* performance and the depletion of the first edition copies at least seven years earlier created a market and the need for a new edition (or at least a reprinting of the old). The manuscripts reveal that the principal changes to be incorporated into this second edition, eventually published in 1947, were for the most part conceived before the first edition was published in 1920 and executed before 1926. As Harmony Ives indicated in her 1939 letter to Lehman Engel quoted earlier, the primary impetus behind the new edition was the restoration of material from the *Emerson Overture*, abandoned between 1911 and 1914 (and possibly the 1919 autograph ink score of the *Concord Sonata*), mainly as it had been consolidated in the *Four Transcriptions from "Emerson"* (1921–26). Other changes from the revised first edition copies (R^1–R^{17}) entered between 1921 and 1940 would also be adopted, although the most dramatic changes Ives considered in his "sketches" on these copies would not be used.

---

[50] Sinclair, The John Kirkpatrick Papers, 359–62, and Clark, "The evolving *Concord Sonata*," passim.

In addition to restoring previously discarded earlier ideas, Ives in his second edition was motivated to correct errors of pitch and rhythm and to offer more precise notational and other user-friendly performance directions, especially dynamics, indications for right- and left-hand positions, and agogic accents. To help him achieve this latter goal he added numerous and frequently detailed notes offering specific solutions and alternatives to some of the thornier technical problems pianists might face in negotiating and interpreting the work. Especially significant among the many changes of the second edition are those that enhance (and in one case obscure) the Beethoven motive at strategic places, mainly in "Emerson."

The second edition marks a return to the somewhat thicker and consequently more dissonant texture of the *Emerson Overture* and the 1919 autograph ink score. In stark contrast to the belated and gratuitous tone cluster that he added in the late 1940s to conclude the tonal Second Symphony,[51] however, Ives's dissonances in the 1947 second edition of the *Concord Sonata* were for the most part created in close proximity to the first edition. Perhaps more important, the orchestral nature and dissonant level of the changes are congruent and compatible with the almost equally high dissonant and atonal content of the first edition. Even the added left-hand octaves filled in with fifths above and fourths below in "The Alcotts" (page 54, systems 1–2) were derived from the autograph ink score, and the other denser chords added in the left hand in the "fugal" passage in "Emerson" (page 13, systems 4–5), which Kirkpatrick refused to play, support rather than contradict the dissonant norms established in the first edition.[52] In short, Ives's dis-

---

[51] See *Memos*, 155 and J. Peter Burkholder, *Charles Ives: The Ideas Behind the Music* (New Haven and London: Yale University Press, 1985), 145, n. 9.

[52] These chords are analogous to the "power chords" described by Robert Walser in connection with heavy metal. In Walser's description, power chords are "produced by playing the musical interval of a perfect fourth or fifth on a heavily amplified and distorted electric guitar . . . used by all of the bands that are ever called heavy metal and, until heavy metal's enormous influence on other musical genres in the late 1980s, by comparatively few musicians outside the genre." One of these few was Ives, who, although he did not use an amplified and distorted guitar, certainly exhibited a precocious predilection for piano power chords. Robert Walser, *Running with the Devil: Power, Gender, and Madness in Heavy Metal Music* (Hanover and London: Wesleyan University Press, 1993), 2.

sonances in the second edition of his *Concord Sonata* were not added indiscriminately to give the aging composer a cachet with the avant-garde; they represented a remembrance and an embrace of dissonances past.

3   Editing Ives's *129 Songs*

H. WILEY HITCHCOCK

This essay might be titled "Editing Ives's *114 Songs* + 15." Mention of songs by Charles Ives immediately brings to mind the collection of one hundred fourteen that he had privately engraved and printed by the firm of G. Schirmer, Inc., in 1922. I have for some time been occupied by the preparation of critical editions of *114 Songs* – also of thirteen others that were published after the songbook appeared, plus two that were never published. And it is hoped that the whole group of one hundred twenty-nine songs will be published as a unit. Hence my title.

It may be difficult to believe that Ives's book of *114 Songs* has existed for almost three-quarters of a century without a proper editing of *any* kind, critical or otherwise. But that is true, as I will suggest here; I will also explain why I believe a critical edition is badly needed and describe some of the problematic aspects of such an edition. My other aims are to suggest the nature of the sources for Ives's songs, since a critical edition must be based on study of them; to suggest something about Ives's revisions of his songs in the book of *114*, since the revised versions must also be consulted for any proper new edition; and to suggest my reaction, after studying Ives's song revisions, to some criticism of Ives in recent years, relating to his "tinkering" with earlier compositions by way of "jacking up the dissonances" and "silently modernizing" them, and even engaging in a "systematic pattern of falsification" about their dates of composition.

Figure 3.1 illustrates the publication history of Ives's *114 Songs* and others. To summarize: After having had *114 Songs* printed in 1922, a year later Ives had Schirmer reprint fifty of its songs in a smaller volume (Figure 3.1,

51

Figure 3.1 The solo songs of Charles Ives and their publication

A   *114 Songs* (privately engraved and printed for Ives by G. Schirmer [not copyrighted], 1922).
    See also §D.j below.
    a   *50 Songs* (privately printed for Ives by G. Schirmer [not copyrighted], 1923): all repro-
        duced from *114 Songs*, unchanged
B   *7 Songs* (Cos Cob Press, 1932): all reproduced from *114 Songs*, unchanged
C   *New Music* editions, ed. Henry Cowell (San Francisco: New Music Society):
    a   *34 Songs* (1933): 31 from *114 Songs* (3 unchanged, 25 with revisions), 3 new
    b   *18 Songs* [*recte* 19] (1935): 14 from *114 Songs* (4 unchanged, 9 with revisions, 1 with words
        added), 5 new
D   Commercial publications (all reproduced from *114 Songs*, *34 Songs*, or *19 Songs*, except as
    noted):
    a   *4 Songs* (Mercury Music, 1950): all unchanged
    b   *10 Songs* (Peer, 1953): all unchanged
    c   *12 Songs* (Peer, 1954): all unchanged
    d   *14 Songs* (Peer, 1955): all unchanged
    e   *9 Songs* (Peer, 1956): 8 unchanged, 1 revised minimally (but with new words)
    f   *13 Songs* (Peer, 1958): 12 unchanged, 1 new
    g   *[11] Sacred Songs* (Peer, 1961): all unchanged
    h   "Flag Song," "Vote for Names" (Peer, 1968): new (separate songsheets)
    i   *3 Songs* (AMP, 1968): all unchanged
    j   *114 Songs* (AMP, Merion, Peer, 1975): all unchanged (except for added copyright notices)
E   Critical editions by John Kirkpatrick (none previously printed):
    a   *11 Songs and 2 Harmonizations* (AMP, 1968)
    b   "Sunrise," with violin obbligato (C. F. Peters, 1977)
    c   *40 Earlier Songs* (AMP, Merion, Peer, 1993)
F   Critical edition by H. Wiley Hitchcock (all but two previously printed):
    a   *129 Songs* [i.e., *114 Songs* + 15] (AMP, Merion, Peer, forthcoming)

§A.a).[1] In 1932, Aaron Copland sparked the reprinting of seven songs of the
114 that he and the baritone Hubert Linscott had performed earlier that
year, with great success, at the First Festival of Contemporary American
Music, on the "Yaddo" estate near Saratoga Springs, New York (Figure 3.1,
§B). For two collections of Ives songs published in Henry Cowell's *New
Music – 34 Songs* (1933) and *19 Songs* (1935) (Figure 3.1, §C) – Ives revised

---

[1] The *New York Evening Sun* of 29 August 1922 reported that Ives would send a
    copy of *114 Songs* to anyone who requested one. Ives telegraphed and wrote to
    the *Sun* asking that it not print such a report again, saying that "I cannot afford
    to supply a public demand . . . even if this were desirable (for the public!)." He
    also said, however, that in view of the "hundreds" of letters he had received in
    answer to the newspaper notice he might have "some of the songs of more
    general interest" reprinted. This he did, in the form of a collection of *50 Songs*

thirty-four of the *114* (but only a few significantly); the remaining eighty of the *114 Songs* have remained unchanged to this day, even though many were reprinted in small commercial collections, along with a few songs published for the first time (Figure 3.1, §D.a–i). In 1975, an integral reprint of *114 Songs* itself was published, altered only by citation of the copyrights that had been assigned over the years to three American music publishers (Figure 3.1, §D.j).

John Kirkpatrick had by then begun to work at editing (as well as frequently performing) songs by Ives and eventually produced the first critical editions of any of them. None of these, however, were from *114 Songs* (Figure 3.1, §E): *11 Songs and 2 Harmonizations*, "Sunrise," and, posthumously in 1993 (Kirkpatrick died in 1991), *40 Earlier Songs*, revised by James B. Sinclair and with a preface by myself.

To return to the book of *114 Songs*:

Early in 1920, in some notes to himself about "things to be done" during the year, Ives wrote: "Select & correct 25 or 30 songs for printing – also set English words for some of the German [songs] (Oct. or Nov.)."[2] He apparently began such a selection according to plan, and 1921 saw many "corrections" of earlier songs – also a burst of composition of new ones, as well as arrangements as songs of material from earlier chamber, orchestral, and choral compositions. In the spring of that year, Ives negotiated with the firm of G. Schirmer, at the time America's biggest music publisher and the one with the best music engravers and printing plant, to engrave, print, and bind a collection of his songs.[3] Schirmer did the job as work for hire, not as a

---

(*recte* fifty-two, though "Old Home Day" and "The Circus Band" are lacking in some copies). *50 Songs* was reproduced from the plates of *114* (in the order in which the songs had appeared there, including the original page numbers). See *Memos*, 153; and for a transcript of Ives's letter to the *Sun*, see *Essays*, 132–33.

[2] Quoted by Boatwright in *Essays*, 121. The "German [songs]" were primarily ones he had written while at Yale, under the tutelage of Horatio Parker, who often asked his composition students to write new settings of texts already well known in lieder by European masters such as Schubert, Schumann, Brahms, and others.

[3] Ives wrote a note on 24 May 1921 to H. J. Strohm, a Schirmer executive, covering his transmission of "the first instalment of the songs – from No. 2 to No. 6. I haven't decided what to put first." About a year later, Strohm was able to confirm that the engraving was finished and that he understood Ives wished

commercial venture, and the songbook that they printed, bound, and delivered in 1922 to the composer – entitled simply *114 Songs by Charles E. Ives,* with the G. Schirmer firm name nowhere in sight – was neither submitted for copyright nor put up for sale.

My conviction is that G. Schirmer, Inc., having made the deal with Ives and accepted his sheaf of manuscripts, turned to their music engravers and said (in effect), "Here: engrave this stuff. Don't ask any questions. Don't fuss with it. Don't worry about inconsistency in it or illegibility or incomprehensibility. Just do the best you can." The engravers went to work. Proofs were pulled. Oddly, however, among the voluminous sources in the Charles Ives Archive of the Music Library at Yale University, proof-sheets are extant for only one of the *114* Songs (no.19, "The Greatest Man"); one imagines that Ives, excited about finally getting a substantial volume of his songs actually in print, may not have cared about proofs and threw them out – or perhaps told Schirmer not to bother returning them to him.[4] Similar lacunae obtain for a considerable number of the actual manuscripts – that is, the autographs or copyists' copies that Ives must have presented to Schirmer for engraving, especially manuscripts of the songs that Ives enthusiastically composed or arranged in 1921, in his excited activity toward a printed songbook.

For that first printing of *114 Songs,* Ives was effectively his own music editor – and, by definition, an inexperienced and unprofessional one. Not only did he serve as his own music editor, but the character and quality of the printed songbook, though superficially an exquisite job of music engraving, suggest very strongly that Ives's proofreading was extremely skimpy and erratic, as was Schirmer's. The same can be said of the songs by Ives that Cowell issued in the two *New Music* collections: Cowell wielded extremely light *editorial* authority over his publications, and it is clear that

more copies than originally planned: ". . . [I] would advise you that we have changed your order for your 'Song' Book to 1,500 copies – 1,000 to be bound in full cloth; 500 with board cover." (Yale University, Charles Ives Archive, Box 35, Folder 11)

4   It was Schirmer's policy to send corrected proofs, but also to request that they be okayed and sent back: in a letter to Ives of 28 February 1922, Strohm reported that he was forwarding separately revised proofs of songs numbered 2–97 and that "we trust that you will find all the corrections have been made, as noted, and that you will forward the O.K'd proofs to us." (Ives Archive, Box 35, Folder 11)

he left the Ives songs, for the most part, essentially unedited and poorly proofread. The songs Cowell published for the first time were, of course, newly engraved, but those from *114 Songs* were printed from the original plates (altered in the case of those with revisions by Ives – and of a small number of others accorded minimal cosmetic emendations).[5]

Thus most of Ives's songs have never undergone even the regular music-editing process of commercial publication, let alone a critical scholarly editing. For singers, pianists, scholars, students, and listeners alike, they desperately need such editing: though Ives's genius is apparent everywhere, so are idiosyncratic and ambiguous musical notations, puzzling inconsistencies, and textual irregularities, besides a myriad of typographical errors. Virtually every page cries out for revisions. Ives commented, in the so-called "postface" of *114 Songs* (printed at the end of the book, instead of a preface at the beginning), that he had "not written a book at all, [but] merely cleaned house [and put everything] out on the clothes line."[6] One might add that he left it to others to do the ironing and folding (which to this day has not been done).

I have said that virtually every page of *114 Songs* cries out for revision; at least, virtually every page raises questions. One representative page is that of "The Cage," no. 64 of *114 Songs* (Example 3.1). Ives's date of 1906 (at the top left) is open to question: it is probably not the song's date but that of an earlier chamber piece entitled *In the Cage*, from which he arranged the song version. (I shall return to this later.) Let me just tick off other questions that arise from a quick look at the page:

1   What is the tempo? Or does it not matter?
2   Why should the piano's chords be double-stemmed?
3   Why, after the introduction, is there only a single barline (third system,

5   The songs that first saw publication in the *New Music* collections are: (in *34 Songs*) "Soliloquy," "Song for Harvest Season," and "At Parting"; (in *19 Songs*) "General William Booth Enters Into Heaven," "A Farewell to Land," "Requiem," "Aeschylus and Sophocles," and "On the Antipodes." (Also, to the unchanged music of "Tarrant Moss," which lacked words in *114*, Ives added a text of his own invention, titling the "new" song "Slugging a Vampire.") Rounding out the forthcoming collection of *129 Songs* are "They Are There!" (1956; in *9 Songs*), "Abide With Me" (1958; in *13 Songs*), and two songs issued in 1968 as separate songsheets, "Flag Song" and "Vote for Names" – all first published by Peer – plus two unpublished "songs without words."

6   Ives, *114 Songs* (Redding CT: by the author, 1922), unnumbered pp. [261–62]; reprinted with editor's introductory note in *Essays*, 120–31.

before the word "wonder")? And why, since the song is essentially unbarred, is that barline there?

4   Why is there no beaming in the voice part – not even in the last phrase, for the setting of "Is"?

5   After the introductory vamp, just before the voice enters, why is the piano's chord notated in whole notes? (It underlies only five eighth notes in the voice.)

6   In the first system, is not a value dot missing after the middle C in the piano's last chord?

7   In the second system, the piano's second and third chords raise a question: the second chord (in dotted half notes) seems (if we check against the voice part) to be followed by the third chord after only three eighth notes, not three quarters.

8   In the third system, are not both the piano's first chord and its third-from-last chord one eighth note too short? – again, check against the voice part they underlie – or should there be eighth-note rests following them?

9   Also in the third system, the same sort of question arises concerning the big rolled chord: should it have value dots to make it a dotted half note? Or should it be a half note plus a quarter rest?

These are among the many questions that may have arisen – must have arisen – in performers' minds for decades. They may have occurred to Schirmer's music engraver, also – but they evidently were not asked of Ives. Nor, apparently, if Ives was asked them, or if he proofread Schirmer's engraving, did he consider anything amiss.

With a comment such as the last one, we approach an area of great difficulty for an editor of Ives's music: to decide whether a notational "error" or a notational "problem" is in fact an Ivesian leap into the notationally unconventional, unprecedented, unknown, in the interest of achieving his private vision.[7]

---

[7] One thinks immediately of the oft-quoted note Ives wrote to his copyist George Price on the manuscript score-sketch of "The Fourth of July": "Mr. Price: Please don't try to make things nice! All the wrong notes are *right*. Just copy as I have – I want it that way." Quoted in *JKCat*, 11. (As is well known, for Ives "nice" was a damning epithet implying pussyfooting, conventional, proper, even cowardly.)

    Ives fulminated elsewhere against Price's editorial intrusions: "Price never made a mistake! What mistakes he made were yours. If he thought you had put down the wrong note, he would put it *right* (right or wrong), and blame you when you had the audacity to say that, not every time there's a C natural, all C sharps that happen on the same beat in the chord should be scrapped. . . . I know many Prices" (*Memos*, 65).

Example 3.1 "The Cage." *114 Songs*, no. 64

NOTE:- All notes not marked with sharp or flat are natural.

Example 3.2 "The World's Highway," piano only, mm. 3–4, 11–12, 45–46
(*114 Songs*, no. 90)

Let me suggest a few such Ivesian notational "problems" that show up in his songs.

One of the most common is inconsistency and illogic of *phrase-slurs*. These would seem to arise from copyists' and/or engravers' overly punctilious reproduction of the merely suggestive – not to imply careless or slipshod – slurs in the manuscripts they were given by Ives. A typical instance is shown in Example 3.2, which reproduces the piano accompaniment of "The World's Highway" (*114 Songs*, no. 90) in three statements of the same cadential phrase. Every one is phrased differently, as they are also in both Ives's pencil sketch and his ink copy – the former dashed off rapidly and, not unexpectedly, lacking in precision, the latter closer to a fair copy but still with many details only suggested or implied. These suggestions or implications would surely have prompted a music editor to make queries of the composer, if not to carry out the composer's apparent wishes carefully and consistently. (But, as I am at pains to emphasize, Ives's songs never had such an editor.)[8]

Example 3.3 illustrates Ives's practice of what might be called *double notation*. Example 3.3a greets one on the very first page of *114 Songs*, near the beginning of "Majority." The boxed cluster-chords are striking enough, but the second one, double-notated as both half and quarter notes, is doubly striking – and problematic. Example 3.3b, the end of "Premonitions" (*114 Songs*, no. 24), is barred as if in 4/4 followed by 5/4 (see the voice part), though there are no meter signatures; both hands of the piano part are double-notated, again in half and quarter notes, as they are also in Example 3.3c, from the end of "Afterglow" (*114 Songs*, no. 39). Example 3.3d, the conclusion of "Immortality" (*114 Songs*, no. 5), is slightly different: again unbarred, but in 4/4 (at least in the voice and the piano's left-hand parts); but the right hand has half notes moving in synchrony with the quarter notes above and below. Since in some songs Ives included notations for sostenuto pedaling and could have done so here, he must have had some other reason for the contradictory voice and right-hand rhythmic notation.

In fact, Ives himself once offered one, in a discussion of the *Concord Sonata*:

> These longer notes on the lesser beats, of course, are helped by the pedal, but ped . . . .* underneath [i.e., indicated thus beneath the piano part] is a

---

[8] Even greater illogic obtains in the piano part of the tiny song "Remembrance" (*114 Songs*, no.12), which until the very end consists only of arching arpeggios of even eighth notes. One attempts in vain to rationalize their phrasing as printed (and no manuscript of the song is extant). Fortunately, in one of his copies of *114 Songs*, Ives annotated "Remembrance" – mostly just with indications for a possible orchestration of it, but beneath the piano part he showed how he wished its phrases to go, by marking the number of eighth notes each should cover: 8, 10, 6, 10, 11, 3, and 8, a phrasing that makes perfect sense. His intention was honored (in the 1930s or later) by a copyist hired by Ives to make a fair ink copy of *The Pond* – the "parent" piece from which "Remembrance" derived, with piano arpeggios exactly the same as those Ives corrected in the printed song.

Example 3.3 Ives's "double notation"

a. "Majority," page 1, system 4. *114 Songs*, no. 1
b. "Premonitions," last two measures. *114 Songs*, no. 24
c. "Afterglow," last system. *114 Songs*, no. 39
d. "Immortality," last four measures. *114 Songs*, no. 5

(a)

(b)

(c)

(d)

Example 3.4 "Shadow parts" in "So May It Be!" or "The Rainbow." *114 Songs*, no. 8

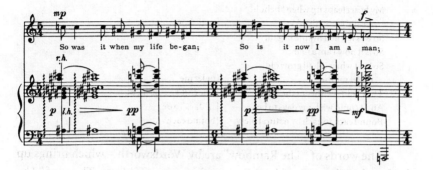

poor substitute for what I had in mind—(that is, what Emerson, Thoreau, etc. had in mind, and what I tried to get out of my system in "tones" or in "sounds" if you like—call it music or not, it makes no difference)—and then the pedal, unless used in long or whole-phrase passages, when lifted, stops the thought-sounds, which ought to be thought of [as] continuing to their natural ends. So to write them, usually the more fundamental themes, somewhat in this way is nearer to what the music (?) should be to the ear and the in-mind than the limited but more conventional (more proper) way.[9]

Ives used the term "shadow parts" to describe one aspect of his Third Symphony: "the final score, now lost, had (I think) a few of the off shadow parts in, and also church bells, crossed out in the old score" (*Memos*, 55). He was referring to barely audible parts co-existing with other, different, more prominent ones.[10] The piano part of Example 3.4 ("So May It Be!" or "The Rainbow" [*114 Songs*, no. 8, mm. 8–9]) is probably an instance of this – the *pianissimo* chords in each measure floating in above the preceding whole-note chords – though the notation perhaps does not make this as clear as it might. The passage reminds us of one of the problematic moments we noted in "The Cage" (see Example 3.1): the second and third piano chords in the second system. Is the third chord a "shadow chord," floating in on top of the second one?

---

9 *Memos*, 189; the bracketed interpolations are mine.
10 See the critical edition by Kenneth Singleton of Ives's Third Symphony (New York: Associated Music Publishers, 1990), especially iv and ix.

Figure 3.2 Text comparison for "The Rainbow"

Wordsworth:	[Ives:
My heart leaps up when I behold	
A rainbow in the sky:	[a rainbow…
So was it when my life began;	
So is it now I am a man;	
So be it when I shall grow old,	
Or let me die!	[or let me…
The Child is father of the Man;	[The child…the man;
And I could wish my days to be	[…days To be
Bound each to each by natural piety	[bound each…

The words of "The Rainbow" are by Wordsworth – which brings up the fact that the *texts* of Ives's songs often raise problems. Those of "The Rainbow" are minimal – orthographic only – if we compare the text as printed in *114 Songs* with the text of a good critical edition of Wordsworth (see Figure 3.2).[11] But what are we to do about "Evening" (*114 Songs*, no. 2), a setting by Ives of a few lines of Milton's *Paradise Lost*? Mostly, Ives's textual variants from Milton are insignificant (see Figure 3.3). He may have borrowed from a slightly corrupt version – reading, in line 9, for example, "but the…nightingale" instead of "all but…the nightingale."[12] And in the last line, perhaps he used "is" instead of Milton's "was" for the same reason (or inadvertently) – but might he have had a private and purposeful reason for doing so?[13]

A few comments about "critical editions" are perhaps in order. One of the most succinct definitions is that of Don Cook, editor of a critical edition of the writings of William Dean Howells, who has written:

11 *The Poetical Works of William Wordsworth*, ed. E. De Selincourt (Oxford: Clarendon Press, 1940), I, 226 (untitled; headed only "[Composed March 26, 1802. – Published 1807.]").

12 John Milton, *Paradise Lost: An Authoritative Text*, ed. Scott Elledge (New York: Norton, 1975), book IV, lines 598–604.

13 One possibility, perhaps far-fetched: the book of *114 Songs* is basically organized as a retrospective collection, working back from the songs most recently composed to the earliest, "Slow March" (no.114) of ?1887. "Evening" was to have been first (see *Memos*, 127), implying it was the last song Ives had composed up to that time. Is Ives suggesting himself as the "nightingale" who has sung "all night long" but is now silent – now (in the present) pleasing Silence?

Figure 3.3 Text comparison for "Evening"

Milton:	[Ives:
Now came still Evening on,	
and Twilight gray	
had in her sober livery	
all things clad;	
Silence accompanied;	
for the beast and bird,	
They to their grassy couch,	
these to their nests were slunk,	
all but the wakeful nightingale;	[but the...
She all night long	[...all night long, all night long
her amorous descant sung;	
Silence was pleas'd.	[...is pleased.

The critical edition aims to present a text that reflects the intention of the author at a chosen moment. . . . Those setting out to produce critical editions must be very circumspect, attempting at all times to adhere to the author's intention so far as it is recoverable, recording fully the evidence on which the editorial decisions are made. . . . Other reasonable scholars examining the same evidence might arrive at other interpretations and conclusions. . . . But the established text [– the critical edition –] rests on the editor's conscientious interpretation of all the discoverable evidence, supported by cogent argument. That, and only that, is what critical edition means.[14]

Cook's comment about "other reasonable scholars [who] might arrive at other interpretations" reminds one of Richard Taruskin's remarks about the paradoxically *interpretive* nature of critical editing:

I am . . . more aware than I have ever been of the irreducibly *sui generis* nature of editorial problems, ergo the necessarily provisional and tentative nature of all editorial precepts, and hence . . . the necessarily personal nature of editorial decisions. . . . For editing is interpretation. Period.[15]

---

[14] Don Cook, "Preparing scholarly editions," *Humanities* [periodical of the National Endowment for the Humanities] 9/3 (1988): 14–17.

[15] From Taruskin's review of John Caldwell's *Editing Early Music* (1985) in *Notes* 42/4 (1986): 775–79. Other thoughtful writings on the aims and limits of critical editing are those of Howard Mayer Brown, "Editing," in *The New Grove Dictionary of Music and Musicians,* and Harold E. Samuel, "Editions, historical," in *The New Harvard Dictionary of Music.*

(I say "paradoxically interpretive" since of course one primary goal of critical editing is for editors not to interpret – that is, *not* to inject their own personalities into the music – not, in sum, to assume they know more than the composer.)

Getting at all the *sources* of a work is the first step toward a critical edition of it. What kinds of sources do we have for the songs of Ives? They differ in quantity and quality from song to song – but they are more extensive and numerous than is generally realized. There are *direct* and *indirect* sources for the music, and similar sources for the texts.

The direct musical sources include:

1   manuscripts by Ives, ranging from preliminary sketches to final complete scores – his characteristic practice being to make pencil sketches, then a more or less clean ink score, followed often by second or later thoughts, embodied in manuscript "patches" (John Kirkpatrick's term) with revisions of details;
2   fair ink copies by one or more of the many professional music copyists whom Ives employed from the late 1890s on;
3   the published versions of songs, and any revised reprints of them;
4   proofsheets toward those publications with markings by Ives (although, as mentioned, there are proofsheets toward only one of the *114 Songs*, and, though proofsheets survive for eleven of the *19 Songs*, none are extant for the *34 Songs*);
5   eight copies of *114 Songs* that were in Ives's possession, in which he jotted indications for corrections or changes, and a few copies of *34 Songs* and *19 Songs* with similar indications by Ives himself. These are what we might call "pseudo-sources" – sources that postdate the works involved – which sounds oxymoronic, but, as we have seen (with the piano's phrase-slurs in "Remembrance"), such pseudo-sources can indeed be helpful, and valid.

For some songs there are also indirect musical sources, such as manuscripts or copyists' copies (or, for that matter, publications) of instrumental or vocal works by Ives that he *arranged as songs*. These can be very important in the editorial process, as we shall see.

For the song texts there are also direct sources, of different kinds – primarily published poetry (or other printed sources from which Ives got song texts, especially newspapers and magazines) and a few manuscripts (besides, of course, Ives's own, some forty lyrics of his invention), especially of poems by his wife Harmony Twichell, eight of which Ives set and in at least two of which they collaborated. Indirect textual sources might include good modern critical editions of published authors, even though Ives may have used others, some now considered corrupt.

Let us return to "The Cage" again (many questions were left unanswered).

For "The Cage" we have no direct sources, only the *114 Songs* printing. But there are two indirect sources, a fragmentary pencil sketch and a complete pencil-and-ink score-sketch for *In the Cage*, the chamber piece mentioned earlier as the "parent piece" for the song version. The one-page score-sketch, dated at the bottom left (with other information) "July 28[?] 1906," is shown as Plate 3.1.

Although many details are illegible in a reduced photoreproduction of the sketch – a palimpsest with strike-outs and over-writings in both pencil and ink – enough are visible to make clear how this source can help to answer some of the questions we asked of the *114 Songs* arrangement.

The song (see Example 3.1) lacks a tempo indication. The score-sketch for *In the Cage* has one: $\quarternote=72$, perhaps 80.[16]

The song has only one barline (after the introduction) and no meter signatures. The chamber piece has both barring and signatures (though added belatedly). They are helpful in several ways. But should we meter and bar the song? No. In the first place, as implied by a note of Ives on the score-sketch, the chamber piece's barring was an expedient to help the players to keep together ("This was not divided into measures, but if parts are copied measures may be made as per dotted [bar]lines").[17] Secondly, to adopt Ives's barring would mislead the singer badly. She or he must obviously *declaim*, not in recitative-like rhythmic freedom but shaping the declamation according to the natural accentuation and grammatical structure of

---

[16] Ives decided later, when the chamber-music piece was printed as the first movement of *A Set of Pieces for Theater or Chamber Orchestra* (*New Music* 5/2 [1932]), on a slower tempo of $\quarternote=60$.

[17] The published *New Music* score of *In the Cage* includes, however, both meter signatures and barring – perhaps, though, only as a concession to conductors who, since the score was not accompanied by parts, would have to extract their own parts. And the barring is not felicitous: as John Kirkpatrick put it in an annotation of *Memos* (37), "in the orchestra score, Ives perpetrated an unnecessary metrical difficulty, putting the barlines with the string chords, which are mostly syncopated against the more stable meter of the melody."

Plate 3.1 *In the Cage* (score-sketch)

the song text, which is not by any means a lyric poem but a prose vignette in vernacular speech. More important than these considerations, perhaps, is Ives's conscious, purposeful avoidance of regular barring and meters in the song, as in a number of others. A footnote he added in "August" (*114 Songs*, no.35) includes the following illuminating clause concerning these: "In this and other songs . . . bars mark the phrase[s] or sections instead of measures." An editor ought to honor Ives's intention here, as in other similar meterless and/or barless compositions.[18]

[18] On the other hand, Ives was (as so often) not fixed in his own mind about his intentions. In a footnote to "December" (*114 Songs*, no.37), he invites barring if the performer wishes: "Measures may be marked off to suit the taste." (Oddly, the footnote was not retained in the revised version of "December" in *34 Songs*.)

The score-sketch of *In the Cage* also helps correct one out-and-out error (probably the engraver's) in the rhythm of the piano introduction to "The Cage": the sketch confirms Ives's intention to build, preceding the final whole note, a quasi-serial progression of ever-shorter chords – half note, dotted quarter note, quarter note, dotted eighth note, eighth note, and *sixteenth* note (not, as printed, a second eighth note). Other problematic rhythmic matters are also clarified, to some degree, by the orchestral score:

1   The chord following the introductory vamp is represented in the score as a half note tied to an eighth. This suggests that the song's whole-note chord is not to last beyond the five eighths of "A leopard went" – but also that Ives's whole-note notation of it may have some special meaning (to which I shall return in a moment).

2   The middle C in the piano's first-system last chord should have a value dot (the lack of it was certainly an engraver's error, as one imagined even without the score-sketch's confirmation).

3   In the song's third system, the piano's first, second, and third-from-last chords are all too short by one eighth note, compared to the score-sketch.

Not all the rhythmic problems of "The Cage," however, can be solved from the orchestral sketch of *In the Cage*. For one thing, in the song's second system, the second and third piano chords are both represented in the sketch as dotted quarters. For another, the big rolled piano chord in the third system

And in a copy of *114 Songs* now in the Moldenhauer Collection of the Music Division at the Library of Congress, in "from 'Swimmers'" (no.27) Ives penned barlines (among other things in his hand) from the fifth system on.

Among the *114 Songs* the following lack, wholly or in large part, both meter signatures and barlines: "Religion" (no.16), "Grantchester" (no.17), "Luck and Work" (no.21), "Premonitions" (no.24), "Like a Sick Eagle" (no.26), "from 'Swimmers'" (no.27), "from 'Paracelsus'" (no.30), "August" (no.35), "September" (no.36), "Afterglow" (no.39), "The Innate" (no.40), "Thoreau" (no.48), and "The Cage" (no.64). The following are barred but lack signatures: "Immortality" (no.5), "Ann Street" (no.25), "The Things Our Fathers Loved" (no.43), "Tom Sails Away" (no.51), and "Old Home Day" (no.52, first section). Songs that are significantly meterless and/or barless, arranged by Ives from earlier choral works that are metered and/or barred, include "Majority" (no.1), "from 'Lincoln, the Great Commoner'" (no.11), "Nov. 2, 1920" (no.22), and "December" (no.37). These suggest a different editorial approach: to leave them as is but to indicate editorially the "parent" works' meters and barlines with meter signatures above the voice staff, and barlines with vertical ticks above the voice and below the piano's left-hand staves.

67

Example 3.5 Excerpt from "The Cage," 1932 printing

is represented in the sketch in whole notes (and lengthy *laissez-vibrer* ties extending from each pitch, which raise *new* questions). And the pitch content of that chord in the score-sketch differs from that in the song's chord: the sketch has a G♯ not in the song, and a d and f♯ (not the song's d♯ and f♮).

Two other sources can help with some of these editorial problems. Both are "pseudo-sources" for "The Cage," postdating the song. One is the score of *In the Cage* published in 1932; it is quite faithful to the 1906 score-sketch (though it omits the text), and it was presumably approved and even possibly (though improbably) written out initially by Ives, so we may use it as a sort of check against the song. The other is a new printing of "The Cage," prepared as a separate insert tucked in as a bonus with the *New Music* orchestral score. The song's second-system second and third chords are clarified in both: the third chord is indeed a "shadow chord" intended as floating in around the second, and both are to last until the *third* chord in that system; Example 3.5 shows the passage as printed in the revised edition of "The Cage."[19] (The revised song edition also adds value-dots to the big rolled chord in the third system.)

The indirect source and the "pseudo-sources" for "The Cage" – the parent piece and the two scores that postdate the *114 Songs* version – thus help in the editorial process toward a critical edition of the song . . . but problems still remain. One has to do with the pitch content of the big rolled piano chord in the piece. The chord is different in each of the four available

---

[19] In the score of *In the Cage*, Ives revised his sketch by dividing the strings here, one half of them sounding the first chord as a dotted half, the other as a dotted quarter followed by the "shadow-chord" as a second dotted quarter.

Example 3.6 "The Cage Chord"

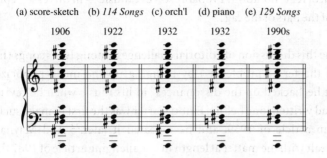

(a) score-sketch   (b) *114 Songs*   (c) orch'l   (d) piano   (e) *129 Songs*

1906   1922   1932   1932   1990s

sources, as shown in Example 3.6. Here, perhaps only careful music analysis can help one to make a defensible editorial decision.[20]

Other aspects of "The Cage" that raise editorial questions, even if they are not "problematic" in the same way as those matters just discussed, are the double-stemming of the piano chords and irrational length of some of them – perhaps also the non-beaming of the two eighth notes setting the word "Is" toward the end. Looking at the *114 Songs* print of the song (see Example 3.1), one cannot help noticing the emphatic *verticality* of the score. There are hardly any contradictions – hardly any typographical usage of horizontals or diagonals or arched slurs – only the tied notes setting "stopped" and the "-der" of "wonder, and two inconspicuous slurs – the one linking the two eighths setting "Is" and the one (with staccato dots) over the last two piano chords. This verticality is of course intensified by the double-stemming of the piano chords (which technically could of course be single-stemmed, the right hand chords stemmed separate from the left hand's). Also, to "correct" the first (vertical) piano chord after the introduction, one would have to notate it in half notes with five (horizontal) ties to eighth notes, as one would similarly have to "correct" the first and third-from-last piano chords in the third system with multiple (horizontal) ties to eighth-note chords. But to single-stem the piano chords and rationalize the durations of all of them with added chords-with-ties-to-other chords would be to destroy one of the most strikingly unique, "Ivesian" aspects of the page, its extraordinary verticality – and an editor had better tread very lightly in

---

[20] Mine is shown in Example 3.6e; Philip Lambert helped me arrive at it (letter of 6 August 1992).

order *not* to destroy this aspect of it. Was Ives after something special here, with his "incorrect" notation? Probably so: "eye music" – in this case, representation of the bars of the cage.[21]

Let me close this discussion of editorial challenges among Ives's songs (not to overuse the term "problems") by bringing up the much-publicized claims that he "jacked up the dissonances" in his music when he revised works he had written long before. Elliott Carter was the first to make such a claim, in an article of 1939, and he repeated it later.[22] And Maynard Solomon dealt with the matter at length in a challenging article of 1987 that even questioned Ives's "veracity."[23] Solomon's hypothesis was that Ives, by "silently modernizing" works – not only by jacking up their level of dissonance but by pre-dating them – staked a claim to modernity that was not

[21] J. Peter Burkholder introduced me to this possibility (letter of 14 December 1993). Another song in which Ives surely intended the *look* of the music (as well as its overall sonorities) to be meaningful is "A Farewell to Land," first published in *19 Songs* (no.[2] in the *New Music* printing; no.[3] in the Merion Music reprint): both the voice and the piano gradually traverse an immense distance notationally, from high to low (the voice from $g\flat^2$ to $g\sharp$; the piano from c^5 – requiring nine ledger lines above the staff – to AAA – requiring six below). This must be Ives's representation of the text's "sun that sets[, which] We follow in his flight." To simplify reading the music by editing it with *8va bassa* or *alta* indications is unthinkable. (Similarly resistant to editorial intervention is the last vocal phrase of the song "Maple Leaves" [*114 Songs*, no.23]: each of the even eighth notes setting the phrase "Like coins between a dying miser's fingers" is flagged, and to beam them would be to destroy completely the imagery probably understood by Ives – of falling leaves, or a handful of coins dropping.)

[22] In "The case of Mr. Ives," *Modern Music* 16 (March–April 1939): 172–76, Carter put it this way: "The fuss that critics make about Ives's innovations is, I think, greatly exaggerated, for he has rewritten his works so many times, adding dissonances and polyrhythms, that it is probably impossible to tell just at what date the works assumed the surprising form we now know." In Vivian Perlis, *Charles Ives Remembered: An Oral History* (New Haven: Yale University Press, 1974; repr. New York: Norton, 1976), 131–45, citing an experience he had on one visit to Ives, Carter reported that he found the composer working at a revision of *Three Places in New England* (perhaps for its 1931 premiere by the Boston Chamber Orchestra under Nicolas Slonimsky) and that Ives "was adding and changing, turning octaves into sevenths and ninths, and adding dissonant notes. . . . I got the impression that he might have frequently jacked up the level of dissonance of many works as his taste changed."

[23] "Charles Ives: some questions of veracity," *Journal of the American Musicological Society* 40/3 (1987): 443–70.

only untrue but was based on what Solomon suggested might be "a systematic pattern of falsification."

My work with songs of Ives and his revisions of them has not borne out Solomon's hypothesis, and I shall suggest, in discussing two songs, that other impulses, not attempts at "modernization" or "falsification," motivated Ives's revisions.

One of these is "Tolerance" (*114 Songs*, no. 59). In the songbook Ives dated "Tolerance" 1909, but in a footnote he explained – with total honesty – "(Adapted, from a piece for orchestra, to the above words, 1921)." As is true of "The Cage," the date Ives gave for "Tolerance" was his recollection of the compositional date of the "piece for orchestra" that he later "adapted" as a song. The parent piece was *A Lecture*, a miniature twenty-five measures long, the last twelve of which Ives arranged as "Tolerance."

We have no direct source manuscript toward the song adaptation, and only one indirect source – a sketch of 1907 or 1908 for *A Lecture*. The other source materials for the song include the *114 Songs* version of 1922; one of Ives's copies of *114 Songs* in which, in the early 1930s, he marked changes he wished made in it toward the *New Music* revision; and the song as printed in *34 Songs* in 1933. Example 3.7 shows the piano part of the ending of the song (mm. 10–12) in those three sources. The *34 Songs* version of 1933, honoring Ives's requests for revisions, is obviously more dissonant than the *114 Songs* version of 1922.

The next example (Example 3.8) suggests why Ives wanted the changes made in "Tolerance." It is a diplomatic transcription of the relevant measures of the strings in *A Lecture* (sketched twelve or thirteen years earlier than its adaptation as the song). Ives's aim here was to make the song closer to the original piece, not to "jack up the dissonance" or to "silently modernize" the music, as is clear from a comparison of Example 3.8 with Examples 3.7a and 3.7c. The revision reinstates material from *A Lecture* that Ives had simplified out of the piece when he arranged it as a song. Ives confirmed his intention in a letter to Herman Langinger, the engraver of *34 Songs*, dated 3 April 1935 (written by Ives's wife but signed by Ives, in the shaky hand he called his "snake tracks"). Addressed to Langinger at his Golden West Music Press in San Francisco, the letter begins:

Example 3.7 Different versions of "Tolerance," mm. 10–12, piano
a. *114 Songs*, no. 59
b. Ives's corrections toward *34 Songs* (made on a copy of *114 Songs*)
c. *34 Songs* (p. 38)

(a)

(b)

(c)

Example 3.8 *A Lecture* (1907–8), mm. 14–21, strings

My dear Mr. Langinger—
Thank you for your letter. As you suggest I will go over the manuscript
(photostat copy) and make the corrections. . . . The other songs will need
but few, if any, corrections – except in those which were arranged from
scores. In a few measures of these it seems that more of the orchestral parts,
which were left out in the old plates [of *114 Songs*,] should go in.[24]

Ives handled similarly the revision of another piece – derived, like
"The Cage" and "Tolerance," from an earlier chamber composition, that
enjoyed a second incarnation as one of the *114 Songs*. That is "Like a Sick
Eagle" (no.26), setting a fragment from Keats. The earliest source we have

24 Yale University, Ives Archive. My thanks to Vivian Perlis for calling my attention
to the Ives–Langinger correspondence, copies of which she acquired for deposit
in the Ives Archive. Langinger had produced the extraordinarily beautiful
engraving of the phenomenally complex second movement of Ives's Fourth
Symphony published as *New Music* 2/2 (1929), reprinted (with ugly handwritten
alterations and additions) as part of the "performance score" of the entire
symphony (New York: Associated Music Publishers, 1965). He is discussed in
Vivian Perlis, *Two Men for Modern Music: E. Robert Schmitz and Herman
Langinger*, I.S.A.M. Monographs No. 9 (Brooklyn: Institute for Studies in
American Music, 1978).

for this song is an indirect one, a pencil sketch toward the chamber version – one of Ives's "songs with or without words." That sketch, datable to 1909, is virtually illegible in reduced reproduction, but a fair ink copy made by George Roberts (much later, in the 1930s) is faithful to it. Example 3.9a shows the beginning of the Roberts copy. Ives explains the plus-signs above the violin and voice parts in a footnote (not seen in the example): "The + + over and between notes mean that between 1/2 tones a slide through a 1/4 tone may be made, and between whole [tones a slide] through a 1/3 tone. This, done in a certain way, gives a more desolate sound." Example 3.9b shows the beginning of the *114 Songs* arrangement (dated 1920 by Ives) in one of Ives's copies of the songbook, in which he had marked the song for revisions toward republication in *34 Songs*.

Ives's marginalia on the *114 Songs* page, probably addressed to an engraver, reads as follows: in the left margin, "F♮/♯ out"; in the right margin, with lines drawn to bass notes in the piano's lower staff, "The Basso held these notes, so it may be well to write them as 𝅗𝅥 or 𝅘𝅥𝅭 notes etc." An inscription at lower left (on a part of the page not shown in the example, but referring to the circled X above the first note in the piano's upper staff), reads: "This part in the score was played by a violin, & a slide down or up through a quarter tone [was made] in a semi tone interval and by 2 third tones in a whole tone, except between the last 5 notes [of the part]." (Ives's past tenses – "The Basso held"; "This part . . . was played" – are referring, of course, to the chamber-music version, the one of 1909, seen in Example 3.9a.)

Example 3.10 shows the beginning of "Like a Sick Eagle" in the *34 Songs* version. Ives's requests for revisions of the *114 Songs* version were honored: the low notes of the piano's left hand have been made more precise rhythmically as pedal tones, and accents have been added to them, so they clash more dissonantly with the other material than in the *114 Songs* version; also, the first F of the piano's right hand has been changed from F♯ to F♮ (as has the same F a few notes later) – creating, of course, the more "modernistic" augmented-octave leap. And so on, including incorporation, as a footnote, of Ives's comment about microtonal performance of the treble instrumental part, with the added remark that "The voice may do similarly" (as indicated some twenty-five years earlier by plus signs in the voice part of the chamber score).

Example 3.9 "Like a Sick Eagle," beginning
a. copyist's copy
b. Ives's corrections, on a copy of *114 Songs*, toward *34 Songs*

(a)

(b)

As is obvious, there are many questions involved in editing Ives's *129 Songs*
– questions raised by the songs themselves in sources and prints alike,
questions that must be asked, and answered conscientiously, by an editor
of a critical edition. The ultimate questions are: In revised versions of
songs such as "Tolerance" and "Like a Sick Eagle" are we confronting an
Ives "tinkering" with an earlier piece? Yes. "Jacking up the dissonances" in

Example 3.10 "Like a Sick Eagle," beginning. *34 Songs*, p. 57

it? Yes. "Silently modernizing" his music? Not at all: we are confronting a composer who is restoring in the 1930s details of his original scores of the 1900s, having decided that his arrangements of them in the 1920s had unnecessarily simplified and weakened them. It seems to me that the answers to *these* questions reveal a case, not of mendacity, but precisely one of "veracity."

4 Redating Ives's choral sources

GAYLE SHERWOOD

In the four decades since Charles Ives's death, scholars, performers, and publishers have worked to secure a distinguished place for him in American culture. Certainly the foremost scholar was John Kirkpatrick, whose 1960 catalogue of the Ives manuscripts (*JKCat*) is the cornerstone of scholarship in the field. The following study is intended to supplement Kirkpatrick's work by suggesting alternative means of dating Ives's manuscripts.

In his 1987 article "Charles Ives: some questions of veracity" and his 1989 reply to Philip Lambert, Maynard Solomon questioned the accuracy of Ives's datings in light of inconsistencies and contradictions.[1] However, as demonstrated in my earlier essay "Questions and veracities: reassessing the chronology of Ives's choral works," many of the apparent contradictions are a result of the limitations of the sources of the established chronology.[2] This chronology was originally presented in Kirkpatrick's 1960 catalogue and was maintained in his subsequent unpublished revisions to that catalogue.

The purposes of this essay are threefold: to review the sources of the established chronology, to outline the supplemental dating method, and to summarize the application of this data to Ives's choral works.

Introduction: the original chronology[3]

Kirkpatrick's chronology was established using three types of evidence: Ives's early letters and diaries, his lists of works, and manuscript

---

[1] Maynard Solomon, "Charles Ives: some questions of veracity," *Journal of the American Musicological Society* 40/3 (1987): 443–70; reply to Philip Lambert, *Journal of the American Musicological Society* 42/1 (1989): 209–18.

[2] Gayle Sherwood, "Questions and veracities: reassessing the chronology of Ives's choral works," *The Musical Quarterly* 78/3 (1994): 429–47.

[3] The following discussion summarizes material from Sherwood, "Questions and veracities."

marginalia. Because of the challenges to the chronology, each of these sources must be re-evaluated.

The letters and diaries date from 1886 to 1895, and contain valuable biographical information. Between 1886 and 1891, Ives sporadically recorded personal and musical events in two separate diaries.[4] The earliest diary dates from 1886, and was reused in 1889 to record such diverse events as the first game of Ives's baseball team and his first Sunday as organist at the Baptist Church in Danbury. The subsequent diary records most of the musical programs for the Baptist Church to 11 October 1891 and information about Ives's thirty-six organ lessons with Alexander Gibson between 22 October 1889 and 4 November 1890. Kirkpatrick used this material for biographical purposes, along with numerous letters from Ives to his family spanning the summers of 1880, 1881, 1886, 1889, and 1890, plus the first year and a half of Ives's period in New Haven, from 18 April 1893 to 29 October 1894.[5]

A few references to Ives's musical compositions and their performances are found in the diaries and letters. For example, the second diary lists two performances of Ives's *Holiday Quickstep* (arranged for organ) in Danbury's Baptist Church on 25 May and 15 June 1890.[6] But for the most part, these contemporary accounts include very few direct references to specific pieces. Although key sources for his early life, the fragmentary, short-term, and musically insubstantial nature of the diaries and letters diminishes their value as a dating tool.

Kirkpatrick's remaining sources are both potentially unreliable. Ives's typed or handwritten lists were prepared between c. 1929 and 1949. For these later sources, Ives's steady mental deterioration during this period is the primary concern. A member of his own family, his nephew Walter Bigelow Ives, once commented on the "senility [that] took its toll in [Ives's] last several years."[7] A more thorough examination of Ives's mental

---

[4] The following information is taken from *JKCat*, vii, and *Memos*, 325–37.

[5] Two other letters from Ives to his mother survive, dated 1895, but these make no significant mention of his music.

[6] Kirkpatrick also proposed that a minimum of three more original works were performed within the two-year period from 1889 to 1891, by interpreting diary entries for 21 December 1890, 12 April 1891, and 24 May 1891 (*JKCat*, vii).

[7] Vivian Perlis, *Charles Ives Remembered: An Oral History* (New Haven: Yale University Press, 1974; repr. New York: Norton, 1976), 80.

condition is presented by Stuart Feder in *Charles Ives: "My Father's Song."*[8] Feder describes Ives's condition toward the late 1920s as follows:

> Successive physical illnesses left him enraged and exhausted. . . . A growing affective instability gave rise to periods of depression and episodes of excitement. His ideation was at times grandiose, and he harbored paranoid suspicions. . . . [A]t some point humor veered into sarcasm, at times vitriolic and uncontrolled, bordering on madness. . . . His habits of speech soon encroached on his writing style, which could scarcely hide the underlying anger; the result was a crazy quilt of word and clang associations.[9]

Feder attributes Ives's "mental disorganization" to "natural or premature aging," and to "the fragmentation of reason by inner rage."

Simultaneously, Ives was creating lists of his works with dates and performance anecdotes, as well as recording autobiographical recollections of specific events and influences. His deteriorating mental condition may well have affected his memory as well as his judgment when composing nine lists between 1929 and 1949–50 and the contemporary *Memos*. Music from the turn of the century or before seems especially vulnerable (for example, his conflicting dates for *Psalm 67* and the First Symphony).[10] This is not surprising, as Ives was recalling events thirty to sixty years removed.

These circumstances may then explain chronological contradictions found in the lists. As the cause of such inaccuracies can be attributed to both physical and psychological factors, Feder's defense of Ives's actions is noteworthy: "if there were distortions [of memory] they were not in the ordinary realm of conscious lying."[11] But given these problems, the second basis for dating Ives's works used by Kirkpatrick, the lists and *Memos*, should be used only as supporting evidence in a study of chronology.

The third source of the established chronology, the datable marginalia (usually dates and addresses) on Ives's manuscripts, is potentially problematic in several respects. Kirkpatrick used Ives's marginalia to date specific

---

8 Stuart Feder, *Charles Ives: "My Father's Song": A Psychoanalytic Biography* (New Haven: Yale University Press, 1992), 259–60.   9 Ibid., 323–24.

10 Solomon mentions a number of contradictions, both within the nine lists themselves and between the dates on the lists and other chronological evidence.

11 Correspondence, 19 August 1993; see also Feder, *Charles Ives*, 354.

sources, stating, "So few of Ives's [manuscripts] are dated that often a return address is the only source of a date." No fewer than one hundred eighty-two dates in the catalogue are drawn from manuscript marginalia.[12] However, it is likely that several of these notations function to associate musical works with biographical events, as suggested by Solomon, Lambert, and my own research, rather than as return addresses or specific source dates.[13] That is the reason for questioning the accuracy of dates drawn from this source.

Solomon questions the purpose of manuscript notations, suggesting that Ives may have added marginalia to provide chronological "evidence" to pre-date works.[14] His skepticism relies in part on statements made by Kirkpatrick about Ives adding addresses retrospectively to manuscripts (*JKCat*, viii). For example, one of Solomon's questions concerns notations on the sketches of "Putnam's Camp," a movement of the First Orchestral Set (*Three Places in New England*). The score-sketch includes the notation "Whitman's House Hartsdale NY Oct 1912," while a more extensive, but incomplete memo on a piano score "patch" reads, "Wanted in these you-beknighted States!—More Independance Election Day 1908—Taft. Today—What Are Vo[ters] . . . More Gumption! Less Parties Politics." Solomon interprets the "Election Day—1908" memo as an "attempt to pre-date 'Putnam's Camp' to 1908," as an exercise in distortion that Ives subsequently abandoned with the "Whitman's House" inscription.[15]

In his 1989 communication, Lambert suggested that the "1908" memo may be associative rather than descriptive, and therefore retrospective instead of contemporary.[16] Solomon's response is as follows:

> Lambert has unwittingly opened up a general objection to all of Ives's marginal notations as predicates for dating his works: for if "Election Day 1908" is not to be considered a plain dating of *Putnam's Camp* why should we regard the score-sketch entry "Whitman's House, Hartsdale, N.Y., Oct. 1912" – or any similar notation on other works – as a dating rather than a free association or nostalgic notation?[17]

---

[12] Based on a survey of the "Table of contents (List of works)" (*JKCat*, xiii–xxxi).
[13] Philip Lambert, "Communication," *Journal of the American Musicological Society* 42/1 (1989): 207; Solomon, reply to Lambert, 211–12; Sherwood, "Questions and veracities," 432–33.
[14] Solomon, "Charles Ives," 457–58.   [15] Ibid.
[16] Lambert, "Communication," 207.
[17] Solomon, reply to Lambert, 211–12.

Solomon's suggestion that all non-functional addresses may serve an associative purpose is intriguing and should be investigated through an analysis of Ives's notational habits.

The majority of Ives's manuscript notations include address references, such as "Hartsdale N.Y." or a street address in Manhattan. That Ives used location as an aid to memory is apparent in both the private diary that he shared with his wife Harmony, called "Our Book" (where most entries in Ives's hand include a specific address), and in Ives's public autobiography, *Memos.* In fact, business and residence addresses, and not dates, provide the standard form of recollection to such an extent that Kirkpatrick has indexed Ives's remembrances in *Memos* (348) under the addresses themselves.

Essentially, Ives remembered *where* something happened, but not always *when*. The forms of the memories range from specific (for example, "While we were living at 70 West 11th St.," or "while living in Hartsdale") to fragmentary and disjointed ("I remember starting the first theme [of the second Violin Sonata], just the first Sunday after [I] gave up playing in church, June 8, 1902, 65 Central Park West.").[18] Addresses then played a central role in Ives's remembrance and autobiography.

In several of Ives's larger works, residential and business addresses are used to retrace stages in the development of a piece, and thereby function as recollections. For example, an ink copy of the fourth movement ("Thoreau") of the *Concord Sonata* reads, "finished May 30 1915 from some ideas—'Walden Sounds—Ch Bells, Flute Harp (Aeolian) to go with Harmony's Mist . . . Elk Lake 1910)." "Elk Lake 1910" is not an attempt to pre-date the manuscript, which Ives dated as 1915 at the top of the memo. The location Elk Lake and its date of 1910 are both indicators of the provenance of the work's original ideas.

This associative reference does not function as a source date. Similar notations appear on all of Ives's orchestral scores, possibly serving as reminders of the compositional evolution of each piece rather than as a date for an individual manuscript. Returning to the "Putnam's Camp" notations, for example, the "Election Day—1908" memo presents a wealth of extraneous information and opinions, and its expulsive, vitriolic tone is consistent with Ives's writings of the late 1920s and 1930s. It does not repre-

---

18 *Memos*, 68.

81

sent a dating (or redating) of the source, but is certainly associative. The "Whitman's House" notation may be related to a separate memo, on a sheet of paper that was detached from the same manuscript and used for a score-sketch of "Housatonic at Stockbridge." The detached page includes the following memo: "... Same 3 ... After leaving the polls on Nat'l Election Day of 1912 walking back over Healey Chicken Farm," which Kirkpatrick identified as Hartsdale. The form of the entry and the lack of significant music on this page illustrate that this is most likely a diaristic, retrospective entry: its original presence in the same manuscript could indicate a relationship to the "Hartsdale NY Oct 1912" reference. As part of a recollection, the Hartsdale reference would serve an associative, not a chronological purpose. If taken out of context however, the address or the date alone could be misinterpreted as a source date.

Multiple dates of association (as in the 1908 and 1912 "Putnam's Camp" dates) do not indicate falsification on Ives's part. Yet they also cannot be used as source dates, given the likelihood of associative functions. Thus the two central sources for Kirkpatrick's dates – the lists and manuscript marginalia – are both problematic. In order to confirm or amend the current chronology, I have proposed supplementary dating methods, including analysis of music paper type and handwriting.

Methodology

My methodology is based on studies of other composers by Alan Tyson, Douglas Johnson, Robert Winter, Wisso Weiss, and Yoshitake Kobayashi.[19] To study Ives's music-paper types I correlated the dates of operation of paper manufacturing companies with securely dated manu-

[19] Douglas P. Johnson, *Beethoven's Early Sketches in the "Fischhof Miscellany,"* Studies in Musicology 22 (Ann Arbor MI: UMI Research Press, 1980); Douglas Johnson, Alan Tyson, and Robert Winter, *The Beethoven Sketchbooks: History, Reconstruction, Inventory*, ed. Douglas Johnson (Berkeley: University of California Press, 1985); Alan Tyson, *Mozart: Studies of the Autograph Scores* (Cambridge MA: Harvard University Press, 1987), and "Watermarks," in *Haydn Studies: Proceedings of the International Haydn Conference, Washington, D.C., 1975*, ed. Jens Peter Larsen, Howard Serwer, and James Webster (New York: Norton, 1981), 90–93; Wisso Weiss and Yoshitake Kobayashi, *Katalog der Wasserzeichen in Bachs Originalhandschriften*, in Neue Bach-Ausgabe, Series IX, vol. 1 (Kassel: Bärenreiter, 1985).

scripts of other composers working in the New Haven and New York area between 1881 and 1941. I was able to determine the earliest date of manufacture, earliest documented use, latest date of manufacture, and/or latest documented use. With this methodology, it is possible to provide a range of dates for almost all the music paper used by Ives and his copyists.

But paper dating, while extremely useful, cannot necessarily indicate the period of Ives's use of specific papers; for this reason I have also employed handwriting analysis. My work expands Carol Baron's preliminary research into Ives's handwriting.[20] Baron's study compared handwriting elements from three securely dated manuscripts as follows: 1902 (*The Celestial Country*, ink scores); c. 1914 (Third Violin Sonata, ink copy); and c. 1929 ("Putnam's Camp" revisions). Although useful as a general survey, Baron's study was limited by its reliance on only these three sources, and by a somewhat unsystematic approach to detailing the changes in Ives's handwriting.

My study of Ives's handwriting draws on analytical techniques used in studies of other composers by Georg von Dadelsen, Yoshitake Kobayashi, Wolfgang Plath, and Alan Tyson.[21] To create a more diverse and reliable database, I have added the following seven sources, all of which are dated through paper type and/or additional correspondence:[22] 1892 (*Variations on "America,"* ink score); 1898 (Organ Fugue in E♭ Major, ink score); 1907 ("The World's Highway" and "Spring Song," ink scores); 1919 ("In Flanders Fields," ink score); c. 1923 ("The One Way" and "Yellow Leaves," ink scores); 1934 ("General William Booth Enters Into Heaven," patches); and 1942 (Ives's parody of Paul Dresser's "On the Wabash"). Baron's criteria – treble clefs, naturals and sharps, black and white noteheads and stems, flags,

[20] Carol Baron, "Dating Charles Ives's music: facts and fictions," *Perspectives of New Music* 28/1 (1990): 20–56.

[21] Georg von Dadelsen, *Bemerkungen zur Handschrift Johann Sebastian Bachs, seiner Familie und seines Kreises*, Tübinger Bach-Studien, ed. Walter Gerstenberg (Trossingen: Hohner, 1957); Yoshitake Kobayashi, *Die Notenschrift Johann Sebastian Bachs: Dokumentation ihrer Entwicklung*, Neue Bach-Ausgabe, Serie IX, vol. 2 (Kassel: Bärenreiter, 1989); Wolfgang Plath, *Mozart-Schriften: Ausgewählte Aufsätze*, Schriftenreihe der Internationalen Stiftung Mozarteum, ed. Marianne Danckwardt, vol. 9 (Kassel: Bärenreiter, 1991); Alan Tyson, "Notes on five of Beethoven's copyists," *Journal of the American Musicological Society* 23/3 (1970): 439–71.

[22] As outlined in Sherwood, "Questions and veracities," 413–14.

beams, and general size and spacing – have been methodically compared and presented in chart form for easy comparison.[23] Based on this data, I have delineated several different periods of Ives's handwriting for comparative use.

The combined paper type and handwriting data represent an objective supplementary dating method. I chose to apply this methodology to the sources for Ives's choral works because, according to Kirkpatrick's chronology, the choral sources span Ives's entire compositional period (pre-1890 through post-1920). This distinction is unique to the choral music and songs. Furthermore, unlike Ives's songs, many of the choral works were "reconstructed." According to Kirkpatrick, when Ives left Central Presbyterian Church in 1902, he left most of his music for chorus and organ in the choir library. The church threw the music out eventually, perhaps when it moved in 1915.[24] Ives returned to many of these works and attempted to reconstruct them from memory and from extant sketches, the clearest examples being *Psalm 24*, *Psalm 25*, and the *Harvest Home Chorales*. Reconstructions present the most acute chronological problem because they involve unclear and contradictory datings from Ives himself, and years or even decades of intervening musical growth between the original and reconstructed versions. Since reconstructions are found exclusively among the choral works, a chronological study of this genre must address this problem.

The revised chronology of Ives's choral works

An appendix to this essay (pp. 96–101) presents a timeline comparison of datings of the choral works (identified by their list number from Kirkpatrick's catalogue and an abbreviated title). The chart compares datings from the revised chronology with datings by Kirkpatrick and Ives. Kirkpatrick's datings are taken from the 1960 catalogue unless followed by "REVCAT" (from Kirkpatrick's revisions to the catalogue) or "AMGROVE"

---

[23] See Gayle Sherwood, "The choral works of Charles Ives: chronology, style, reception" (Ph.D. dissertation, Yale University, 1995), 322–23, 366–70.

[24] See *Memos*, 148n. The editors' notes to *Psalm 90* state that the music was thrown out when the church moved in 1915. See Ives, *Psalm 90*, ed. John Kirkpatrick and Gregg Smith (Bryn Mawr: Merion Music, 1970), 3.

(from the Ives article in the *American Grove*).[25] Ives's datings are taken primarily from the lists, although some dates for the choral songs are found in the index to *114 Songs* (indicated as "114").[26]

Only the earliest source for each work is listed, except when there is a significant difference between sources (as in *Psalm 24*, *Psalm 25*, and the *Harvest Home Chorale* reconstructions). Manuscripts used as dating benchmarks in the revised chronology (such as the ink copies of *Variations on "America"* of 1892 and the Third Violin Sonata of c. 1914) are listed in bold capital letters. Dates that are questionable or open to interpretation, such as those drawn from Ives's manuscript inscriptions, are preceded by a question mark.

Based on this comparison, some observations can be made about the differences between the revised and original chronologies. First, many works originally dated by Kirkpatrick between 1890 and 1898, such as the anthems *Turn Ye, Turn Ye* and *I Come to Thee*, appear to have later datings. Second, an overview of the revised chronology indicates that not all sacred choral works were written before 1902.[27] Instead, Ives continued to compose, reconstruct, and rearrange in this genre throughout his creative life with only one brief hiatus (c. 1903–c. 1909). Third, the revised chronology shows a noticeable increase in Ives's scribal activity in the 1920s, including the arrangements of *Majority*, *Lincoln*, and *An Election*. Although there is no concrete evidence, this could have been related to early performance or publication opportunities, or was possibly a result of Ives's lessened duties in his insurance firm at that time.[28]

With this data, it is possible to suggest two choral style periods. During

---

[25] Kirkpatrick's revisions to the catalogue are preserved in James Sinclair, "Microfilm concordance to the Kirkpatrick Catalogue" (unpublished, 1975), and in Kirkpatrick's and Paul C. Echols's work list in *The New Grove Dictionary of American Music*.

[26] See *Memos*, 147–66 (the lists) and 167–77 (Ives's datings for *114 Songs*).

[27] Wendell Clark Kumlien, "The sacred choral music of Charles Ives: a study in style development" (Ph.D. dissertation, University of Illinois, 1969), 9, groups all forty sacred choral works within three style periods from 1885 to 1902. J. Peter Burkholder, "The evolution of Charles Ives's music: aesthetics, quotation, technique" (Ph.D. dissertation, University of Chicago, 1983), 156, states "Ives wrote no more music for organ solo or church choir after 1902, although he later reconstructed from memory the lost *Psalm 90*."

[28] See Feder, *Charles Ives*, 300, 305.

the first (c. 1887–c. 1903) Ives wrote a large number of smaller works, while in the second (c. 1909–c. 1927) he produced fewer but larger works. Certain works, including the psalm and chorale reconstructions, date from both periods. In such instances it is difficult to assign a single date.

The first choral period: c. 1887–c. 1903

Included within the first choral style period are Ives's earliest hymn settings, his service music and protestant anthems, and the psalm and chorale settings, some of which are fragmentary. The revised chronology clarifies some controversial datings, while it also reflects Ives's circumstances in the 1890s. One of the most significant results of the revised chronology is a clear correlation between Ives's church positions between 1893 and 1902 and the performing forces and genres of the sacred choral works.

The close relationship between music and circumstances is supported through supplementary dating of one early work, the *Nine Experimental Canticle Phrases* (as named by Kirkpatrick). The sketch of this work was part of Ives's introduction to "pointing chant" at St. Thomas's Episcopal Church in New Haven. This technique involves unmeasured or free declamation by the congregation of parts of the liturgy. Pointing is essentially an oral tradition, and can vary greatly from congregation to congregation (and from week to week). Not surprisingly, Ives expressed confusion with the pointed chants in a letter to his father of 9 May 1893, describing his first Sunday at St. Thomas's: "I had the most trouble with the chants, and found the best way to learn them was to commit the music [to memory] and then follow the words."[29]

In the *Nine Experimental Canticle Phrases* Ives assimilated this oral tradition into his written music. The more specific purpose of this setting is recounted in a letter to his father of 24 February 1894:

> During Lent all the chants that are sung are founded on the Gregorian tones. The choir sings them in unison, and so I have to change the harmonies. It is rather awkward to do as the air has to be kept on top. The best way I have found is to use diminished chords in the same key, or go to the [first] ♭ or ♯ remove[d].[30]

[29] Yale University Ives Archive, Box 33, Folder 1.   [30] Ibid.

The nine extant harmonizations present two separate melodies, labeled "Venite" and "Magnificat."[31] Each phrase uses progressively more adventurous harmonies to accommodate the pitch-consistent melodic presentation, including several diminished-seventh chords as Ives mentioned in his letter. This confirms a dating of 1894 for the canticle phrases.

An instructive comparison can be made between the established and revised chronologies using the 1894 *Nine Experimental Canticle Phrases* manuscript as a reference point. On the basis of handwriting analysis, Kirkpatrick dated the work from 1891–92, a difference of two to three years from its actual date. In the revised chronology, other works dated by Kirkpatrick from 1891–92 have been redated at least two or three years later by paper and handwriting analysis. For example *Crossing the Bar* was dated by Kirkpatrick in the catalogue as 1891, and as 1890 in *American Grove*. The revised chronology redates this work to c. 1894 based on both the handwriting (as compared with the *Nine Experimental Canticle Phrases*) and the use in the first ink score and tenor part of a paper type usually found in New Haven sources.

In fact, almost all choral sources dating from 1893–94 are service music, including the *Nine Experimental Canticle Phrases* and a full *Communion Service*. This period corresponds exactly with Ives's tenure at St. Thomas's Episcopal Church in New Haven from 7 May 1893 until 29 April 1894 (see *Memos*, 326). The nature of the Episcopalian service probably encouraged these specifically liturgical settings that could not have been used at previous or later churches.

Similarly, the revised datings for sacred anthems such as *Crossing the Bar, Turn Ye, Turn Ye*, and *Easter Carol* place them within Ives's tenure as organist at Center Church on the Green, New Haven, between 1894 and 1898.[32] This venue provided not only encouraging support from the choir director (Dr. John Cornelius Griggs) but also an available group of qualified performers. According to Lewis Bronson, a member of the choir,

---

[31] The "Venite" (phrases 1–4) is untitled but texted, while the "Magnificat" (phrases 5–9) is titled on the last page of the sketch.

[32] Ives's predecessor at Center Church was Harry B. Jepson, the organ teacher at Yale (*Memos*, 183), while his successor, David Stanley Smith, followed Horatio Parker as head of the Yale School of Music. See Elizabeth Goode, "David Stanley Smith and his music" (Ph.D. dissertation, University of Cincinnati, 1978), 29.

> Center Church . . . at that time [1896] had the best church quartet that I knew about. . . . [W]e had choir rehearsals and gave some fairly substantial pieces with Mr. Ives playing the organ and the quartet and chorus directed by Dr. Griggs. We had a rehearsal every week, and the members of the chorus received lessons in return. We had a good quartet, so that we could really do some pretty elaborate pieces.[33]

This description confirms that the choir of Center Church was a "quartet choir," consisting of a professional quartet in addition to the amateur chorus. Choruses organized in this manner were common in many American churches in the late nineteenth century. Quartet choirs were closely associated with Dudley Buck, one of Ives's organ teachers and a major composer of amateur-level choral music.[34] In fact *Easter Carol*, Ives's largest anthem from this period (according to the revised chronology), includes an interlude for solo quartet in its central fugato.

Surviving choral sources from the years 1898–1902 are exclusively sacred and systematically experimental, again reflecting the nature of Ives's employment during that period. Following two years at the First Presbyterian Church in Bloomfield, New Jersey (1898–1900),[35] Ives relocated to Central Presbyterian Church in New York, where he remained until June 1902. This was Ives's only position where he served as both organist and choir director.[36] During these two years, for the first and last time in his life, Ives had a performing ensemble completely at his disposal, as opposed to his previous access to choirs only through Dr. Griggs's influence at Center Church or his father's ambiguous church positions in Danbury. The New York position presented a significant advantage that may well have proved crucial to the development of Ives's experimental choral style, for he could now try out his own compositions as he wrote them.

At least a few of these works were dated by Kirkpatrick on the basis of

---

[33] Perlis, *Charles Ives Remembered*, 20–21.

[34] See William Kearns, "Horatio Parker 1863–1919: a study of his life and music" (Ph.D. dissertation, University of Illinois, 1965), 585.

[35] Two settings using boys' choirs may date from the period when Ives was at Bloomfield (*Psalm 67* and *Psalm 150*, both c. 1898), suggesting that such a choir may have been available there, though there are no records to confirm this. There are no indications that any of Ives's other churches had a boys' choir. Yale University Ives Archive, Box 50, Folder 1 (Programs).

[36] *Memos*, 57, 68, 237, 262, and 327–28.

manuscript memos that he interpreted as performance dates. On closer examination, however, Ives's memos seem unclear in meaning and inconsistent in presentation. One example is his memo on the source of *Psalm 150* (5C26), which according to handwriting analysis dates from around 1898. A memo on the sketch reads as follows: "Dr. Griggs and Choir sing in part[?] verse in Praise Service in Centre Ch. New Haven Sunday M[?] 14 1896" (*JKCat*, 137). This memo makes use of the present tense, contrary to what one would expect in a performance recollection entered contemporaneously. As a result, the memo may instead be a retrospective entry. Similar vague references are found on the manuscripts of *I Come To Thee* (formerly entitled *God of My Life*), *Turn Ye, Turn Ye*, and *Crossing the Bar* (see *JKCat*, 130, 132, 133).

Ives's settings of *Psalm 67*, *Psalm 150*, *Psalm 54*, and *Psalm 24* were dated by Kirkpatrick between 1894 and 1897 in the 1960 catalogue, and redated to the summer of 1894 in the revised catalogue and *American Grove*. In the revised chronology these works have been redated to 1898 and later, through paper analysis and handwriting comparison with the Organ Fugue source of 1898 and *The Celestial Country* scores of 1902. Kirkpatrick's original placement of these psalms as a group within a few years remains valid: only their dates have changed.

The redating of *Psalm 67* represents a significant difference from the established chronology. In Ives's lists from at least forty years after the likely date of composition, he dated the work as 1898 (*Memos*, 153–54). This date accurately reflects, for the most part, the source's handwriting.[37] However, in his prose writings Ives dates the work from around 1894 or even earlier. Twice he recalls his father conducting the piece with a choir in Danbury, thereby dating *Psalm 67* before November 1894. The sources for these recollections are significant, since both date from the 1930s: one is in *Memos*, which Ives began in 1931, and the other, which is sketched on a piece of staff paper, contains the "snake tracks" and wobbles characteristic of Ives's handwriting beginning in the mid-1930s.[38] As discussed above, Ives's worsening condition during this decade may account for inaccuracies in these references.

[37] Some revisions on the manuscript date from c. 1902.

[38] *Memos*, 47. The second recollection is preserved in the Ives papers, and was transcribed by Kirkpatrick in *Memos*, 178–79.

The inconsistent datings of *Psalm 67* have been the subject of debate. Lambert suggests that George Ives's performances may have been merely "read-throughs" of an earlier version of the work that Ives then completed in 1898, while Solomon noted the lack of a "preliminary sketch" that would support Lambert's defense.[39] But it is the absence of a preliminary sketch that makes *Psalm 67* an interesting case. On one hand, if Ives copied this work from a pre-existing sketch (as seems likely based on page layout and lack of structural revisions), then there must have been an earlier manuscript that has not survived. On the other hand, if Ives wrote this manuscript without first sketching the work, it is a remarkable achievement indeed. The extant manuscript clearly lacks an exemplar; that would account for the discrepancy between the date in Ives's recollections and the period of the extant manuscripts. However, there is no way of knowing what such a lost exemplar might have contained. In any case, the work did not exist in its preserved form until at least around 1898.

To sum up, the revised chronology of Ives's choral works in this early period leads to a number of preliminary conclusions. First, compositions dating from before and during his Yale period are clearly conservative, including secular choral songs (such as *For You and Me* and *The Bells of Yale*) and sacred service music and anthems. Second, the forms and genres of these works reveal a consistently utilitarian approach. Third, the sophisticated compositional techniques of the psalms and chorales emerged only after Ives's study with Horatio Parker, and therefore suggest a greater degree of influence than previously recognized.

The second choral period: c. 1909–c. 1927

The works of Ives's second choral period include reconstructions or completions of earlier works (*Psalm 24*, *Psalm 25*, *Psalm 135*, the interludes for *The Celestial Country* and the first and third *Harvest Home Chorales*), as well as entirely new compositions (the second *Harvest Home Chorale*, *Psalm 90*, and choral songs such as *December* and *The New River*). According to the revised chronology, Ives returned to both hymn texts and

---

[39] Lambert, "Communication," 204; Solomon, "Charles Ives," 462, and reply to Lambert, 210.

the choral genre around 1909 with his setting of *Serenity*. Perhaps his renewed interest was connected to the most significant event of Ives's life in these years, his marriage to Harmony Twichell on 9 June 1908 (*Memos*, 277). The importance of religion in her life could have revived Ives's interest in sacred and religious texts.[40]

Harmony's influence was probably supplemented by renewed contact between Ives and Dr. Griggs as early as 1911 or 1912 (at which time the third *Harvest Home Chorale* and *Psalm 135* were reconstructed).[41] As traced by Burkholder, Griggs had been influential in the development of Ives's Transcendentalist views while at Yale. Later, from the mid-teens to at least the early 1920s, Griggs communicated with Ives on philosophical, religious, and musical matters.[42]

The revised chronology is particularly significant for clarifying dates of reconstruction for several larger choral works, including *Psalm 24*, *Psalm 25*, and the first *Harvest Home Chorale*, all of which may be connected with a source for the First Piano Sonata. Kirkpatrick suggested 1910 as a date for the second ink copy of the first movement of the First Piano Sonata.[43] He believed that the pages for the reconstructions of *Psalm 24*, *Psalm 25* (both of which he dated "after 1910"), and the first *Harvest Home Chorale* (which he dated "1910?") were drawn from the same source as that of the First Piano Sonata. He then used the same date for the choral sources.[44] However, the 1910 date is probably inaccurate, given that one of the paper types of the sonata source was not in use before 1911, and others were not in use before 1917. A redating of this original source by several years then affects the

---

[40] Harmony may have been responsible for Ives's renewed church attendance following their marriage. No references are made to Ives's attending services between 1902 and 1911–13, when he apparently heard a sermon by Rev. Daniel Ernest McCurry in Hartsdale, New York. See the memo on the score of *Two Slants* (sketch), transcribed in *JKCat*, 124.

[41] Kirkpatrick suggests that Ives may have played the "Emerson" movement of the *Concord Sonata* for Griggs at about this time (*Memos*, 202, 255).

[42] J. Peter Burkholder, *Charles Ives: The Ideas Behind the Music* (New Haven: Yale University Press, 1985), 68–72, 135.

[43] *JKCat*, 83. The source is redated 1909 in the revised catalogue for reasons unknown.

[44] *JKCat*, 121, 138. After examining these sources closely, I must suggest that some of Kirkpatrick's conclusions regarding manuscript relationships between the choral sources described here and the First Piano Sonata source are questionable. They are included in this study pending further research.

91

dependent datings of the choral reconstructions, all of which have been moved forward into the mid to later teens in the revised chronology.

The revised datings of the reconstructions of *Psalm 24* and *Psalm 25* may be supported by further evidence placing them in the mid teens. Kirkpatrick states in *Memos*:

> When Ives resigned as organist from the Central Presbyterian Church (then at Broadway and 57th Street), he left all his best choir and organ music there, and in subsequent moves it was all thrown out.[45]

In the editorial notes to *Psalm 25* and *Psalm 90* Kirkpatrick states that the church threw out Ives's music (including copies of *Psalm 25*) in a 1915 move.[46] If that is the case, Ives's reconstructions of *Psalm 25*, and possibly his completions of *Psalm 24* and the first *Harvest Home Chorale*, must date from at least 1915. Since the church was still in midtown Manhattan where Ives lived, he would certainly have tried to recover the originals before reconstructing works from scattered sketches and fragments. However, earlier reconstructions (*The Celestial Country* interludes from c. 1909 and *Psalm 135* from around 1912) indicate that Ives's reconstructions were not limited to the mid teens.

Several choral songs have been significantly redated, including *Lincoln* (1912, revised to 1920–21) and *An Election* (1920, revised to 1924–25). Both works lack exemplars for their choral arrangements: therefore, earlier sources must have existed, but are not extant. Without these earlier choral sources neither Kirkpatrick's 1920 date for *An Election*, nor Ives's 1912 for *Lincoln* can be confirmed.[47] In the case of *The New River*, the dating problem is compounded by the multiple arrangements of the work, and by the numerous datings provided by Ives and Kirkpatrick. There are three separate arrangements: for chorus and orchestra; for solo voice and piano (published in *114 Songs*); and for chamber orchestra (without text), as the third of six movements in Set no. 1, under the alternative title "The

---

[45] *Memos*, 148, n7. Kirkpatrick's source for this information is unknown.

[46] John Kirkpatrick and Gregg Smith, Editors' Notes to *Psalm 90*, 3, and Editors' Notes to *Psalm 25*, 3. Kirkpatrick's source for this information is unknown.

[47] *JKCat*, 128, and *Memos*, 164, respectively. In *114 Songs* Ives dated *Lincoln* from 1921. This is probably the date of the voice and piano arrangement, since the paper of that source dates from between 1919 and 1923. There is no extant source for the song arrangement of *An Election*.

Ruined River." Furthermore, there are two separate datings from Kirkpatrick (1911 in the 1960 catalogue, and 1906 in the revisions to the catalogue),[48] while Ives provided the date "before the spring of 1913" in *Memos* (60). Given these variables, the compositional chronology of the work could not possibly be characterized by a single dating.

Kirkpatrick's date of 1911 in the 1960 catalogue is questionable, since it is taken from a non-functional, probably associative memo on the manuscript of the voice and piano arrangement (*JKCat*, 196, 6B49). His 1906 date stems from Ives's description in *Memos* (59) of a set "for cornet solo (with or without voices) and small orchestra . . . made in 1906." Kirkpatrick identified this work as Set no. 1 and thus suggested a date of 1906 for "The New River"/"The Ruined River." But Ives was certainly not referring to the set as it is preserved (since he mentions a seventh movement), and "The New River" is not mentioned specifically in his description. Thus "The New River" may not have belonged in the set as it was "made" in 1906. This movement is mentioned, however, on the next page of the *Memos* manuscript, where it is grouped with another set and given the date "written before the spring of 1913, at least before we were in Brattleboro in January 1913" (*Memos*, 60).

Therefore Ives's date of "before 1913" is most defensible for this work. The revised chronology places the sources for "The Ruined River" (from Set no. 1) and separate sketches of the choral parts for "The New River" around 1915–16. However the manuscript is carefully copied out with little revision, indicating a missing exemplar. The difference between the most likely date provided by Ives and the revised datings of the sources is then negligible.[49]

Apart from these considerations, one source redating merits closer attention since it represents in microcosm the challenges facing an accurate reassessment of the Ives chronology. That source is the three *Harvest Home Chorales*. Ives provided several apparently contradictory dates for this work in his lists: 1897 for the first and second chorales, and 1902 for the third (in

---

[48] *JKCat*, 196, and Sinclair, "Microfilm concordance," 196.

[49] The song arrangement of "The New River" appears to be slightly later: the paper is unidentified, while the hand dates from 1914–19, closer to 1919. In *114 Songs* Ives dated the song arrangement of "The New River" as 1921, which postdates the extant source (*JKCat*, 151).

the 1935 list); 1898 for the second, and "dates uncertain" for the first and third (1937 list); before 1912 for all three (1943 list); before 1902 for all three (1945 list); and 1898 for the first and "dates uncertain, some time before 1902" for the second and third (1949 list).[50] Ives's confusion is justified, however, in light of the composite nature of the source. The original opening material of the first chorale is from c. 1902 or slightly later, based on handwriting comparison with the 1902 sources from *The Celestial Country*; since it is impossible to know how much other material from this early source does not survive, this fragment is enough to support tentatively Ives's datings in the 1945 and 1949 lists. The remainder of the work postdates 1902, based on handwriting comparison with 1907 and 1914 sources. Of these, the third chorale source may date from c. 1912, thereby confirming the 1943 list date. Like the later completions of *Psalm 24* and *Psalm 25*, the reconstructions of the first and second chorales (dated by handwriting comparison around 1915–16) are not mentioned in Ives's list dates. Therefore most of Ives's contradictory dates – stretching from before the turn of the century up to 1912 – are reflected in the manuscripts' physical structure, while his remark "dates uncertain" may be related to the confusion of the source.[51]

To summarize, the revised choral chronology illustrates the importance of recognizing the psalm and chorale reconstructions as products of Ives's mature-period compositional style. This second choral period also represents a continuation of Ives's previous secular style; the choral songs *December*, *An Election*, and *Johnny Poe* are arranged for male chorus, the only settings of this type to postdate Ives's Yale days. Of these, *Johnny Poe* (concerning a popular Princeton man who died in World War I) is particularly close in spirit to Ives's college choruses, as its text was written by a Yale alumnus and published in the Yale magazine (*JKCat*, 128).

---

[50] *Memos*, 154. Kirkpatrick suggests that the 1912 date is an error.

[51] Kirkpatrick acknowledged the different stages of each composition dating from different periods in the catalogue. This knowledge is not reflected, however, in the singular date assigned to each work at the beginning of every catalogue entry and is therefore subject to misinterpretation.

Conclusions: questions and veracities

The revised chronology of the choral works leads to two significant conclusions. First, although the alterations to the established chronology are extensive, the general ordering of works by Kirkpatrick is supported.[52] Second, the revised chronology supports Ives's reputation as a compositional innovator.

In addition to revised datings of particular works, the new chronology necessitates some alterations in our view of Ives's development. To start, the conservative service music, sacred anthems, and secular songs dominate the first decade of a creative career that lasted just over forty years at the most (c. 1887–1928). Therefore Ives spent one quarter of his compositional life writing almost entirely in a conservative style. The usual portrait of Ives as an independent innovator decades ahead of his European contemporaries necessarily reduces or neglects this first, conservative decade. Yet most of Ives's conservative choral works remain unpublished, unrecorded, and unperformed, unlike the exclusively experimental choral works (the psalms and choral songs) that postdate his graduation from Yale. The placement of the anthems within Ives's Yale years justifies a treatment equal to that already given to compositions previously assigned to this period, such as the First String Quartet and the First Symphony.

In closing, it should be noted that these alterations to the chronology of Ives's works will not threaten his position as one of America's greatest composers. On the contrary, a comprehensive revised chronology will undoubtedly result in a more complete, and possibly more provocative, view of Charles Ives.

---

[52] As suggested by J. Peter Burkholder, "Charles Ives and his fathers: a response to Maynard Solomon," *Newsletter of the Institute for Studies in American Music* 18/1 (1988): 11.

Appendix: Timeline Comparison, 1885–1942

	Revised chronology	Kirkpatrick	Ives
1885			5C3 *Psalm 42*
1887	5C1 *1st Hymn* 5C2 *Chant*	5C3 *Psalm 42*	5C1 *1st Hymn* 5C2 *Chant* 5D1 *The Year's*
1888		5D1 *The Year's* (1888–89) 5C3 *Ps. 42* (AMGROVE)	5C9 ?*Benedictus* (1888–89) 5C13 ?*Benedictus* (1888–89)
1889		5D1 *The Year's* (AMGROVE) 5C10 *I Think* (AMGROVE)	5C10 *I Think* 5C11 ?*Turn Ye* 5C18 ?*I Come to Thee*
1890	5C5 *[Easter]* (1890–91)	5C5 *[Easter]* 5C7 *Crossing* (AMGROVE) 5C9 *Benedictus* 5C10 *I Think* 5C11 *Turn Ye* 5C4 *Gloria* (1890–91)	
1891	5C16 *Be Thou* (1891–92) 5C17 *Oh God My* (1891–92)	5C7 *Crossing* 5C12 *Communion* 5C13 *Benedictus* 5C14 *Bread* (AMGROVE) 5D2 *Serenade* 5D3 *Partsong* 5C6 *Nine Exper.* (1891–92) 5C15 *Search Me* (1891–92) 5C14 *Bread* (1891–92)	

Revised chronology	Kirkpatrick	Ives
1892 3D6 VARIATIONS ON "AMERICA," Ink Score	5C16 *Be Thou* 5C17 *Oh God My* 5C18 *I Come to Thee*	5C19 *?Easter*
5C3 *Ps. 42*		
5D1 *The Year's*		
5C4 *Gloria* (1892–93)		
5C13 *Benedictus* (1892–93)		
5C15 *Search Me* (1892–93)		
1893 5C9 *Benedictus* (1893–94)	5C20 *Life of* 5C21 *Lord God* (1893–94)	
5C12 *Communion* (1893–94)		
5C14 *Bread* (1893–94)		
1894 5C7 *Crossing*	5C24 *Ps. 67*	5C24 *?Ps. 67*
5C6 *Nine Exper.*	5C26 *Ps. 150* (REVCAT)	
	5C27 *Ps. 54* (REVCAT)	
	5C30 *Ps. 24* (REVCAT)	
	5D4 *Love* (1894–95)	
1895 5C10 *I Think* (1895–96)	5C25 *Light That* 5D5 *The Boys*	
5D2 *Serenade* (1895–96)	5D6 *Partsong* 5D7 *For You* (1895–96)	
1896 5C11 *Turn Ye*	5C26 *Ps. 150*	
5C19 *Easter*	5C30 *Ps. 24*	
5C20 *Life of*	5D8 *Age of Gold*	
5C18 *I Come to Thee* (1896–97)	5D9 *Partsong* 5D10 *Song of*	
5D5 *The Boys* (1896–97)		
5D6 *Partsong* (1896–97)		
5D10 *Song of* (1896–97)		

97

Revised chronology	Kirkpatrick	Ives
1897 5D3 *Partsong* (1897–98)	5C28 *Kyrie*	5C34 ?*Ps. 23* (1897–98)
5D8 *Age of Gold* (1897–98)	5C29 *Ps. 25*	
5D9 *Partsong* (1897–98)	5C30 *Ps. 24*	
	5D11 *Bells of*	
	5D11 *Bells of* (1897–98) (AMGROVE)	
	5D12 *O Maiden* (1897–98)	
1898 3D15 ORGAN FUGUE, Ink Copy	5C31 *All-Forgiving*	5B2 *Harvest I*
5A1 *Celestial* (1898–99)	5D13 *My Sweet*	5C24 *Ps. 67*
5C24 *Ps. 67*	5C33 *Ps. 100* (1898–99)	5A1 *Celestial* (1898–99)
5C25 *Light That*	5C34 *Ps. 23* (1898–99)	
5C26 *Ps. 150*		
5C31 *All-Forgiving*		
5D11 *Bells of*		
1899 5D12 *O Maiden* (1899–1900)	5C35 *Ps. 14* (AMGROVE)	
5D13 *My Sweet* (1899–1900)	5C29 *Ps. 25* (1899–1901) (REVCAT)	
	5C35 *Ps. 14* (1899–1900)	
	5C36 *Ps. 135* (1899–1900)	
	5C37 *Ps. 90* (1899–1900)	
1900 5C29 *Ps. 25*	5C36 *Ps. 135* (AMGROVE)	
5C30 *Ps. 24*		
5C21 *Lord God* (1900–01)		
5C28 *Kyrie* (1900–01)		
1901		5B2 *Harvest II* (before 1902)
		5B2 *Harvest III* (before 1902)
		5C38 ?*Processional*

Revised chronology	Kirkpatrick	Ives
1902 5A1 CELESTIAL COUNTRY, Ink Scores	5B2 *Harvest I* 5B2 *Harvest II*	
5B2 *Harvest I*		
5C27 *Ps. 54* (1902–03)		
5C33 *Ps. 100* (1902–03)		
5C35 *Ps. 14* (1902–03)		
5C36 *Ps. 135* (1902–03)		
5C38 *Processional* (1902–03)		
1906	5B4 *New River* (REVCAT)	
1907 6B43 "SPRING SONG" 6B42c "WORLD'S HIGH"		
1909 5A1 *Celestial* (Interludes)	5B3 *Serenity* 5C29 *Ps. 25* (recon.) (after 1908)	
5C34 *Ps. 23* (recon.)		
5B3 *Serenity* (1909–10)		
1911	5B4 *New River* 5B7 *Two Slants* (1911–13) 5C34 *Ps. 23* (recon.) (after 1910)	5B2 ?*Harvest II* (before 1912) 5B2 ?*Harvest III* (before 1912)
1912 5B2 *Harvest III* 5C36 *Ps. 135* (recon.)	5B2 *Harvest I* (recon.) 5B2 *Harvest II* (recon.)	5B5 *Lincoln* 5B6 *December* (1912–13)
1913 5B6 *December* (1913–14)	5B8 *Walt Whitman*	
5B7 *Two Slants* (1913–14)		

99

Revised chronology	Kirkpatrick	Ives
1914 2C6 THIRD VLN. SONATA, Ink Copy	5B9 *General Booth*	5B9 *General Booth* (114)
5B9a *Sneak Thief*	5B9a *Sneak Thief*	
5C29 *Ps. 25* (recon.) (1914–15)	5B10 *Majority*	
5C30 *Ps. 24* (recon.) (1914–15)	5B10 *Majority* (1914–15) (AMGROVE)	
5B8 *Walt Whitman* (1914–15)		
5B9 *General Booth* (1914–15)		
1915 5B2 *Harvest I* (recon.) (1915–16)		5B10 *Majority*
5B2 *Harvest II* (recon.) (1915–16)		
5B4 *New River* (recon.) (1915–16)		
5B10 *Majority* (1915–16)		
1917		5B11 *He Is* (114)
1918 5B11 *He Is* (1918–19)		
1919 6B56 "FLANDERS"	5B11 *He Is*	
1920 5B5 *Lincoln* (1920–21)	5B12 *An Election*	
1923 6B72 "ONE WAY"		5C37 *Ps. 90* (1923–24)
6B73 "YELLOW"		
5C37 *Ps. 90* (1923–24)		

Revised chronology	Kirkpatrick	Ives
1924 5B12 *An Election* (1924–25)		
1926	5B13 *Johnny Poe* (after 1925)	
1927 5B13 *Johnny Poe* (1927–28)		
1942 1C34iii WABASH 5B14 *They*	5B14 *They*	

Historical and biographical contexts

5   The idea of potentiality in the music of Charles Ives

WOLFGANG RATHERT

> *Sea, earth, air, sound, silence.*
> *Plant, quadruped, bird,*
> *by one music enchanted,*
> *One deity stirred,*   Emerson, "The Sphinx" (1841)

I

In spite of intensive research since the 1970s, the music of Charles Ives remains enigmatic in many respects. Now as ever, it continues to challenge customary notions of what music really is and should be, and continues to resist integration into an easily mastered and commonly accepted history of composition. There is likewise little consensus on what Ives himself saw as the ultimate goal of his artistic aspirations. Although in his writings and postfaces to his compositions he commented extensively on his musical, aesthetic, and philosophical premises, no coherent picture emerges from them. The reception history of his music is even more confusing: while the Europeans have been fascinated by Ives's ostensible carelessness, with which he freed himself from stylistic constraints, Americans themselves are divided over the significance of his achievements. Leading composers of the generation following Ives either criticized his lack of compositional craft (as did Aaron Copland, Virgil Thomson, and Elliott Carter) or considered his approach too dependent on traditional (European) formal concepts (as did John Cage), thus questioning his place in the autonomous avant-garde. Ives's music has fallen into the cracks, and the composer has been branded an exotic. He remains an outsider, excluded from the Eurocentric version of music history and from the academic mainstream of

105

American modern music.[1] One is reminded of Ives's famous split existence
and his struggle between romantic and modern values, confronting the
fundamental duality of the American "Gilded Age" in which he found
himself immersed.[2]

Thus Ives's personality and art are filled with elusive paradoxes. His
music contains a remarkable variety of styles, levels of difficulty, and stages
of refinement, even among works written in close chronological proximity. The common view of an artist's development as a straight, teleological
process can be applied to Ives only within certain limitations. Although it is
of course possible to establish style periods for his music, as demonstrated
for example by J. Peter Burkholder,[3] we must not forget that the music Ives
composed between 1890 and 1925 is consistent in only one respect, namely
in its constant fluctuation among expressive extremes and diverse
compositional procedures. Did Ives intend to underline fluctuation and
diffuseness and to elevate these aspects to central artistic principles? The
unusual overall forms and incongruous stylistic worlds of his major works,
such as the *Concord Sonata* or Fourth Symphony, hint at such an intention.
It would be incomprehensible for a composer following aesthetic conventions to juxtapose a monumental sonata movement in the tradition of
Beethoven ("Emerson") with stylized but nevertheless sentimentally
affecting nineteenth-century parlor music ("The Alcotts"), or to follow a
unique phantasmagoria of sound ("Comedy") with a classicist, even epi-
gonous imitation of Brahms ("Fugue").

The incongruities and paradoxes constitute one of the main obstacles
to a profound understanding of Ives's music, and have inspired a variety of
scholarly responses and interpretations. One perspective that has been
offered originates in the unique circumstances of turn-of-the-century
America, when composers were confronting both an insufficiently developed nationalist identity and an overbearing European tradition. In con-

[1] See Wolfgang Rathert, *Charles Ives*, 2nd edn, Erträge der Forschung, vol. 267
(Darmstadt: Wissenschaftliche Buchgesellschaft, 1996), 154–65.
[2] See Frank R. Rossiter, *Charles Ives and His America* (New York: Liveright, 1975),
and Peter J. Conn, "Innovation and nostalgia: Charles Ives," in *The Divided
Mind: Ideology and Imagination in America, 1898–1917* (Cambridge: Cambridge
University Press, 1983), 230–50.
[3] J. Peter Burkholder, *All Made of Tunes: Charles Ives and the Uses of Musical
Borrowing* (New Haven: Yale University Press, 1995), 6.

trast to most composers of his or the preceding generation, this unbalanced self-image of the American art music did not lead Ives to a "national" or "academic" point of view.[4] Horatio Parker, John Knowles Paine, Edward MacDowell, and Arthur Farwell decided in favor of either a crypto-European Americanism or a folklorism (a belated attempt to develop a national style) in order to avoid the aesthetic dilemma that had characterized American art music. (H. Wiley Hitchcock used the terms "genteel" and "vernacular" to describe this antagonism between a "high," cultivated style borrowed from European art music and a "low," indigenous style drawn from the various ethnicities and popular cultures, an antagonism that comprises the substantial conflict between "written" and "oral" spheres of music.[5]) Even before the turn of the century, Ives looked for another more radical solution, a response that would ultimately assume responsibility for his isolation from his contemporaries: he made the antagonism itself his artistic subject.

Ives decided to ignore the barriers between the "high" and "low" styles and to use "foreign" musical objects such as quotations, borrowings, and allusions to form his artistic identity and as points of creative departure. The technique of using such heterogeneous materials serves a twofold musical and symbolic function, underlying two fundamental characteristics of Ives's style: on the one hand an integration and dissolution of the "foreign objects" through motivic-thematic procedures in the form of musical puns, and on the other hand a music "about" music, or style "about" styles. This richness of borrowed musical sources and phenomena on the one hand transfers colloquialisms to a kind of "anonymous" compositional idea, while on the other hand it leads to a strangely hermetic, almost incomprehensible personal musical language. The idea of authenticity, which Ives drew from the renunciation of thematic originality and the superiority of stylistic eclecticism, reveals a dialectical dilemma. Therefore Ives continuously tried to replace eclecticism with innovative musical forms, either as abstract, "objective" structures or in fusion with other artistic means of expression. This becomes apparent both in numer-

---

4   For more information, see Barbara Zuck, *A History of Musical Americanism*, Studies in Musicology, vol. 19 (Ann Arbor MI: UMI Research Press, 1980).

5   H. Wiley Hitchcock, *Music in the United States: A Historical Introduction*, 3rd edn (Englewood Cliffs NJ: Prentice-Hall, 1988).

ous constructivist approaches at the levels of pitch systems and temporal organization, and in the strong literarization of music, which the term "programmaticism" can capture only insufficiently. This literarization received its ultimate realization in the simultaneous publication of the *Concord Sonata* and the *Essays Before a Sonata* (meant to clarify the compositional intentions at the unambiguous level of language) and confirms Ives's "unfinished" concept of music. It reveals an important Romantic heritage, namely the increasing questioning of a work's expressive power, which for clarification needs the author's own interpretation.[6]

II

Can Ives's music be analyzed sufficiently by a thorough investigation of the "foreign objects," or is there another key to understanding his intentions? To answer this question, we must first consider exactly how borrowings operate within Ives's compositional philosophy. First of all, we must recognize that the identification of sources for borrowed material has contributed significantly to the unveiling of Ives's private mythology and its autobiographical, historical, and local sources. In J. Peter Burkholder's view, Ives's techniques of integrating borrowed material place him squarely within the mainstream of the nineteenth-century European tradition, serving merely to refine and individualize stylistic practices that had been common for generations. From that perspective, Ives would be an original contemporary of Brahms, Richard Strauss, or Sibelius, from whom his compositional technique and style would differ not in substance but only by degrees, through the abundance of quotations and incorporation of popular tunes. This view carries with it two assumptions: first, that a coherent concept of style exists in both American and European music since the end of the eighteenth century; and second, that Ives, in spite of his undoubtedly innovative compositional methods, subscribed to the powerful European notion of "music as music."

[6] This does not only pertain to Romantic program music since Berlioz, but also, for example, to the Pre-Raphaelite school of painting, where the title or the commentary on the frame becomes an integral part of the artwork. The long original title of the *Concord Sonata* or the title of the finale of the Second Orchestral Set, "From Hanover Square North, at the End of a Tragic Day, the Voice of the People Again Arose," betrays exactly this insecurity.

But in spite of Ives's association with Horatio Parker, and his emphatic admiration of Beethoven – perhaps more a reflection of the American Beethoven cult of the nineteenth century than of actual compositional influences – any suggestion of an unequivocal connection between Ives's and European ways of musical thinking is open to question. In fact, Ives no longer felt obliged to follow classical and romantic compositional theory, with its reliance on the paradigm of major-minor tonality, tempered tuning, and the rhythmic-metric system of *Periode* and *Satz*. Even if drawing from traditional formal and technical functions and models, he is struggling to liberate his music from historical dependence, and from the normative dictates of European music theory. Ives has a view of tradition that is simultaneously "iconoclastic" and "ironic."

A perspective that focuses exclusively on normative and historical limitations of Ives's technique of modeling fails to recognize his unique position in early twentieth-century music. Such a perspective would barely distinguish Ives from many European composers of the late nineteenth and early twentieth centuries, who – with the exception of Mahler – were captivated by historicism. Compared with neoclassicism, for example, particularly Stravinsky's formalism and sense of order in the revaluation and actualization of older models, Ives's procedures appear nostalgic and without direction. But Ives's music does not participate in the formalist tradition of European art music, which leads from the idea of "absolute music" to Eduard Hanslick's *tönend bewegten Formen*. Form in Ives's way of thinking emerges from a symbolic idea of music that is based on complex romantic aesthetic theories and means something entirely different from Stravinsky's or Schoenberg's definition of musical form as the "result of 'logical elaboration' of the musical material."[7] Such "elaboration" has nothing in common with the "creative eclecticism" to which Ives, inspired by Emerson's transcendentalism, paid homage. Even the other aspect of Ives's composing – the constructivist experimentation with tonal and temporal systems – relies much more on "extra-musical" mathematical principles than on the dialectical revaluation and replacement of major-minor tonality (Schoenberg), or classic accent-based rhythmic structures (Stravinsky).

---

[7] Igor Stravinsky, "Antworten auf 35 Fragen," in *Leben und Werk – von ihm selbst* (Zurich and Mainz: Schott, 1957), 252.

Ives's relation to notation strongly confirms this point. While European art music shows the tendency to determine all aspects of structure and sound by notational means, Ives turns in the opposite direction toward a new "orality" and "directness" of artistic content that is opposed to the finality of conventionally conceived notation. In this respect Ives follows in the Puritan tradition of the orator and preacher, for whom the effect of the spoken word directed toward the community or audience is of primary importance.[8] Paradoxically, because of Ives's historical situation this attitude and practice led to an overload of writing, even to an implicitly "oral" writing, including multiple versions of the same piece and an extremely unstable concept of the "work."

III

If we agree that the European model of a formalistic and abstract "music as music" can describe Ives's musical and aesthetic thinking only insufficiently, we must search for an alternative, indicated here by the concept of "potentiality." This concept attempts to accommodate the differences between Ives and his European contemporaries, and the inherent peculiarities of his aesthetic approach. The idea of potentiality interprets the discrepancies in Ives's style not as a deviation or extension of a universally valid aesthetic, but as an intrinsic characteristic of his music.

The *Essays Before a Sonata*, published in 1921, may be considered a focus and summit of Ives's views. The *Essays* demonstrate the fundamental influence of ideas from the worlds of Romanticism and American Transcendentalism, along with connections to other more obscure literary and aesthetic sources of the nineteenth and early twentieth centuries. Since the most profound literary influences on the *Essays*, particularly the early English Romantics and the American Transcendentalists, have already been extensively investigated,[9] it must suffice here to mention the important idea

---

[8] See Bronson Alcott's comment: "Only the living, spoken, answered word is final." Quoted in Lawrence Buell, *Literary Transcendentalism: Style and Vision in the American Renaissance*, 2nd edn (Ithaca NY: Cornell University Press, 1973), 81.

[9] See Audrey Davidson, "Transcendental unity in the works of Charles Ives," *American Quarterly* 22/1 (1970), 35–44; Wolfgang Rathert, *The Seen and the Unseen: Studien zum Werk von Charles Ives*, Berliner musikwissenschaftliche Arbeiten, vol. 38 (Munich: Emil Katzbichler, 1991), 36–60; and David Michael

of "potentiality" as it applies to the philosophy of Ralph Waldo Emerson. Ives himself alludes to this concept when he characterizes the great transcendentalist as an "invader of the unknown – America's deepest explorer of the spiritual immensities" (*Essays*, 11). The organicist model of a symbolic and real interlocking of art and nature, "word" and "world," which Emerson – drawing from and misreading Kant's critique of transcendentalism – develops in his writings from the very beginning, has its foundation in the autonomy of the mind, the absolute "I," through which the external world is then determined. (The phenomena of the "outer" world are available only to the mind and do not have any provable reality outside of its sphere.) Emerson's aesthetic theory – which absorbs essential impulses from Samuel Taylor Coleridge's poetics of imagination and Percy Bysshe Shelley's stylization of the poet as seer of the absolute – values not only the form of the artwork but also the conditions of its creation and reception. Charles Feidelson, following F. O. Matthiessen's landmark interpretation in *American Renaissance*, describes the basis of Emerson's theory of art as the "organic experience [of] which both mind and object are functions."[10] That is, in both form and content the artwork reflects an inextricable unity of "mind" and "object," of the one who perceives and what is perceived. The work is therefore all-inclusive, flowing, organic, and – as a faint reflection of nature's original wealth and variety of correspondence – utopian.

But the organic concept of form suffers from a fundamental contradiction between its boundless "inner" vision and the need for a comprehensive "outer" shape. Emerson tries to resolve this problem by creating analogies. He describes the organic form as a balance of macrocosm and microcosm, often using the rhetorical figure of synecdoche or metonymy.[11] This balance characterizes the process of artistic creation and aesthetic perception as well. In his essay "The Poet" Emerson conceives artistic imagination as a kind of catalyst of the unceasing streams of perception:

Hertz, *Angels of Reality: Emersonian Unfoldings in Wright, Stevens, and Ives* (Carbondale: Southern Illinois University Press, 1993), 114–59.

[10] Charles Feidelson, *Symbolism and American Literature* (Chicago: University of Chicago Press, 1953), 121.

[11] See Lawrence Buell's interpretation of the transcendental concept of form as "a structure which will be atomistic, discontinuous, yet comprehensive and essentially unified by the artist's vision of the cosmic order" (*Literary Transcendentalism*, 157).

But the quality of the imagination is to flow, and not to freeze. The poet did not stop at the color or the form, but read their meaning; neither may he rest in this meaning, but he makes the same objects exponents of his new thought. Here is the difference betwixt the poet and the mystic, that the last nails the symbol to one sense, which was a true sense for a moment, but soon becomes old and false. For all symbols are fluxional; all language is vehicular and transitive.[12]

In further essays (such as "Poetry and imagination" and "The method of nature") Emerson generalizes and mystifies this theory to the extent of granting every human being artistic potential: the individual becomes the "vessel" that merges, in an ecstatic state, with divine streams of perception.[13] For this reason Emerson's theory of art is also bi-polar: the "flowing," transitory character of the artwork preserves the transition from diffuse perception to molded form in a *statu nascendi* and becomes actualized in the perceiver. In a compensating act, the spectator must become free from passivity of reception, while on the other hand the artist must become immersed in passivity to reach a state where inspiration is possible. It thus comes as no surprise that the concept of "repose" plays an important role in Emerson's aesthetics, reflecting his intensive dealing with Buddhism.[14] Emerson's "repose" erases the "absolute mind," reinstating the original unity of subject and object. Imagination of this unity represents the highest goal of the transcendental artist. This form of aesthetic "passivity" is related to transcendentalism's fundamental attitude of

---

[12] Ralph Waldo Emerson, "The poet," in *Selected Essays, Lectures, and Poems*, ed. and with a foreword by Robert D. Richardson, Jr. (New York: Bantam, 1990), 220.

[13] "[Man's] health and greatness consist in his being the channel through which heaven flows to earth, in short, in the fulness in which an ecstatical state takes place in him. It is pitiful to be an artist when by forbearing to be artists we might be vessels filled with the divine overflowings, enriched by the circulations of omniscience and omnipresence." From "The method of nature," in *The Collected Works of Ralph Waldo Emerson*, vol. 1 (Cambridge MA: Belknap Press of Harvard University Press, 1971), 130. Another point worth mentioning concerns the "intentional" artistic attitude, which stands in the way of true inspiration. Cage's concept of a "non-intentional" art reflects this idea, and we might wonder whether the same holds true for Ives's criticism of the *déformation professionnelle* and his renunciation of a career as a composer.

[14] For more information on this subject, see Wolfgang Rathert, "Der amerikanische Transzendentalismus," in *Musik und Religion*, ed. Helga de la Motte-Haber (Laaber: Laaber, 1995), 191–214.

eclecticism: it focuses not so much on the originality of one's own ideas but on one's ability to absorb and amalgamate those of others. In this context we must understand the extensive use of quotations in Emerson and Ives as an aesthetic passivity, a willingness to be influenced, which later would also distinguish Cage's aesthetic.

Emerson's aesthetic theory of the organic and "potential" artwork belongs to a broad movement in nineteenth-century philosophy that seeks to elevate art to new forms of perception. Drawing on all available artistic means, the theory holds that a work of art should encompass a maximum richness of corresponding phenomena while still remaining in some sense "deficient" or "transitory." This duality of Romantic thought – which on the one hand led to historicism and the concept of "style," but on the other dreamt of an "immediate" art free of all historical shackles and conventions – culminates in the idea of the sublime. Kant characterized the sublime as a feeling of "boundlessness" and "totality" of a subject; it is the essence of the Romantic aesthetic of the "infinite," influencing all aspects of the fine arts, literature, and music.[15] It also marks the culmination of M. H. Abrams's procession from the "mirror" to the "lamp," from the mimetic to the expressive concept of art first introduced by the early English Romantics.[16] In his essays Ives regularly refers to those poets, philosophers, musicians, and artists besides Emerson and Thoreau who represent this change: William Wordsworth, Thomas Carlyle, John Ruskin, and Robert Browning.

Ives's reception of Romanticism, his literary and musical metaphors, and his metaphysics of art all belong to this aesthetic of the infinite and sublime, which is part of a transatlantic history of ideas. His view of Beethoven at the end of his Emerson essay, his reverence for the imagery of landscape and mountains, inspired works such as the short study *From the Steeples and the Mountains*, the last movement of the Second String Quartet ("The Call of the Mountains"), and, above all, the *Universe Symphony*. And even the ethical and aesthetic judgment behind the seemingly strange confrontation of the "rare country man" Thoreau with the "city man"

---

[15] See Marjorie Hope Nicolson, *Mountain of Gloom and Mountain Glory: The Development of the Aesthetics of the Infinite* (Ithaca NY: Cornell University Press, 1959).

[16] M. H. Abrams, *The Mirror and the Lamp: Romantic Theory and the Critical Tradition* (Oxford: Oxford University Press, 1953).

Debussy (*Essays*, 82) was influenced by this metaphysics. Ives wanted to imbue his music with that presence of the "sublime" he admired not only in the expressive and metaphysically charged art of Beethoven and Browning, but also in the "nature-like," organic-formless artistic conception of Thoreau. Behind Ives's celebrated dualism between "substance" and "manner" stand the antipodes of "nature" and "history," of "expression" and "style," of "truth" and "appearance."

The equally complex history of Beethoven reception in nineteenth-century America, which can be directly linked through John Sullivan Dwight and Margaret Fuller to the rise of Transcendentalism,[17] involves the presence and eventual subsumption of the same antitheses, upholding the music of Beethoven as the epitome of a "metaphysical" work of art. The *Concord Sonata* reflects in a twofold way this strong influence: as a monumental homage to Beethoven the sonata looks for a naive and direct communication with his spirit and the musical past; its "transcendental tunes" represent icons of a European metaphysical burden. But since Ives tries to avoid any stylization and aesthetic mediation, the homage cannot bring to closure the aura connected with a Beethoven-like "opus." Rather, it abides in an undefined zone of a modern "work in progress," whose richness of associations does not allow for completion. And Ives's choices of orthography and notation intensify this twilight, leaving the character of the sonata in an ambiguous *statu nascendi* between an "oral" *Klangrede* and a "written" *opus perfectum*.

It is not surprising, then, that the use of quotations in the *Concord Sonata* generates an inherent ambiguity that obscures clear musical or symbolic allocations. Its central interval, the falling third, is an allusion to Beethoven's Fifth Symphony and to *Missionary Chant*, but at the same time to neither one nor the other. Such an allusion leads to a hermeneutic circle of references, aiming at several ways of perception that simultaneously allow multiple interpretations. Ives's procedure of superimposing perspectives (not to be mistaken for a "collage" in the sense of a surrealistic montage and deconstruction of meaning[18]) thus anticipates the avant-

---

[17] See Ora F. Saloman, *Beethoven's Symphonies and J. S. Dwight: The Birth of American Music Criticism* (Boston: Northeastern University Press, 1995).

[18] For this reason, J. Peter Burkholder's reinstatement of the term "collage" to describe one of Ives's central techniques strikes me as problematic. See *All Made of Tunes*, 369ff.

garde principle of an "impure," non-polar art. Referring to paintings by Jasper Johns, John Cage described this principle as a decisive factor in an avant-garde and non-hierarchical aesthetic of perception.[19]

IV

The English historian of philosophy Leon Vivante has argued that the concept of potentiality – because of its Romantic and ultimately Platonic origins – is grounded in the act of transcending the constitutive, formal, and content-related boundaries of art. Potentiality thus necessarily refers to an "inner form" that could be described as "thought in its ever immediately created existentiality," or "nakedness, a value of presence and promptness." The artist no longer views this type of form as *res facta* or as an unchangeable object, but rather as an "absolute presence" and therefore in principle infinite.[20] Such a concept of form is inevitably deeply paradoxical because it tries to capture what is possible only beyond imaginable forms. It lives in the absence of any form, or in a negation, which can be realized in several ways. Emerson had in mind an "encyclopedic" or "total" art work absorbing an abundance of phenomena and as such resembling a catalogue. Thoreau talked of the "epiphany" of the phenomenal world, which should be explored in art as another form of life.

In Browning's complex and allegorically rich philosophical dramas – which Ives obviously knew very well – the poet created a "form of formlessness" resulting from the confrontation of diametrically opposed forces. His dramas pursue utmost mental presence in spite of their use of distant historical images and figures. In the words of J. Hillis Miller, "Browning's aim is to get the whole meaning of a life into the most concentrated form. . . . All Browning's art is based on the paradoxical attempt to give form to the formless."[21] Certainly Ives's most ambitious symphonic conceptions, such as the "Comedy" from the Fourth Symphony, "Putnam's Camp" from *Three*

---

[19] "The situation must be Yes-and-No not either-or. Avoid a polar situation." Quoted in John Russell, *The Meanings of Modern Art*, rev. and updated edn (New York: Harper & Row, 1981), 336.

[20] Leon Vivante, *A Philosophy of Potentiality* (London: Routledge and Kegan Paul, 1955), 61, 64.

[21] J. Hillis Miller, *The Disappearance of God: Five Nineteenth-Century Writers* (Cambridge MA: Belknap Press of Harvard University Press, 1963), 126, 159.

Places in New England, the finale of the Second Orchestral Set ("From Hanover Square North, at the End of a Tragic Day, the Voice of the People Again Arose"), and "The Fourth of July" from the *Holidays Symphony*, all show an affinity with "formless form," confronting listeners with an all-embracing universe of sounds that is to be experienced as a "stream of consciousness" or "*monologue intérieur*." In these movements, which outline a concept of a purely rhetorical and potential form, Ives creates a unique tension between centrifugal and centripetal forces, between the heterogeneity of the quoted musical objects and the homogeneity of the dramaturgical and compositional strategies.[22]

We can best define the Romantic concept of "inner form" in Thoreau's and especially in Whitman's transcendentalism as "imminent fulfillment," as an overly full and, it seems, associatively assembled "catalogue rhetoric."[23] Ives's concept of art links up those ideas; at the same time, however, potentiality in his music encompasses much more. The external shape of many of his works and his seemingly unsystematic way of confining them to paper – an aspect that still awaits thorough investigation – result from two tendencies that in part negate traditional procedures. One is the habit of deliberately leaving major works unfinished; the other is the abundant intermingling of thematic ideas and compositional techniques between different works.[24] Behind these tendencies stands the silhouette of a "total composition" spanning all style periods and concretized in separate works as its excerpts and fragments; perhaps the book of the *114 Songs* can be seen as the "secret" center, since it obviously collects all styles, techniques, and quotations Ives had used during his compositional career. From this point of view we can also better understand Ives's unremitting urge to revise. Fragmentation and incompletion do not apply only to the *Universe Symphony*, a work that marks an extreme point of Ives's compositional aspirations, both through the enormous challenge of its program

---

[22] The difference between Ives's approach and that of his European contemporaries is substantial and should not be overlooked. Burkholder's comparison of Ives with Richard Strauss (*All Made of Tunes*, 411) seems questionable because it takes for granted a universal musical aesthetic.

[23] Buell, *Literary Transcendentalism*, 165ff.

[24] Stephen Blum speaks of an "intricate web of interrelations stretching across his work." See Stephen Blum, "Ives's position in social and music history," *The Musical Quarterly* 63/4 (1977): 459–82.

as "cosmic landscape"[25] and through the obvious choice of the particular "catalogue" of sounds and temporal structures for the foundation of the work.[26] Similar conditions can be found in the *Concord Sonata*, whose many stages and versions create a kind of "quarry" of musical ideas, and the diverse variants of the "Comedy" movement of the Fourth Symphony.

Ives draws on this reservoir of ideas, which he had laid out already in the1890s, in a very flexible manner and subjects it to permanent transformation. This practice directly reflects his working methods, which are reminiscent of James Joyce's use of "notesheets."[27] First he collects and registers acoustic sources and other models (i.e., all material to be quoted or paraphrased); later he assigns them to specific works. His compositional development is characterized by amalgamation and constant refinement of diverse borrowings and their integration into higher programmatic and symbolic contexts. Ultimately Ives refers to his own music as a source or model, creating new, surprising structures and connections like the "auto-eclectic" design of the Fourth Symphony.

On the other hand, Ives refused to end the process of amalgamation. To do so would have been for him a contradiction of the nature of artistic imagination, a denial of the experience of playing and resounding in favor of a fixation on lasting, unchanging works. In an often-cited sentence, Ives himself confirms this view: "In fact, as soon as music goes down to paper, it loses something of its birthright" (*Memos*, 189). He elaborates on these ideas in revealing comments on the "Emerson" movement of the *Concord Sonata*, attesting not only to this movement's key role in his music but also to the importance of the idea of mutability, organic growth, open-endedness, and potentiality:

> This is, as far as I know, the only piece which, every time I play it or turn to it, seems unfinished. . . . Some of the passages now played haven't been

---

[25] This aspect perfectly exemplifies the iconology of the sublime and Ruskin's glorification of the mountains. See Wolfgang Rathert, "Paysage imaginaire et perception totale: L'idée et la forme de la symphonie *Universe*," *Contrechamps* 7 (1986): 129–54.

[26] See the essays by Larry Austin and by Philip Lambert elsewhere in this volume.

[27] See Philip F. Herring, "Zur Textgenese des *Ulysses*: Joyces Notizen und seine Arbeitsmethode," in *James Joyces Ulysses*, ed. T. Fischer-Seidel (Frankfurt am Main: Suhrkamp, 1977), 80–104.

written out . . . and I don't know as I ever shall write them out, as it may take away the daily pleasure of playing this music and seeing it grow and feeling that it is not finished. (*Memos*, 79–80)

Ives's relationship to musical notation warrants a separate investigation. His deviations from convention reflect an urge to realize a certain distinctive but vaguely defined conception that merges notation and sound. He tries to record music that originally exists only in performance (or imagination) rather than to define an abstract compositional structure by notational means. His concept of notation is therefore characterized by a paradox resembling that of the "inner form": it is at the same time deficient and overdone, refusing as notation to make the step from an ambiguous process-driven orality to a clear fixation. Moreover, he ennobles irregular notation – according to his praise of vagueness in the *Essays* – as a symbol of greater artistic truth. Also interacting with the irrationality of notation are the numerous literary allusions, whether texts, programs, marginalia, or even extra-notational symbols, such as the letters indicating dynamic levels in the score of "Comedy." Ives's annotations become an integral part of the core of the work, as if trying to specify what the musical notes themselves can express only inadequately. That they do not in reality diminish but rather heighten ambiguity further exemplifies the intentional instability of Ives's concept of "the work."[28] Finally, Ives turns the usual sequence of sketching and then realizing a composition upside down: the actual notation of the work relapses into a preliminary state merely intending "to get the gist and swat" (*Memos*, 191), as Ives observes in connection with "Hawthorne," to trace the motion of the sound. This priority of sketchiness and incompleteness over any stable musical shape represents a nearly unsolvable problem for the editor of Ives's works,[29] but it corresponds to the importance John Ruskin assigns to

[28] The only aspects that can be clearly determined are the extramusical, philosophical, and religious frameworks of Ives's concept of the work. These forces involve a metaphysical and romantic idea of the beautiful that concerns not the tangible world but something absolute. In this respect, Ives comes very close to the convictions of the European symbolists, some of whom ranked among his favorite poets. See C. M. Bowra, *The Heritage of Symbolism* (London: MacMillan, 1947), 11–13.

[29] See Wolfgang Rathert, "The unanswered questions of the Ives edition," *The Musical Quarterly* 73/4 (1989): 575–84.

the sketch as a "metaphysical" form of art and thus as the truest measure of the depth of artistic imagination.[30]

V

There remains one other important aspect of "potentiality" in Ives, namely the relation between music and program and thus the overt auto-biographical orientation of his works. I do not wish to raise the issue of the degree to which Ives's actual autobiography reveals the uniqueness of his art. Stuart Feder and Jan Swafford have done this from different points of view, with special attention to the roles of George Ives and Harmony Twichell, and to Ives's later state of health.[31] Rather, I will examine the general aesthetic function of the autobiography as an expansion of the artistic conception. Through Transcendentalism and an exaltation of the subject among the Romantics, the strong traditions of autobiography and self-examination in American cultural history became a dynamic force that influenced some of Ives's greatest works.[32] These include not only the *Concord Sonata*, with its deliberate correlation between "movement" and "portrait" (as opposed to the more abstract formal schemes of the still underrated First Piano Sonata), but especially the innumerable real and

---

[30] See Robert Hewison, *John Ruskin and the Argument of the Eye* (London: Thames and Hudson, 1976), 65ff. The following passage from the epilogue of Ives's *Essays* sheds light on this issue: "Perhaps [substance] is an unexplained consciousness of . . . approaching truth or approaching unreality; [it is] a silent something felt in the truth of nature in Turner against the truth of art in Botticelli – or in the fine thinking of Ruskin against the fine soundings of Kipling" (*Essays*, 75). The opposition of "art" and "nature" immediately returns here as one of the categories.

[31] Stuart Feder, *Charles Ives: "My Father's Song": A Psychoanalytic Biography* (New Haven, Yale University Press, 1992); Jan Swafford, *Charles Ives: A Life with Music* (New York: Norton, 1996).

[32] On the nature of autobiography, see the collection of essays in *Autobiography: Essays Theoretical and Critical*, ed. James Olney (Princeton: Princeton University Press, 1980), especially the contribution of Robert F. Sayre, "Autobiography and the making of America," 146–68. One is reminded of the famous paraphrase of Rousseau at the beginning of *Walden*: "In most books, the *I*, or first person, is omitted; in this it will be retained." See Henry David Thoreau, "Walden," in *Thoreau: Walden and Other Writings*, edited and introduced by Joseph Wood Krutch (New York: Bantam Books, 1962), 107.

fictionalized autobiographical references Ives makes in the programs of his orchestral works and in his songs.

These references are approximations of personal or aesthetic experiences, through which the artwork becomes a symbolic reenactment of life. Again and again Ives portrays primal events intended to startle the listener into an "epiphany" or mystic moment, as "flashes of transcendent beauty, of such universal import, that they may bring, of a sudden, some intimate personal experience" (*Essays*, 30). He creates models of experience and perception that serve as aesthetic motifs and achieve a symbolic union of individual and collective experiences, irrespective of actual autobiographical events. Prominent examples include "From Hanover Square North," "Decoration Day," and "The Fourth of July." What these and other similar works display are musical structures of many perspectives, along with superimpositions of fragments of consciousness and perception, of remembrance and present. Musical language and individuality are here – to borrow Kenneth Burke's comment on *Finnegan's Wake* – of "equal substance."[33] Burke's observation, that each literary work contains a number of implicit "equations" and "association clusters" that hint at the author's motivation, but are not identical with the literary motifs,[34] can be applied to Ives's musical phantasmagorias to great benefit. Considering the technique of fragmentation, we can realize that fragmentation not only constitutes a technical principle, but itself becomes a central aesthetic and symbolic issue, as exemplified most impressively by the figure of the "open" endings.[35] In this process the quotations and pre-existing formal models, which for Ives serve as points of departure, lose their familiarity and become insignia of an "inner" autobiographical motivation, and perhaps an unconscious artistic message of the work in its entirety. Thus fragmentation builds the bridge between the composer's conception and the listener's perception and represents Ives's idea of potentiality in its most advanced state.

[33] Kenneth Burke, *The Philosophy of Literary Form: Studies in Symbolic Action* (Baton Rouge: Louisiana State University Press, 1971), 44.
[34] Ibid., 20.
[35] See Wolfgang Rathert, "Zur Entwicklung des symphonischen Werkes von Charles Ives," in *Bericht über das Internationale Symposion "Charles Ives und die amerikanische Musiktradition bis zur Gegenwart," Kölner Beiträge zur Musikforschung* 164, ed. Klaus Wolfgang Niemöller (Regensburg: Bosse, 1990), 53–70.

VI

In the remainder of this essay I will discuss two aspects of Ives's music that exemplify its uniqueness and individuality and that thereby highlight basic differences between Ives and nineteenth-century European composers.[36] The first is the notion of "open" form; the second is the interchangeability of formal parts.

The project of the *Concord Sonata*, with its maze of uncertainties about multiple versions, notational practices, and interconnections with other Ives works (especially the Fourth Symphony, *The Celestial Railroad*, and some songs) perfectly demonstrates the intentional instability of Ives's formal conception.[37] Taken as a whole, Ives's handling of the sonata exhibits a seemingly inexhaustible amount of ambivalence, regarding the balance and the sequence of movements, the cyclic role of the "human faith melody," and ultimately the structures of individual movements. In a way, the *Concord* is already an adaptation, a transcription (in the sense of Busoni) of some larger imaginary work that brings together

---

[36] It is, of course, beyond question that Ives shared many similarities with some Europeans, especially Berlioz, who pushed forward the emancipation of musical space, and Mahler, who successfully mediated between "high" and "low" styles. Ives's role in the emancipation of the "landscape of sound" and musical space during the nineteenth century, as well as his relation to the question of Romantic synaesthesia have been investigated systematically by Robert P. Morgan, "Spatial form in Ives," in *An Ives Celebration: Papers and Panels of the Charles Ives Centennial Festival-Conference*, ed. H.Wiley Hitchcock and Vivian Perlis (Urbana: University of Illinois Press, 1977), 145–58. Two writers have made preliminary contributions toward a general theory: Stefan Kunze, "Raumvorstellungen in der Musik," *Archiv für Musikwissenschaft* 31/1 (1974): 1–21, and David Matthews, *Landscape into Sound* (St. Albans: Claridge Press, 1992). For comparisons of Mahler and Ives, see also Robert P. Morgan, "Mahler and Ives: mutual responses at the end of an era," *19th-Century Music* 2/1 (1978): 72–81; Wolfgang Rathert, "Mahler und Ives: Gibt es eine 'geheime Zeitgenossenschaft'?" *Neue Zeitschrift für Musik* 151/10 (1990): 7–12; and Leon Botstein, "Innovation and nostalgia: Ives, Mahler, and the origins of modernism," in *Charles Ives and His World*, ed. J. Peter Burkholder (Princeton: Princeton University Press, 1996), 35–74.

[37] On multiple versions, see Sondra Rae Clark, "The elements of choice in Ives's *Concord Sonata*," *The Musical Quarterly* 60/2 (1974): 167–86; and the essay by Geoffrey Block elsewhere in this volume. On notational issues in the *Concord*, see Rathert, *Seen and Unseen*, 110ff. On interconnections with other works, see Burkholder, *All Made of Tunes*, 350–59.

ideas from sources such as the incomplete *Emerson Overture*. Such a conception is evident in Ives's description of the original sound design (*Essays*, 84):

> The first movement (Emerson) . . . was first thought of (we believe) in terms of a large orchestra; the second (Hawthorne), in terms of a piano or a dozen pianos; the third (Alcotts), an organ (or piano with voice or violin); and the last (Thoreau), in terms of strings, colored possibly with a flute or horn.

We can sense such origins not only in the various pianistic idioms of the sonata but also in Ives's suggestion that other instruments might participate. A viola part represents a vestige of an orchestral version of "Emerson," and a flute part adds a programmatic and coloristic element to "Thoreau." Only the "Hawthorne" movement (which also forms the backbone of the "Comedy" movement of the Fourth Symphony, where it is again assigned to the piano) has a genuinely pianistic conception.

Among the four movements, however, it is "Emerson" in which the overall conception of "transcription" and the construction of a "super-form" come to a head. In one respect this movement is an attempt by Ives to re-create the original orchestral sound of untempered strings, evident in his strangely contradictory notation of accidentals.[38] In another respect, which Ives suppressed in the 1947 edition, it is an imitation of a literary speech, with alternating sections in "verse" modeled on Emerson's poetry, and "prose" modeled on Emerson's essays.[39] It furthermore shares elements with Liszt's "multifunctional form," since the formal

---

[38] See Rathert, *Seen and Unseen*, 265ff.

[39] For more on this aspect see Giselher Schubert, "Die *Concord Sonata* von Charles Ives: Anmerkungen zu Werkstruktur und Interpretation," in *Aspekte der musikalischen Interpretation: Sava Savoff zum 70. Geburtstag*, ed. Hermann Danuser und Christoph Keller (Hamburg: Karl Dieter Wagner, 1980), 121–38, and Felix Meyer, *"The Art of Speaking Extravagantly": Eine vergleichende Studie der* Concord Sonata *und der* Essays Before a Sonata *von Charles Ives*, Publikationen der schweizerischen musikforschenden Gesellschaft, Series II, vol. 34 (Bern: Haupt, 1991), 141–66. The parallelism of musical and literary strands within one overall form offers a striking affinity between Ives's sonata and some of Schumann's early piano music.

Figure 5.1 Form chart of "Emerson"

Page/Staff System*	Literary Form (1st edn)	Sonata Form	Multifunctional Form
1/1	Prose	*Introduction/* *Exposition* (1st/2nd/3rd themes)	Cadenzas/ First mvt
5/1	Verse	2nd theme	Second ("Slow") mvt
5/4	Prose	Transition	
8/1	Verse	? (Interpolation/ Final section)	Third mvt ("Scherzo")
12/1	Prose	*Development:* 1st theme ("as a Song")	
13/4		2nd/3rd themes	
[16/1]		*Recapitulation:* 1st theme	
15/4 [16/3]	Verse	2nd theme	Last mvt
16/1 [17/1]	Prose	*Coda:* 1st theme	

* different location in 2nd edn in brackets

process suggests a "sonata within a sonata."[40] Finally, it reflects Ives's pre-occupation with the idea of a teleological and dynamic sonata form in the spirit of Beethoven, which he transforms and finally negates. These various formal interpretations are summarized in Figure 5.1.

As might be expected, an analysis of thematic processes in the sonata reveals an intricate layering of cyclic and movement-specific thematic ideas that are held together by basic and thus sufficiently flexible motivic cells. The most important cell is the interval of the third; it predominates in the cyclic "human faith melody," mediates between the Beethoven motto and

[40] Ives mistakenly speaks of three movements of the original *Emerson Overture* but continues to enumerate four that supposedly became part of the "Emerson" movement of the *Concord Sonata*: "the first (the cadenzas)—then the slow movement (starting with the theme at the top of p. 5 of the printed sonata)—the scherzo was about the same as from p. 8 to 11 . . . —the last movement was about [from] the middle of p. 16 to the end, but this was much longer than in the printed copy" (*Memos*, 77).

the *Missionary Chant,* and characterizes in inversion the second (lyrical) theme of "Emerson." The thematic unfolding both of "Emerson" and of the whole sonata exemplifies a striking rethinking of thematic process in the classic–romantic sonata form; it does not lead from the exposition to the development but – in a dramaturgical reversal – from the part to the whole. In terms of the overall melodic architecture, this process mainly applies to the "human faith melody," which appears in the first two movements only in fragments, in "The Alcotts" almost complete, and is finally disclosed and completed in the flute theme at the end of "Thoreau." But on the other hand this "cumulative setting" (as aptly characterized by Burkholder[41]) is thwarted by a formal principle common to the classic period which Charles Rosen once described as "the gradual loosening of the formal tensions" from the first toward the final movement.[42]

But such a reversal also characterizes themes within "Emerson" itself. First a cadenza-like and rhapsodic opening features an expansion of the tonal space through whole tones and by diffuse paths through widening registers, and the emergence of the third as a motivic nucleus. Within this texture Ives presents three movement-specific themes in a manner typical of conventional development sections: the first – with its characteristic combination of seconds and fourths – is hidden among the massive chords of the right hand in the second system of the first page, and the second (lyrical) and third (accompanying) themes emanate from the contrapuntal layering at the beginning of the third system.[43] The dramaturgical plan of the movement repeatedly tends toward clarification or formal "exposi-tions," often following the outlines of the original "Emerson" movements and the verse–prose sectionalization. As defined by a "multifunctional" form, the combination of the second and third themes (top of p. 5) could thus be seen as the "slow" movement, whereas the material of pages 8–11 might be considered a kind of "scherzo." The first theme reappears dis-guised as a "song" in a new prose section beginning at the top of page 12.

Viewing the movement as a single sonata form, one might expect the development at this point. But the "song" section appears instead as a kind

[41] See *All Made of Tunes,* 137–60.

[42] Charles Rosen, *The Classical Style* (New York: Norton, 1972), 423.

[43] Page numbers and staff system numbers refer to the sonata's second edition (New York: Associated Music Publishers, 1947).

of re-exposition of the first theme, which leads to the actual development section (starting with the second and third themes) at the fourth system of page 13. This exchange in the placement of "development" and "exposition" demonstrates that there is no real connection between thematic processes and formal construction. Their dialectical relation is replaced by a paradoxical "regression" of the themes, supported by their song-like melodic structures that render them unsuitable for long-range motivic and thematic developments. In the end, thematicism and form are at variance with each other, a continual undermining of a "logical" process.[44]

Notably, the "song" passage, through its evocation of a "timeless" mood lost in dreams, anticipates the gesture of the "human faith melody" at the end of "Thoreau," just as the opening broken chords of that movement are anticipated earlier in "Emerson" (p. 7, third system). The fact that thematic ideas in "Emerson" initiate developmental processes that achieve completion only at the end of the sonata illustrates more than the principle of thematic metamorphosis; it also reveals the dominance of the "Emerson" movement as the "microcosm" and "poetics" of the entire work.

We can thus understand the "Emerson" movement as a compositional "entelechy" that nevertheless eschews common principles of the European sonata form, including consistent motivic-thematic development, functional major-minor tonality, and correspondences of theme and form. Pitch structure and sound organization in the sonata, for example, are based largely on hexachordal extracts of the whole-tone and half-tone shifts (major/minor triads), perhaps following a rigorous yet unexplained compositional system.[45] In contrast to this, triadic harmony functions for purposes of coloring or – most notably in "The Alcotts" – as an object of distortion. Overall, Ives aspires toward a symbolic form-world, which because of its ambiguity cannot be narrowed down to either an absolute or a programmatic essence. Precisely because of its remarkable individuality, Ives's "inner form" has no defining formal principle.

[44] The same could be said of Ives's choice of the Beethoven motto. Whereas in the first movement of Beethoven's Fifth Symphony the motto's rhythmic energy persists throughout, in the musical prose of the "Emerson" movement it is strangely neutralized and lyricized in an impressionistic manner.

[45] See the discussion of a whole-tone organization in the *Concord Sonata* by Michael J. Babcock, "Ives' 'Thoreau': a point of order," *American Society of University Composers Proceedings* 9–10 (1974–75): 89–102.

Form arises from connections among the various thematic, formal, and historical elements and associations, the latter conjured up by the quotations. Ives's use of the Beethoven motto in connection with the portrait of Emerson parallels his association of Stephen Foster's "Massa's in de Cold Ground" with Thoreau. With this constellation he contrasts the European historical and metaphysical implications of the Beethoven motto with the innocence and "local" American authenticity of the Foster theme. Since musical factors alone cannot explain the sudden appearance of the Foster theme exclusively in the last movement, we must assume that Ives uses this and other quotations in order to suggest an imaginary discourse or even reconciliation between two aesthetically remote worlds. The quotations function as emblems in the same way as overall form is created by a sequence of "pictures" or "scenes."

From a rhetorical point of view, the *Concord Sonata* is more adequately interpreted as an "open" text than as a "closed" form. This text, which subdivides into several "sub-texts" corresponding to individual thematic strands, opens up an entire panorama of styles, forms of perception, and thus also of compositional attitudes. It is technically organized by an equally basic and intricate principle of metamorphosis that generates "puns," one of which appears in the "human faith melody."[46] Larry Starr has written of Ives's "meta-style" and "style about styles" that result from overcoming and "democratizing" stylistic barriers.[47] But does not Ives in the imaginary, potential form of the *Concord Sonata* go beyond this "meta-style" by presenting "style" as a result of various contexts? Does not such a view lead to a modern critique of our concept of style, and does it not demonstrate the ambivalence of all aesthetic perception?

Ives's laconic invitation for "somebody" or anyone to complete his unfinished compositions then begins to make sense.[48] It challenges us to free ourselves from the dogma of the individual author and from the aesthetic autonomy of the work. Whereas such autonomy is a central feature of

---

[46] That is, the conflation of the Beethoven motto with the similar beginning of the hymn tune *Missionary Chant*.

[47] His most recent discussion of this idea appears in *A Union of Diversities: Style in the Music of Charles Ives* (New York: Schirmer, 1992).

[48] In his *Memos* (108), Ives says in connection with the *Universe Symphony*: "I am just referring to the above because, in case I don't get to finishing this, somebody might like to try to work out the idea."

European musical aesthetics, with its more rigid conception of form and motivic-thematic development, it does not exist in the *Concord Sonata* and its new concept of form as text. Not only has Ives continuously "recomposed" the sonata, but he has also enabled listeners constantly to make surprising intertextual connections with music history (as an "imaginary museum"), or to follow their own musical associations and newly complete the work or perceive it in its "incompleteness" as text. In the same way that Emerson in his essay "Quotation and originality" already understood tradition as a "book" or "catalogue" that can be used without inhibition, Ives absorbed musical tradition as "text," which he then varied and transformed into new forms of perception. This relation to tradition requires a certain distance and at the same time a playful openness, which is something fundamentally different from the attitude of most European composers up to 1945. For them tradition remained a normative concept, and they did not abandon the aesthetic and technical canon of "music as music."

VII

The interchangeability of themes, formal elements, and complete movements, characteristic of much of Ives's work, represents another important break with the Classic–Romantic tradition. This break, however, is inherently different from Liszt's, for example, who newly arranged his *Hungarian Rhapsodies* mainly for pragmatic reasons. Especially in music based on motivic-thematic development, the interchangeability of formal elements jeopardizes a fundamental postulate of "logical" formal structure or – in the theories of August Halm and Heinrich Schenker after the turn of the century – of *Zeiten der Form*. According to these theories form is "energy" and consists of a sequence of stages that cannot easily be exchanged; further, the physiognomy of the themes must conform with their respective formal locations.

In Ives, on the other hand, interchangeability is evidence of the tentativeness of the form and thus of its potentiality. In the *Concord Sonata* and its symphonic counterpart, the Fourth Symphony, this principle becomes recognizable in the changes that separate the respective closely related second movements. "Hawthorne" features a kaleidoscopic construction, a loose sequence of individual sound images that seem to emerge from a phantasmagoric and creative fantasy rather than from the idea of a scherzo, the place it occupies within the sonata. The "Comedy" is also a kaleidoscope, but it is not merely an orchestration of "Hawthorne." Rather, it is a broad recomposition based on a complex program in the narrative form of a dream that brings together various pictorial, literary, and religious motifs, many suggesting a Puritan pilgrimage inspired by Bunyan's *Pilgrim's Progress* and Hawthorne's *The Celestial Railroad*. The topic of the machine or, more accurately, the railroad, is of similar importance.[49] Thus the sound shape is dominated by percussive effects: the metrical basis consists of mostly simple march rhythms and ostinati, which establish the background of a heterogeneous, broken perception of time.

Striking episodes from "Hawthorne" resurface in the "Comedy," providing important components of a phantasmagoria in two large spans, ultimately leading to catastrophe and awakening from the dream. The first (rehearsal numbers 1–21) includes two marches, "Country Band March" (a pseudo-quotation of Ives's own earlier composition), and "Columbia, Gem of the Ocean"; the second (rehearsal numbers 22–47) juxtaposes quotations of the hymn-tune *Martyn* at half-step intervals (G major vs. F♯ major). More important than the adaptation itself is the question of why it works, why it does not diminish the musical effect. Here, too, the answer lies in the uniqueness of Ives's formal conception, which is not oriented around any "logical," non-reversible thematic execution but rather unfolds a prismatic tableau of images and perceptions. Within this musical space the listener can move, so to speak, freely and "against" time, dwelling on individual sound events.

One of Ives's greatest musical achievements was to advance, in works such as the "Comedy," beyond imitations of existing models stipulated by normative aesthetics. He aspires not simply to convert established models, but to imagine a holistic form of perception that reflects both the "natural" way we perceive things and the distorting forces of the dream. Here we find the difference between Ives's concept of form and "collage": a collage tries to break down perception, whereas form in Ives remains integral in the sense

---

[49] See Roy V. Magers, "Charles Ives's optimism: or, The program's progress," in *Music in American Society 1776–1976*, ed. George McCue (New Brunswick NJ: Transaction Books, 1977), 73–86; Rathert, *Seen and Unseen*, 209–46; and Burkholder, *All Made of Tunes*, 389–410.

of Emerson's aesthetic theory of organicism, and therefore values the unity of perception and experience. For Emerson and Ives fragmentation always implies the "not yet" of an artwork, but never the "no more" of European philosophers and theories of art from Nietzsche to Adorno.

Thus it seems difficult to characterize Ives's music as "amorphous." On the contrary, intensive study of his compositions makes us more and more aware of the degree of elaboration that forms the basis of his associative connections, and the ingenious way he selects and combines quotations. In the "Comedy," for example, he associates musical quotations with citations from the Bible, thus suggesting in sound the stations of the pilgrimage. But his principles of connection have little in common with formalistic models of "comprehensibility" valued by nearly all important composers of European art music since the classical period, including Brahms, Schoenberg, Webern, Hindemith, and Stravinsky. To find a spiritual kinship, it makes more sense to look to James Joyce, who described the crucial parameter of his literary technique as follows: "I have the words already. What I am seeking is the perfect order of the words in the sentence."[50] Ives, too, had already found his "words," namely all those melodies and forms taken from a collective musical memory or dictionary, which he continually arranges in different orders and exchanges with one another without obscuring their identity or etymology.

Further, Ives follows such formal principles irrespective of the role of quotations. To demonstrate, let us finally compare his *Robert Browning Overture* with its derivative, the song "from 'Paracelsus'" (*114 Songs*, no. 71). As a musical portrait of the complex personality and poetry of Browning the overture is one of the most difficult of Ives's works to approach and interpret. It is dominated by an abstract, highly dissonant, and nearly always atonal language. Rather than relying on development and interrelation of quoted tunes, its structure is created by intervallic and rhythmic patterns similar to those in "On the Antipodes" and *In Re Con Moto Et Al.*

A comparison of the overture with the song reveals surprising similarities and differences. As a miniature drama the song almost presents a condensed version of the overture, and as such brings together several motives of "Paracelsus." Browning's drama strongly relies on Shelley's

---

[50] Quoted in Herring, "Zur Textgenese des *Ulysses*," 85.

Prometheus Unbound and the theme of human arrogance. Ives, who described the overture as an attempt "to catch the Browning surge into the baffling unknowables" (*Memos*, 76), reinforces this motive through textual compilation. The power of the human spirit, its "potency," is at the same time its doom. The passage compiled from verses 807, 846, and 847 ("I gazed on power till I grew blind. / What wonder if I saw no way to shun / despair? The power I sought for man, seemed God's") marks the climax of Ives's song. The symbolic context is again remarkable but it does not become clear without knowledge of the overture. Ives not only projects the musical search for the "unknowable" and the "unknown fields" onto the text, but he also creates a compositional parallel by transforming the overture into a song. Even more rigorously than in the "Comedy," he cuts the material and pastes it into a new context, which – beyond all aesthetic and technical concepts of traditional "logic" – follows its own precepts.

The comparison of the overture and song in Figure 5.2 shows that with the exception of m. 107, Ives derived the song material exclusively from the slow introduction and the exposition of the subsequent allegro (mm. 1–54) of the overture. After that point, the overture turns into a homogeneous march and becomes less appropriate for the texture Ives had established for the song. By exchanging single measures or groups of measures, the composer alters not only the original temporal structure of the overture material but also the vertical relationships through the isolation of bass and upper parts. Again, this reworking does not disturb the musical cohesion of "from 'Paracelsus.'" However, here it is not stylistic changes that demarcate structure, as in the "Comedy," but it is rather subtle intervallic constructions and an extended tonal language, providing a stronger kind of unity than do motivic and thematic elements.[51] In comparison to "formal" composition based on a normative compositional technique, Ives's approach appears to be illogical and unjustifiable. With this song he proves, however, that the individual pitch-interval organization can alone determine the value of a composition and that many such musically satisfying constellations exist. Here, too, though at another level, we recognize "potentiality" as an essential driving force in Ives's compositional thought.

[51] See detailed analyses in Rathert, *Seen and Unseen*, 247–56.

Figure 5.2 Comparison of *Browning Overture* and "from 'Paracelsus'"

Browning Overture (Measures)	"from 'Paracelsus'" (Phrases)
42–44	1–2
45	3
46, 48	4
49–52	5–7
53–55 (freely), 107	8–10
27–29 (freely, upper parts)	11–12
38–41	13
_____	14
27–28 (bass parts), 31, 33 (freely)	15
_____	16 "Andante molto"
7–8, 10 (freely)	17–19
_____	20

VIII

When Stravinsky observed – with part respect, part envy – that Ives "set about devouring the contemporary cake before anyone else had even found a seat at the same table,"[52] he had in mind the almost unbelievable spectrum of diverse compositional procedures that Ives had developed. But when Stravinsky in virtually the same breath referred to Ives as a "no doubt soon-to-be overrated composer," he implicitly criticized a lack of systematization. Yet Stravinsky surely hit upon a fundamental feature of Ives's music, namely its "potential," open character, which was a prerequisite for the abundance of procedures and also for the richness of connections between the individual compositions themselves. Ives's works have always been separate "texts" of one comprehensive "infinite text"[53] of musical and acoustic structures that he explored throughout his life. That is how his music can encompass the conventional, even the trivial, as well as the progressive, both extreme subjectivity and strict objectivity through the use of mathematical and acoustic laws and processes, the dimensions of which

---

[52] Igor Stravinsky, *Retrospectives and Conclusions* (New York: Knopf, 1969), 30.

[53] For this poetological problem, see the contributions of Hans-Jost Frey, *Der unendliche Text* (Frankfurt am Main: Suhrkamp, 1990), and George Steiner, "Das totale Fragment," in *Fragment und Totalität*, ed. L. Dällenbach and C. L. Hart Nibbrig (Frankfurt am Main: Suhrkamp, 1984), 18–29.

131

have only begun to be explored.[54] Ives realized the limitations of musical language and expanded his vocabulary in all directions: he dealt with tradition, he questioned it, and he experimented with a new and speculative syntax. The potentiality of his musical and aesthetic thought therefore represents not only a fascinating challenge to performers, listeners, and scholars, but also a powerful and inviting legacy of music still to come.

(Translated by Andreas Giger)

[54] See Philip Lambert, "Interval cycles as compositional resources in the music of Charles Ives," *Music Theory Spectrum* 12/1 (1990): 42–82.

6   Charles Ives and the politics of direct democracy

JUDITH TICK

America needs more direct democracy. It is a way in which we can
restore meaning to our democracy and truly give the people the
opportunity to control their own destiny.   Mark Hatfield, 1979[1]

The National Voter Initiative offers the people an unimpeded end-run
around that liberal establishment [in Washington]. Now is the time for
the brothers to put up or shut up.   Patrick Buchanan, 1977[2]

The judgment of the American people is extraordinarily sound.
                                        George Gallup, 1984[3]

My grandfather was a quiet man, but you could always get him to talk
by interjecting certain words into any conversation: "Republicans,"
"Roosevelt," "labor unions," "liberals," "conservatives." Sometimes during a long family meal I deflected uncomfortable questions about myself
with, say, "McCarthy," whom he cursed into the ground. I think Charles
Ives was like that, only his words were different: "party politics," "property," "majority" "the masses," "world government."

Such powerful words: words whose meanings everyone knows and

I would like to thank several colleagues for their assistance with this essay. Carol
Baron and Larry Starr offered comments on the ideas in the paper in its early
stages; David Nicholls, Carol Oja, and Mark Tucker also gave me many helpful
suggestions. This essay is dedicated to my mother, Miriam Tick.
[1] Thomas E. Cronin, *Direct Democracy: The Politics of Initiative, Referendum, and*
    Recall (Cambridge MA: Harvard University Press, 1989), 157.
[2] Ibid., 173.   [3] Ibid., 180.

nobody knows, because we are not supposed to know them if by that knowledge we fix their meanings forever. "Political labels are image-laden, appealing as much to the emotions as to the intellect," David Green writes. "Because politics is an ongoing struggle for power, the competition to define political terms is constantly being renewed.... The long-run effect of the process is that the popularly accepted meanings of political terms constantly change."[4]

Surely this is one reason why the literature on Charles Ives's political ideas has been slow to emerge.[5] Just as politicians compete to define the labels according to their needs, so we scholars compete to find the proper labels for this citizen-artist (was he Populist, Socialist, Progressive?) according to our own political culture at a time when some of the meanings of these "image-laden" words have dramatically changed. In Ives's time, populists stood on the left; today's populists are on the right.[6] In Ives's time, opponents of majoritarianism came from the right; today most come from the left.[7] Furthermore, our own attitudes toward the issues that occupied Ives have shifted as well.

The issue Ives cared about most was "direct democracy"—the empowerment of voters to bypass their elected representatives in making, approving, or revoking laws, recalling officials, electing senators, or nominating political party candidates. Friends and relatives would later recall how "he sincerely felt that the basic decisions of great moment in our political lives

---

[4] David E. Green, *The Shaping of Political Consciousness: The Language of Politics in America* (Ithaca NY: Cornell University Press, 1987), 2–3.

[5] Carol Baron mentions the absence of any serious discussion of Ives's political ideas in "What motivated Charles Ives's search for time past," *The Musical Quarterly* 78/2 (1994): 206–19. Michael Broyles states, "a reconsideration of the roots of Ives's beliefs is long overdue." See Broyles, "Charles Ives and the American democratic tradition," in *Charles Ives and His World*, ed. J. Peter Burkholder (Princeton: Princeton University Press, 1996), 118–60. I began to think about Ives and politics when asked to respond to a paper Broyles presented at the national meetings of the Sonneck Society in 1994. Although I disagree with some of his interpretations, I would like to acknowledge the stimulus of his finely argued essay.

[6] Michael Kazin calls the "migration of populism" a "major alteration in national politics" that began in the late 1940s. See Michael Kazin, *The Populist Persuasion: An American History* (New York: Basic Books, 1995), 4.

[7] Derrick Bell, for example, believes that the referendum facilitates bias and racial discrimination (Cronin, *Direct Democracy*, 94).

should be made by the people rather than the politicians."[8] In his essay "The Majority" Ives wrote that the question of a national constitutional amendment providing the procedures of initiative and referendum for all states was "one of the most, if not the most, important questions before Congress today" (*Essays*, 162). In this belief Ives hardly stood alone.

His political consciousness developed during a period of democratic experiments. The notion of a gap between "procedural and substantive democracy," as the political historian Aileen Kraditor has written, was "far more plausible between 1890 and 1919 than it has been at any other time [because of] the raw power of the big capitalists and their corruption of legislatures, by the disfranchisement of a large number of white male workers who often moved from job to job or who were recent immigrants, and by the precariousness of unskilled workers' employment."[9] Many states enacted measures to allow for the initiative, referendum, and recall, and debate over these issues filled the press. The year 1912, a high-water mark for reformist activity, brought a bibliography on the topic that listed 788 items; between 1910 and 1914 no fewer than eighty-seven articles on initiative and referendum (often abbreviated as I & R) appeared in the American periodical press.[10]

As we shall see, Ives produced both words and music about the ideals and values of direct democracy. He wrote songs responding to election campaigns. He sent letters to prominent politicians and opinion pieces to New York newspapers promoting direct democracy on the national level. He fused his Emersonian optimism with the ideology of direct democracy into what I have come to call "transcendental majoritarianism"; this

---

8 Ives's nephew, Brewster Ives, quoted in Vivian Perlis, *Charles Ives Remembered: An Oral History* (New York: Norton, 1974), 77. See also Amelia Van Wyck's comment on the "knock-down-and-drag-out fights" she had with her uncle over "his belief that the people should vote on important issues directly and not turn things over to the politicians" (ibid., 11–12).

9 Aileen S. Kraditor, *The Radical Persuasion 1890–1917: Aspects of the Intellectual History and the Historiography of Three American Radical Organizations* (Baton Rouge: Louisiana State University Press, 1981), 269.

10 Hermann Meyer, *Select List of References on the Initiative, Referendum and Recall* (Washington: Government Printing Office, 1912) includes historical documents as well as references to about 120 books and 200 articles that were published since 1889. My tally of articles comes from the *Reader's Guide to Periodical Literature* for those years.

idiosyncratic vision illumines the longest essay he ever wrote, "The Majority," a partner to the similarly titled song, "Majority," which he placed first in his *114 Songs*. The song and essay thus join the *Concord Sonata* and the *Essays Before a Sonata* as manifestations of beliefs and values so powerful that they produced two forms of creative representation: words and music.

He cared so much, and we care so little. Today the topic that was in 1915 "so much a feature of recent political discussion in the United States"[11] is a "neglected aspect of American politics"[12] – even after some revival in the mid 1970s. The United States is now one of the very few western industrial democracies without the possibility of a national referendum on any issue; not all states, moreover, have I & R provisions. This makes it challenging to have intellectual empathy for Ives's political ideas.

Compounding that challenge is the historical interpretation of the Progressive Era that we have inherited. Richard Hofstadter, who finds reform zealousness "naive and misguided," calls the Direct Democracy movement "the culmination of the Yankee-Mugwump ethos of political participation without self-interest."[13] Frank Rossiter, Ives's important early biographer, followed suit, styling the composer's political thought "rather naive for a man of his discernment," revealing an "isolation from the political thought and the other intellectual currents of his time."[14] Stuart Feder has written that Ives's political ideas "invariably had a sentimental basis in the past."[15] Unwilling to distinguish between "Populist" and "populist" and limiting terms like "Progressive" to strict party definitions rather than general persuasions, Michael Broyles minimizes the contemporary nature of Ives's thinking, labels him a "republican," and

---

[11] Frederick Davenport, "On the trail of progress and reaction in the West," *The Outlook*, 21 July 1915, 677.   [12] Cronin, *Direct Democracy*, 6.

[13] Hofstadter, *The Age of Reform*, cited in Cronin, *Direct Democracy*, 57–58, who observes that "these criticisms of the populist and progressive movements raise some valid points; yet several exaggerate the naive or irrational tendencies in these protest efforts." The late-nineteenth-century insult "Mugwump" refers to a person who affects neutrality on controversial political issues.

[14] Frank Rossiter, *Charles Ives and His America* (New York: Liveright, 1975), 143.

[15] Stuart Feder, *Charles Ives: "My Father's Song": A Psychoanalytic Biography* (New Haven: Yale University Press, 1992), 276.

anchors him in nineteenth-century myths of American identity.[16] Which way do we turn Ives's face? Back to tradition or forward into modernity? That opposition, which plays itself out across the spectrum of the Ives scholarly literature, manifests itself here as well.

Perhaps because I am writing this essay during the 1996 American election campaign season, I find Ives's political language jumping out of its historical frame; I try to turn this man of many faces away from the past not only into his present, but into ours as well. That process has already begun in the work of Ives's most recent biographer Jan Swafford, who writes so insightfully about Ives's political "pattern of reasoning." But even he shows limited interest in the pragmatic politics of Ives's time.[17] Therefore, my main intention in this article is to contribute historical nuance to our understanding of Ives's political discourse, and to lend intellectual credibility to the ideas themselves.

Perhaps for some composers we might stop there. But not surprisingly, this composer who talks politics around the margins of his music manuscripts subverted my intention to deal just with the writings.[18] So, in

---

[16] Broyles writes, "I will argue that Ives was neither a populist nor a progressive, and that his political roots draw on quite different traditions, which were prevalent in late nineteenth-century America but have been totally ignored in Ives scholarship" ("Ives and the American democratic tradition," 120). This just may be a battle of the upper and lower cases – "Populist" versus "populist." Kazin makes the distinction that I follow here: the "mass movement that arose in the 1880s in the West . . . is the upsurge that gave Populism its name, and it deserves to be the only one graced with a capital P" (Kazin, *The Populist Persuasion*, 5). He uses "populist" to mean a "persistent yet mutable style of political rhetoric with roots deep in the nineteenth century; a language whose speakers conceive of ordinary people as a noble assemblage not bounded narrowly by class, view their elite opponents as self-serving and undemocratic, and seek to mobilize the former against the latter" (ibid., 1). My use of the term "progressive" also follows the spirit of Kazin's thinking. J. Peter Burkholder talks about Ives's progressive or populist political ideas in a similar fashion: see Burkholder, *Charles Ives: The Ideas Behind the Music* (New Haven: Yale University Press, 1985), 106–07.

[17] Jan Swafford, *Charles Ives: A Life with Music* (New York: Norton, 1996), 314–15.

[18] Ives's writings to be discussed in this essay are: text for the song "Vote for Names" (1912); original work toward "A People's World Nation" (1914); text for the choral work *The Masses* (1915–16); portions of the essay "The Majority" (1915–16); "Stand By the President and the People" (1917); "George's Adventure" and "Majority" (1919–20); "Concerning a Twentieth Amendment"; and the text for the song "Nov. 2, 1920" (1920). Dating information from *Essays*

the second part of this essay, I connect the image-laden political vocabulary of a citizen with some of its musical representation.

I speak of a Direct Democracy "movement" (also known as the "I & R" movement after its two most effective tools – the initiative and referendum)[19] because its early advocates formed organizations (such as the Non-Partisan Federation for Securing Majority Rule, the National Popular Government League, the National Direct Legislation League, the National Federation for People's Rule, the Short Ballot Organization); published various journals, papers, and magazines (such as *Equity* and *Referendum News*); lobbied and spoke before Congress; and took positions on many controversial issues of the day apart from their main focus on legislative electoral reform.[20]

Like most reform movements, the Direct Democracy movement first emerged on the activist fringe, moving closer to established political parties over time and gaining consensus (and therefore respectability) as the momentum of reform gathered strength. Accordingly, its pioneering

and John Kirkpatrick's article on Ives in *The New Grove Dictionary of American Music.*

[19] The initiative allows a percentage of the voters (rather than legislative representatives) to generate new laws by petitioning to have measures placed on the ballot. The referendum allows for laws passed by representatives to be reviewed (rejected or approved) by voters as well. A third practice, "recall," allows for the removal from office of elected officials.

[20] In addition to Cronin, *Direct Democracy*, 164ff, I have relied on David Schmidt, *Citizen Lawmakers: The Ballot Initiative Revolution* (Philadelphia: Temple University Press, 1989). As a statement of the movement, here is what was printed on the inside title page of *Equity*:

Equity [formerly *Equity Series*]. Including the *Direct Legislation Record* and *Referendum News*. The purpose of this publication is to improve the machinery for self-government, to promote honest and efficient government, and to place public affairs and public officials under direct final control of the electorate. The ideal is: that every American community— town, city, and county—shall have the freest and simplest plan of self-government possible, resulting in the most efficient government possible; that every state shall have a short and simple constitution, fewer and better laws, and a more efficient government; that the national constitution shall be more easy [*sic*] to amend than at present; and that it shall be possible for the people of the nation to express themselves definitely concerning national issues whenever they wish to do so: that the civilized governments of the world shall cooperate through a central organization to conserve life and property, replacing the wanton destruction of war.

figure, James W. Sullivan, started the People's Power League in the 1890s to mainstream its ideas, finding allies in the Populist and Socialist Labor Parties by 1900.[21] When the National Direct Legislation League was founded in 1896, the Socialist leader Eugene V. Debs and the Populist-leaning Democrat William Jennings Bryan supported it. In 1898 South Dakota became the first state to approve a constitutional amendment making I & R state policy. Then in 1902 Oregon established what the historian Charles Beard describes as a "complete and thoroughgoing system" of I & R, including an important provision for the publication and distribution of arguments for and against propositions submitted to the voters.[22] By 1912 a number of the movement's goals had been main-streamed, and two of the three presidential candidates that year endorsed them. (Theodore Roosevelt, the Progressive, and Woodrow Wilson, the Democrat, but not William Howard Taft, the Republican.) By 1918 twenty-eight states had passed I & R provisions. Other reforms were enacted as well, including the direct election of state senators and the establishment of direct "primaries" to enable the electorate rather than party convention delegates to nominate presidential candidates.

Given the prominence of the Direct Democracy movement in a for-mative period of Ives's political consciousness, it is not surprising to find affinities between the movement's ideology and several dimensions of his thought: his rejection of doctrinaire party allegiance, his sense of social justice, the kinds of evidence he marshaled for his arguments, the nature of his internationalism, and the foundational value of majority rule. At the highest level Direct Democracy supported Ives's optimism about "the people." In *Direct Legislation by the People* (1892) Nathan Cree, one of the movement's pioneers, advocated "government by discussion," and accord-ing to Thomas Cronin, "viewed the majority of the people as the wisest, most just, and most conservative political power in the country."[23] Note further the fit between Ivesian values and this contemporary assessment of the emotional qualities of the movement: "The characteristic of direct democracy is its deep-seated distrust of representative leadership, and its

---

[21] See James W. Sullivan, *Direct Legislation by the Citizenship through the Initiative and Referendum* (New York: The Nationalist Publishing Co., 1893). On Sullivan's success see Schmidt, *Citizen Lawmakers*, 6.

[22] Charles Beard, *American Government and Politics* (New York: Macmillan, 1925), 506–08.   [23] Cited in Cronin, *Direct Democracy*, 46.

superior confidence in the instinct, the common sense, and the conscience of the mass of the people."[24] Ives echoed this opinion more aggressively: "To be afraid to trust the mind and soul of the people is a common attribute of the timid.... And we doubt that the quality of the thinking of the masses will be as inferior as some of the practical voices think" (*Essays* ["Concerning the twentieth amendment"], 206–07).

I & R reformers understood majority and minority as terms related to socio-economic class. They contrasted the propertyless majority of wage-earners to what one prominent advocate, Judson King, sarcastically called the "sacred minority" of the "propertied classes."[25] James Sullivan wrote that "the true point of view from which to see the need of the application of this principle [of I & R] is from the position of the unemployed propertyless wage-worker," a "slave of society" whose rights could only be restored by direct legislation.[26] Ives similarly censured the propertied class in the classic Direct Democracy tradition. In "Stand by the President and the People" he criticized the United States Senate and listed the personal income of several extremely rich public figures; he worried about American "reactionaries" who "feel safe in the exploitation of the interest of the large property of this country, because our government is one of representation" (*Essays*, 136–37). In *Essays Before a Sonata* he wrote of the greedy "hog-mind" of the minority, how "the biggest prop to the hog-mind is pride – pride in property and the power property gives" (*Essays*, 28). In "The Majority" the fiscal detail surrounding redistribution of wealth (shortly after the Federal Income Tax became law in 1913) testifies to his seriousness of purpose.

Most I & R reformers expressed indignation at the corruption of the representative system because of "machine rule" and the power of the "plu-tocracy." In 1892 Nathan Cree championed national referenda to "break the crushing and stifling power of our great party machines, and give freer play to the political ideas, aspirations, opinions and feelings of the people."[27] A few years later James Sullivan similarly wrote how through "direct legisla-tion by the citizenship, the political ring, boss, and heeler may be abolished,

---

[24] Davenport, "On the trail," 677.

[25] Judson King, *New Dangers to Majority Rule* (Washington DC: Bulletin of the National Popular Government League, 1912), 3–5.

[26] Sullivan, *Direct Legislation*, 103, 105.

[27] Cited in Cronin, *Direct Democracy*, 47–48.

the American plutocracy destroyed, and government simplified and reduced to the limits set by the conscience of the majority as affected by social necessities."[28] Similarly, Ives explained that the American government is a representative government "only in theory," repeatedly attacking party politics (*Essays*, 136). In "The Majority" he wrote that issues were "always overshadowed by party personality, party tradition (for its own sake), party power and party self-consciousness, and deformed by election campaign hysterics" (ibid., 190).

What followed from this position was a focus on the nature of political communication rather than on policy and a simultaneous rejection of party loyalty. Attacks on Direct Democracy from across the political spectrum proved to its disciples that their values floated above the transient fray of parties. Writers for *Equity* magazine, a leading publication of the movement, frequently pointed out that I & R did not automatically produce progressive or conservative law, and that "the fact that bi-partisan political machines oppose . . . Initiative, Referendum, and Recall proves that they are feared by the forces of evil."[29] In "The Majority" Ives echoed this pattern of thinking in his own work by labeling right to left "personified partisans of the relative, never of the absolute," and "party digits interested in the effect, seldom in the cause," and by creating hypothetical scenarios of incompetence for the capitalist, the syndicalist, the socialist, the Communist (*Essays*, 146–48). In *Essays Before a Sonata* he again plays off "the Bolsheviki and Bourgeois" against each other (ibid., 62). If he has defied today's controlling labels, it is partly because he shares with other proponents of Direct Democracy beliefs and convictions that transcend party categories.

The impact of Direct Democracy ideology also arrives through other aspects of politics in the early 1900s. One of these is the contemporaneous use of the New England town meeting as a paradigm of a political community. Broyles makes much of the influence of New England self-governance in Ives's thinking as a reflection of the cultural mythology of the Colonial Revival.[30] We should also recognize, however, that the image-laden phrase "New England town meeting" played a vital role in the rhetoric of the

---

28 Sullivan, *Direct Legislation*, 5–6. "Heeler" refers to a "ward-heeler" – a minor politician controlled by the party boss or other major politician.
29 "The initiative, referendum, and recall department," *Equity* 17 (January 1915): 30.
30 Broyles, "Ives and the American democratic tradition," 149.

sophisticated politicians who were Ives's contemporaries; they trotted it out to show that direct democracy was not, as the conservative William Taft charged, "a complete negation of the representative system established by the Pilgrims and the Puritans."[31] Sullivan, who studied Switzerland's canton structure and national I & R system, parried accusations of radicalism by making his message seem down-home: "Direct legislation is not foreign to this country. The town meeting of New England is the counterpart of the Swiss communal political meeting."[32] After 1900 Sullivan's words were echoed by mainstream politicians, among them Theodore Roosevelt, who in 1911 wrote that "in one of the oldest and most conservative sections of the country there has existed throughout our National life, and now exists, a form of self-government much more radical where it applies than even the initiative and referendum . . . the New England town meeting. . . . The initiative and referendum represent merely the next stage."[33] Ives's allusions to "the experience of referendum proceedings in Switzerland [that] shows more favorable results than otherwise" reveal his familiarity with traditional I & R argument (*Essays*, 163). If, for Ives, the "ultimate political paradigm was the New England town meeting," this came from the strategy of a contemporary political movement as much as from nostalgia.[34]

Apparently Ives knew the contemporary literature on I & R fairly well, as the data cited occasionally in his writings testify. Articles in *Equity* magazine, for example, analyzed presidential election voting patterns and legislation state by state. Ives cited I & R statistics to refute what Charles Beard calls "the second leading argument against the initiative and referendum":[35] that the minority can tyrannize the majority when too few people vote on propositions, when special interest exploits public apathy. In "The Majority" Ives wrote: "that the non-voters do not throw the results towards

---

[31] "Mr. Taft again," *Equity* 17: 61.   [32] Sullivan, *Direct Legislation*, 72.

[33] Theodore Roosevelt, "Nationalism and popular rule," *The Outlook*, 21 January 1911, 99.

[34] Broyles, "Ives and the democratic tradition," 149. I am not trying to deny the importance of the Colonial Revival or the mythologizing of New England traditions that Broyles convincingly documents. Perhaps it influenced Sullivan and Roosevelt too. But that misses the point of its conversion into politically topical language during Ives's lifetime.

[35] Beard, *American Government*, 510.

Minority rule is shown by the percentages in the returns of the states using the referendum from 1904 to 1916" (*Essays*, 162). Figures on pluralities and percentages followed.[36] Without additional information we can only speculate about the source of Ives's data, but it is conventional I & R argument.

The onset of World War I challenged Ives and the Direct Democracy movement at large. I & R advocates responded to stages of mobilization ("preparedness") and Wilson's eventual declaration of war with varying degrees of pragmatism. Initially, many supported a War Referendum plan as the way to preserve peace, with leading politicians proposing that "Congress shall not declare war except to repel invasion or under circumstances calling for measures of self defense until after a national referendum."[37] However, with the imminence of war, many in the Direct Democracy movement deserted the radical Peace movement and "stood by the president and the people," as Ives wrote in his short position paper on the war. Ives followed the Direct Democracy pattern here – not even mentioning the national war referendum proposal supported by William Jennings Bryan, Jane Addams, and many other progressives. At this crucial time Ives behaved like a left-centrist, recasting the war as a "war for democracy." While Charles Seeger was advocating the Socialist Party's official pacifist position that would eventually get him fired from the University of California, Ives volunteered for six months in France with the ambulance service of the YMCA in 1918.

Even while supporting Wilson, the Direct Democracy movement continued to lambaste familiar enemies: the minority-propertied class, the propaganda surrounding mobilization, and the special-interest groups profiteering from defense spending. When Ives writes of the propertied classes getting control of the "war machinery" of the country, he is on familiar ground (*Essays* ["Stand by the President and the People"], 136). In addition, during the incipient days of the League of Nations movement, Direct Democracy advocates concentrated on international government as a

---

[36] "The important measures submitted received 84.6 per cent of the total vote, and the less important measures 68.3 per cent, making an average of 75.7 per cent. In the vote for President (1916), in fourteen States, 4,355,062 out of the 4,785,783 votes were given to the most important measures" (*Essays*, 162–63).

[37] Ernest C. Bolt, *Ballots before Bullets: The War Referendum Approach to Peace in America 1914–1941* (Charlottesville VA: University Press of Virginia, 1977), 3.

potential deterrent to conflict. The historian Ernest Bolt explains that many leading figures, including some in Congress, called for "substantive reform of war powers enjoyed by the Congress, . . . convinced that international arbitration, disarmament, and world federation offered the best way to prevent war."[38] Others proposed an international naval force to maintain peace. *Equity* magazine ran an editorial in October 1915 entitled "World peace through world power" that proposed an international convention to meet after the war ended. In April 1916 *Equity* quoted Darwin P. Kingsley, President of the New York Life Insurance Company, calling for an "effective union of democratic nations" – a "Union for World Law and Order." In January 1917 their inside front cover proclaimed that "the most rational 'preparedness' against war is to extend the blessings of government to international relations." Ives's ideas about a "People's World Union," including his proposal for a "People's World Nation Army Police Force," come out of this ferment.

I have offered these comparisons to re-create the political consciousness of Ives's time with the intention of making Ives's writings more politically viable and more deeply connected to his political moment. Yet despite all these parallels, I do not claim that the Direct Democracy movement explains Ives completely. There are affinities and influences, shared strategies and common enemies. But there are also crucial differences.

In his ardor for the national application of direct democracy as the way of the future, Ives parted company with the movement's mainstream. Although there was some activity promoting nationwide I & R in the early 1900s, it did not win wide support.[39] I & R writers trod cautiously on ground that seemed to undermine representative values, not wanting to pose a choice of one over the other. In 1912 Senator Jonathan Bourne, Jr. of Oregon, a pioneering I & R state, denied "unequivocally that in effect or substance we in Oregon have abandoned representative government, or that the mass of the people pass upon the intricate details of legislation, execute the laws, or administer justice between man and man."[40] In 1915 an *Equity* writer put it just as plainly: "Everybody knows that nobody wants to

---

[38] Ibid.   [39] Cronin, *Direct Democracy*, 164–65.

[40] Jonathan Bourne, Jr., "A defence of direct legislation," *Atlantic Monthly* (January 1912), as reprinted in *The Initiative, Referendum, and Recall*, ed. William Bennett Munro (New York: D. Appleton, 1912), 204.

make these processes [of I & R] supplant representative government. . . . We do not wish to use these democratic processes except when necessary to correct errors of representative government."[41] But Ives was not "everybody."

Undaunted by neither the shrinking interest in I & R during the war nor the lack of interest in its national application, Ives formulated a proposal for radical investment in legislative self-determination. Perhaps emboldened by the ratification of the constitutional amendment extending suffrage to women on 26 August 1920, he proposed an amendment to establish national direct democracy, with the newly enlarged national electorate voting on substantive policy issues. He printed up flyers promoting his proposal for a twentieth constitutional amendment, even going so far as to have them distributed at the Republican National Convention, with plans for similar action at the upcoming convention of the Democrats. To many people today this aspect of Ives's politics seems particularly quixotic.[42] Perhaps we can give Ives's proposal the hearing that it never got, for, ironically, there is some continuity between Ives's proposal to establish direct legislation at the national level and similarly intentioned realistic measures for a National Initiative and a National Advisory Referendum proposed about sixty years later (as summarized in the Appendix to this chapter, pp. 161–62).[43] (In 1978 a Gallup public opinion poll found about fifty-seven percent in favor of a National Initiative.[44]) I have summarized these plans to suggest that Ives's twentieth amendment has more viability than is commonly assumed, even though his efforts to promote it through leaflets and letters could not possibly compensate for his lack of involvement in conventional political organizations.

Instead, Ives pursued political rumination rather than arguing about policy in "smoke-filled rooms." As Swafford describes it, Ives's politics borrowed ideas from social evolution theory, from a belief in the validity of actuarial probability, and from his "good-hearted faith and idealism [that]

---

[41] "Mr. Taft again," 61.

[42] Perhaps this is so because he saw three constitutional amendments ratified in his lifetime, and we have seen none since 1971.

[43] Some of the information in the Appendix comes from Cronin, *Direct Democracy*, 159–60.

[44] Cronin, *Direct Democracy*, 175–76. By 1987 support had faded to about forty-eight percent in favor and forty-one percent opposed.

God made human beings innately intelligent and good."[45] Ives expressed these ideas in a new political language, adapted from his hero, Emerson. Borrowing such quasi-mystical terms as "Over-soul," the "Common Heart," and the "Universal Mind," he rooted his transcendental majoritarianism back in the past in order to justify his radicalism: "If there is one ideal value which social evolution must have as its cornerstone, it is the belief in the innate goodness of mankind" (*Essays* ["The majority"], 193). He envisioned an extraordinarily idealized version of the masses, whom he prophesied

> will need no intermediary. The many are autogenerating a collective-personal social consciousness. Their governments, by natural processes, are passing from the indirect to the direct; it doesn't take a biologist to observe this tendency... And so the day of leaders, as such, is gradually closing—the people are beginning to lead themselves—the public store is being opened; the Common Heart, the Over-soul and the Universal Mind are coming into their own.   (*Essays* ["The Majority"], 160)

From this followed the spiritual fantasy that ends "The Majority" predicting the coming of the

> Majority giant, this great mass personality.... As it approaches maturity, there will come ... a radiance such as the world has never seen! "Why! Why!" the Pilgrims turn and ask. Man knows not the horizon of the soul—but Faith has yet its Olivet, and Love its Galilee!   (*Essays*, 199)

Springing from a private vision, such charged words make Ives's prose lurch from the mundane to the metaphysical: one minute the accountant writes details of income redistribution; the next minute the seer imagines a majority giant on the horizon. Such juxtapositions disrupt narrative flow (making the essay "The Majority" notoriously difficult to follow), and the millennialist oratory arouses suspicions of *fin-de-siècle* political sensibilities, cognizant of the short step from totalizing rhetoric to totalitarian practice. Indeed, the more extreme the ideas, whether negative (such as the threat of violence against the recalcitrant minority-elite), or positive (such as the eventual enlightenment of the body politic through direct democracy), the more transcendental the vocabulary. Ives thus harnessed his

---

[45] Swafford, *Charles Ives*, 314–15.

political ideology to what Leon Botstein has recently described as "Ives's spiritual universalism," which was "clearly indebted to Emerson's faith in an underlying metaphysical unity."[46]

As Burkholder has noted, Ives's interest in the Transcendentalists, which re-emerged during his courtship and marriage to Harmony Twichell, helped provide "solutions to problems with which he had long struggled.... Emerson's world view provided a framework for resolving the dichotomies of Ives's life and art."[47] Yet the irony is that despite these affinities between them, Emerson did not share Ives's kinship with the masses. Cornel West has written convincingly of Emerson's "political cynicism," his "disparaging of the masses," his lack of faith in "collective political actions," and "at times, like his admirer Nietzsche on 'The Herd,'" his unabashed elitism. Emerson wrote:

> One has patience with every kind of living thing but not with the dead
> alive.... The worst of charity is that the lives you are asked to preserve are
> not worth preserving. The calamity is the masses. I do not wish any mass
> at all, but honest men only, facultied men only, lovely and sweet and
> accomplished women only; and no shovel-handed Irish, and no Five-
> Points; or Saint Gileses, or drunken crew, or mob, or stockinghers, or
> millions of paupers receiving relief, miserable factory populations, or
> Lazzaroni, at all.[48]

Ives transformed Emerson's ideas to fit his vision, leaving his transcendentalism far behind, demonstrating once again that meaning in politics changes with context. He ignored this troubling aspect of Emerson as well as his explicit "armed neutrality" towards practical politics, and made excuses for Thoreau's comparable antipathy towards the mass-ideal in politics.[49] Perhaps he excused them partly because he had the foresight granted

---

[46] Leon Botstein, "Innovation and nostalgia: Ives, Mahler, and the origins of Modernism," in Burkholder, *Charles Ives and His World*, 56.

[47] Burkholder, *Charles Ives: The Ideas Behind the Music*, 107–08.

[48] Cornel West, *The American Evasion of Philosophy: A Genealogy of Pragmatism* (Madison: University of Wisconsin Press, 1989), 24.

[49] Perry Miller writes: "To the distress of his friends – those who developed Transcendental premises into an extreme anarchy of individualism, or those who proceeded from the same assumption toward socialism or authoritarianism – Emerson guarded his 'armed neutrality': 'The relation of men of thought to society is always the same; they refuse that necessity of mediocre men, to take

to him by modern technology (which they could not have imagined), the technology that made his own politics seem plausible to him. The transition from representative to direct democracy could be accomplished because "a man can sit down and talk to his brother in San Francisco, receive a co-daily message from Cape Town, and hear the voice of a dead man make a speech on modern business efficiency – and all in the same three minutes" (*Essays* ["The Majority"], 162). If mass communication posed "the principal difficulty in any plan of functioning mass expression" (ibid., 164), then inventions such as the telephone could make direct democracy practical in the future.

In fact, contemporary technology has done just that. Even though the idea of Congress becoming an Ivesian "clerical machine" sounds bizarre to us today (particularly because of the disrepute into which national direct democracy has fallen), just as Ives predicted, mass communication has made it credible, albeit in a surrogate form. For better and worse, public opinion polls are our current form of national I & R. We follow the polls, we cooperate with all sorts of survey research, we vote on television after political debates. In sum, we live with a market form of direct democracy that influences our political communication on a daily basis, and technology has made this possible. It seems to me that the impact of technology on Ives's thinking might be useful in helping us link the citizen with the composer because it emphasizes the process of communication so germane for Direct Democracy ideology. As we shall see, the process of political communication becomes a dynamic theme in Ives's political music.

How should citizens in a democracy talk politics to one another? A cluster of pieces written by Ives around 1909–12, including the Second String Quartet, the song "Vote for Names," and the chamber orchestra piece "'Gyp the Blood' or Hearst!? Which is Worst?!" engages the process of political communication in varying degrees. We begin with the Second String

sides.'" See Perry Miller, *The American Transcendentalists: Their Prose and Poetry* (New York: Doubleday, 1957), 287. Ives defended Thoreau from the charge that Thoreau "cared not one fig for the people in the mass. . . . He cared *too* much for the masses – too much to let his personality be 'massed' – too much to be unable to realize the futility of wearing his heart on his sleeve but not of wearing his path to the shore of 'Walden' for future masses to walk over, and perchance find the way to themselves" (*Essays*, 64).

Quartet, whose movements have programmatic titles based on the traditional metaphor of this genre as conversation. As Broyles points out, "Ives's commentary about his Second String Quartet articulates his political ideal."[50] In a sketch he wrote "S. Q. for 4 men – who converse, discuss, argue (in re 'Politick'), fight, shake hands, shut up – then walk up the mountain side to view the firmament." In the movement called "Arguments" Ives depicts the process of debate, even representing political stonewalling by assigning a rhythmic ostinato to the second fiddle (mm. 66–79), who beats time apparently unaffected by the complexities in the other parts. In a marginal note Ives elaborates on this bit of musical intransigence: "saying the same thing over & over & louder & louder – ain't arguing" (*JKCat*, 60).

Here is the germ of a crucial leitmotif in Ives's political critique, for he decried the public practice of "saying the same things over and over" as much as he did its private forms as well. The reductionist repetition of slogans and hooks in the public media subverted authentic political dialogue, and that is precisely what Ives found so reprehensible in the mass communication of his own time. He returned to the political-musical implications of "saying the same things over and over" in "Gyp the Blood," a little-known topical piece originally intended as the second movement of Set No. 2 for Theater Orchestra.[51] "Gyp the Blood" was the nickname of Harry Horowitz, a gangster sentenced to death in a murder/police corruption scandal that was major news between August and November of 1912. The facts behind the assassination of Herman Rosenthal, a New York City gambling house owner, were exposed in the press through details of million-dollar payoffs for "protection money" to the police, complicity, and cover-up. Even now the names of Gyp's co-conspirators, "Big Jack" Zelig and "Lefty Louie" Rosenberg (which make this story sound like a Jewish version of *The Godfather*), convey some of its human interest. "Gyp" was a serious political scandal. Every newspaper covered it, but the Hearst tabloid newspapers, the *New York Morning* and *Evening Journals* (which William Randolph Hearst bought in 1895), fueled the flames of public cynicism through their sensational reporting.[52]

---

50 Broyles, "Ives and the American democratic tradition," 150.
51 Details about this piece come from Kenneth Singleton's realization and admirable edition (New York: Peer International, 1974), which includes facsimiles of the sketches and marginal notes.
52 Edwin Emery and Michael Emery, *The Press and America: An Interpretive History of the Mass Media*, 5th edn (Englewood Cliffs NJ: Prentice-Hall, 1984), 284.

It made Ives furious. Like many intellectuals of the time, he was appalled by the success of the tabloids, which were dubbed "yellow newspapers" at the time (a phrase still in use). With "their fake pictures and fake sensations," as Ives's contemporary Hamilton Holt had written three years earlier, they pandered to the worst of public taste. Holt, the liberal editor of *The Independent*, ruefully acknowledged that the yellows

> have come to stay. They serve yellow people. Formerly the masses had to choose between such papers as *The Atlantic Monthly*, *The Nation*, the *New York Tribune*, and nothing. No wonder they chose nothing. In the yellow press they now have their own champion, a press that serves them, represents them, leads them, and exploits them, as Tammany Hall does its constituency.[53]

Because Hearst, who ran for mayor of New York in 1906, epitomized the political clout of yellow journalism, Ives attacked his integrity and his tactics in "Gyp the Blood." Treating Gyp's ensemble of three winds, one brass, five strings, and piano as a concerto grosso of sorts, he labeled a passage of repetitive quarter-note chords:

> Blow HARD – Randolph = Yellow gut. THESE NICE chords are an apology for Hearst <u>Headlines</u>, keep going over + over (whole BAND (Paid by Hearst)

Hearst is like the viola in the Second String Quartet, which "keeps going over and over" its material in futile argument. The soloist, Harry "Gyp" Horowitz emerges in the ragtime figures of the piano – "Just Piano Gyping," Ives wrote in his dark burlesque mode. The composer filled the margins of the score with topical diatribe that he later published in his *Memos*:

> Gyp, a prominent criminal, (legally) gets the gallows – Hearst, another p.c. [prominent criminal] gets the money. Hearst, a prominent criminal, (not legally) gets the money. Hearst's newspapers make Gyps. He sells sensational bunk to the soft-eared [and] soft-headed, and headlines and pictures that excite interest in criminal life among the weak-brained and defectives. An old-fashioned western horse thief is [a] respectable man compared to Hearst. When the American people put Hearst with the horse

---

53 Hamilton Holt, *Commercialism and Journalism* (Boston: Houghton-Mifflin, 1909), 90. "Tammany Hall" was the nickname for the New York state Democratic Party machine.

thief "on the rope," American history will have another landmark to go with
Bunker Hill, and perhaps a new song to go with "The Battle Cry of
Freedom." (*Memos*, 60)

Another shorter note on the score reads: "Hearst sell: touch and color up
news. a lower form of dishonesty even for –." And at the end of the piece, Ives
instructs that "the music stop but not end, just like the commercialists: keep
going over & over ... keep same old bunk going ... over again nice." Thus the
source of Ives's anger against Hearst is not only his identification with
"yellow people," but his resentment at exploitative mass communication.
As contemporary media historians have written, the "new journalism
without a soul . . . trumpeted concern for 'the people,' but choked up the
news channels on which the common people depended."[54]

It was but a short step from this attack on yellow journalism to Ives's
next attack on yellow politics. Gyp the Blood's trial overlapped with the
campaign season for the presidential election of 1912. Ives connected one
with the other in his song "Vote for Names." Among the three legitimate
candidates Ives found mass campaign tactics particularly toxic. On a sketch
Kirkpatrick dates Election Day, November 5, 1912, Ives writes above three
identical chords, "this, this or this??? A Sad chord – a hopeless chord – a
chord of futility – Same 3."[55] These stood for the respective presidential
candidates: Teddy Roosevelt, the sad chord; President Taft, the hopeless
chord; and Woodrow Wilson, the chord of futility. Ives would later clarify
his discontent:

> The ambiguities, personal animosities, eloquent platitudes, mis-statements
> due to party politics and election campaign hysterics would be obviated to
> some extent. . . . It is discouraging for thinking persons and the majority
> (the people) are thinking nowadays – to go to the polls and find nothing on
> the ballots but a mass of names and party emblems staring dumbly up at
> them." (*Essays* ["Concerning a twentieth amendment"], 209)

He represented this communication blockage by denying any
differences among the three candidates, making them "nice men" – never
a compliment. Hearst was "nice" and so are they in Ives's vocal text:

---

54 Emery and Emery, *The Press and America*, 282.
55 Swafford, *Charles Ives*, 256.

Example 6.1 "Vote for Names," mm. 4-6

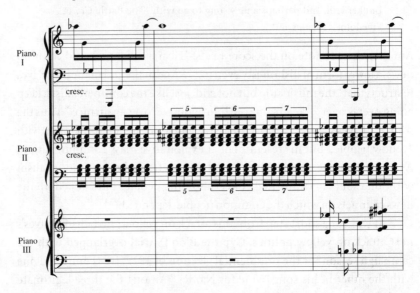

Vote for names! Names! Names!

All nice men!!

Three nice men: Teddy, Woodrow & Bill.

After trying hard to think what's the best way to vote I say: Just walk right in and grab a ballot with the eyes shut and walk right out again.

We hear the "yellow" propagandist standing on a soap-box, barking out the satirical text in a pseudo-election song. With the ostinato as the musical-political metaphor, three distinctive gestures stand for the three candidates (see Example 6.1): the first, an arpeggio of falling and rising ninths; the second, two common triads of e minor and d augmented plus an E♭; and the third, a series of exposed intervals (sevenths and one cluster chord).[56] This take-off on political propaganda music protests false communication

56 My musical example is drawn from Nachum Schoffman's edition, in his article "Charles Ives's song 'Vote for Names,'" *Current Musicology* 23 (1977): 56–65. The standard edition is published by Peer International (New York, 1968). "Vote for Names" appears on the CD *The Complete Songs of Charles Ives*, vol. 3 (New York: Albany Records, Troy 079).

through the separation of the three gestures, which always sound apart, disengaged from real interaction.

At the end of the song, Ives shifts the narrative second-person imperative to himself, the hapless voter. The candidates become products and the voters, responding to the advertisements, either buy or not. "Vote for Names" is a response to the manipulation of public opinion. If, as Hamilton Holt claimed, "public opinion is the ultimate force that controls the destiny of our democracy," then "commercialism," whether promoted by a political party or a tabloid newspaper, threatened its integrity. Like Holt, Ives used "commercialism" as a political buzzword. I do not quote Holt idly. Ives read *The Independent*, and Holt was the first president of the New York chapter of the Direct Legislation League; the title of his book *Commercialism and Journalism* is particularly relevant here.[57]

In Ives's world "commercialism" threatened the culture of politics and the politics of culture. Nothing less than American identity was at stake because of "commercialism, with its influence tending towards mechanization and standardized processes of mind and life (making breakfast and death a little too easy)" (*Memos*, 133). The "soft ears" and "soft heads" of "the yellows" who read Hearst tabloids parallel the more familiar denunciations (about which much has been written) against "yellow" listeners and critics, that is to say, the masses of music-lovers manipulated by the musical "commercialists." Accordingly, critics were "commercial pansies,"[58] in league with the

> business-man-musician-European (with a bigger reputation than anything else) [who] has carefully told them [what] to say, think, deride or approve.

[57] Kirkpatrick points out that Ives used the version of "General William Booth Enters into Heaven" that appeared in a review in *The Independent* on 12 January 1914 as the text for the song of the same name (*JKCat*, 125). The information about Holt being the first president of the New York state chapter of the Direct Legislation League is in Schmidt, *Citizen Lawmakers*, 253. Holt shared Ives's view in the social evolution of man, believing that "from now on, evolution is to be a psychical rather than a physical process. The world is on the threshold of a new era. We see the first faint dawn of universal peace and the brotherhood of man" (Holt, *Commercialism and Journalism*, 104).

[58] *Memos*, 27. Ives's intensification of his political beliefs through gender stereotypes is common. I discuss this in my essay, "Charles Ives and gender ideology," in *Musicology and Difference*, ed. Ruth Solie (Berkeley: University of California Press, 1993), 83–106.

153

> The great trouble is that the commercialists are always (most always) on the side of the conventional and so sellable (*Memos*, 94).

And "commercial monopolists" tell America it is an "unmusical country" (*Memos*, 41). Radio music is "worse than molly-coddle – it's the one-syllable gossip for the soft-ears-and-stomachs, easy for their bodies, and is fundamentally art prostituted for commercialism" (ibid., 134). The hype around presidential candidates satirized in "Vote for Names" corresponds to the hype surrounding celebrity performers.[59]

Ives's phrase, "keeps going, over and over" is code for the process of communication gone awry, which often takes the form of ostinatos sounding apart rather than together, or repetitions of some small musical gesture in robotic fashion. We see this in compositions about musical taste as well as politics. In the winter of 1909–10, when Ives fulminated about the Kneisel Quartet playing Haydn's "nice easy sugar plum sounds for the soft ears pocketbooks," he added, "(nothing but triads ·/· ·/· ·/· ·/· ·/· ·/·)" (*JKCat*, 221). Soon after he produced his take-off of the Andante of Haydn's "Surprise" Symphony, indicating that one measure was to repeat forty-eight times.[60] These literary and musical jibes clarify the analogy between art and politics: just as commercialism in political discourse disrupts the bond between the voter and authentic choice, so commercialism in culture disrupts the bond between the listener and new art. The voter and the listener are the one and the many, the individual and the mass.

After the 1912 election, as Ives grew increasingly fervent about the masses, they emerge ever more forcefully as protagonists in his music. In 1914 they march into heaven behind General William Booth. In 1915 they mourn in a subway station in Hanover Square for the lives lost in the sinking of the *Lusitania*. During these years Ives completed the drama of their apotheosis in his work for chorus and orchestra named after them, writing the text as well as music of *The Masses*. Around the edges of this score in 1914 he scribbled, "The Masses are on the blink! Eddie! They get it in the NECKO!!" (*JKCat*, 127).

[59] See Holt, *Commercialism and Journalism*, 42. Holt actually describes the controversy surrounding Mary Garden and Strauss's *Salomé* as an example of a publicity ploy manufactured by the administration of the Metropolitan Opera.

[60] Information about this sketch from Frank Rossiter, "Charles Ives and American culture: the process of development" (Ph.D. dissertation, Princeton University, 1971), 308.

Ives celebrates their power, turning Emerson's walking "dead alive" into pilgrims of progress. The text is, as Kirkpatrick points out, "in psalm form" (*JKCat.*, 126). Though the music is not antiphonal, it evokes the pace of archaic chant through its 4/2 meter. Both text and music glorify the agency of the masses. As the verbs change, so do meter and tempo: from "have toiled" in half notes to "thinking" in quarter notes, "singing" in 6/8, "yearning" in 4/4, and "dreaming" in 3/4; and in several extreme shifts of metronome marks, as a recently published letter by Harmony Ives indicates.[61]

Ives revised the choral work *The Masses* for solo voice and piano around 1919, retitling it "Majority."[62] Who can forget the visual impact of the opening page of *114 Songs*, even without hearing a note of the music? The monumental chords of its opening piano solo – could these possibly be played by one pair of hands? – have been interpreted differently,[63] but most convincingly as the representation of the masses of humanity (Example 6.2).[64] The final phrase of "Majority" shatters its complexities in a stunning controversial resolution (Example 6.3). Suddenly, a turn towards block tonal chords evokes the musical world of a hymn tune, reaffirming community and optimism as living ideals. An amen cadence is reversed,[65] and a slightly altered quotation from Robert Browning's famous poem "The Year's at the Spring" suggests mindful acceptance of universal order as the spiritual foundation of Direct Democracy: "God's in His Heaven, All will be well with the World." The parallel between the essay "The majority" and the

---

[61] A letter from Harmony Ives to Radiana Pazmor, 10 June 1939, describes the metronome shifts as follows: "at the beginning there is a metronome mark at about 66–72=a quarter note. When the voices begin, at about 52–58=a half note. 2nd verse, 'The masses are thinking,' (previous half note=quarter note) and 68–80=quarter note. 'The Masses are singing,' 54–60=dotted quarter note. 'The masses are yearning,' 52=quarter note. 'The masses are dreaming,' 44–48=quarter note." See Burkholder, *Charles Ives and His World*, 242.

[62] For a discussion of the significant differences between the choral work and the solo song, see Broyles, "Ives and the American democratic tradition," 125–33.

[63] I would like to thank Carol Baron for pointing this out to me.

[64] As Broyles points out, both Larry Starr and Stuart Feder have also made this point. Broyles feels that the huge dissonant chords refer to the act of "toiling." See Broyles, "Ives and the American Democratic Tradition," 131, 133.

[65] Larry Starr makes this point in *A Union of Diversities: Style in the Music of Charles Ives* (New York: Schirmer Books, 1992), 137–38.

Example 6.2 "Majority," page 1. *114 Songs*, no. 1

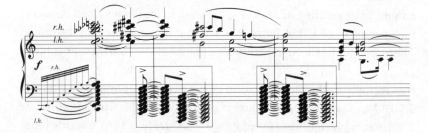

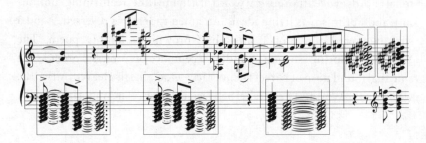

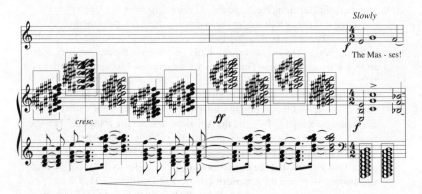

Example 6.3 "Majority," last six measures

song "Majority" is telling: both end with spiritual affirmation and references to hymns.[66]

By the time Ives revised *The Masses* into "Majority," much had changed. In 1914, when he initially wrote the text, he may have been inspired by the popularity of the journal of the same name. Under the editorship of Max Eastman, who attracted a young generation of intellectuals and artists to what became a highly publicized magazine of left-wing

[66] With respect to the Browning quotation, I wonder if Ives knew Amy Beach's famous setting of "The year's at spring." Popular enough to be considered a standard by 1910, it too reaches a triumphant diatonic fullness at this line, and Ives may have been playing against this well-known work as a foil of sorts. The essay "The Majority" ends with a partial quotation of the hymn *Immortal Love* by Whittier. See *Essays*, 199.

opposition, *The Masses* was in its glory days just during these years. And in its pages, "the toiling masses" – a cliché of the left – made their dignity felt. But some six years later, Eastman's revolutionary magazine was defunct. Most importantly, the country had just endured a period of post-war "Red scares." The editors of *The Masses* had stood trial on charges of espionage. Eugene Debs, the Socialist leader, went to prison, and the infamous arrests and persecutions of left-wing radicals culminated in the Palmer Raids of 1919.[67] To many Americans, the masses were synonymous with mob action and with the four million workers who went on 3600 strikes in 1919 as well.[68] At such a time Ives's defense of the masses in words and music is nothing less than courageous. In "The majority" he writes: "That mob action is not uncommon today does not invalidate any of the above theories or expressions or take aught from our hope" (*Essays*, 158). And in *114 Songs* he puts their apotheosis in music at the beginning of the collection.

This act also reaffirmed his faith in transcendental majoritarianism at a time, just after the election of 1920, when it had been sorely tried. Wilson's defeat to Warren Harding and the rejection of membership in the League of Nations produced another election protest song, the memorable "Nov. 2, 1920" (also called "An Election").[69] In it Ives revisits the representation of political communication, which suffuses this extraordinary text with tremendous energy.

It strikes me that . . .

Some men and women got tired of a big job; but, over there our men did not quit. They fought and died that better things might be! Perhaps some who stayed at home are beginning to forget and to quit. The pocketbook and certain little things talked loud and noble, And got in the way; Too many readers go by the headlines, party men will muddle up the facts, So a good many citizens voted as grandpa always did, or thought a change for the sake of change seemed natural enough. "It's raining, lets [*sic*] throw out the weather man, Kick him out! Kick him out! Kick him out! Kick him out!

---

67 Eugene Leach, "The radicals of the masses," in *1915: The Cultural Moment*, ed. Adele Heller and Lois Rudnick (New Brunswick NJ: Rutgers University Press, 1991), 42–43.

68 Robert K. Murray, *Red Scare: A Study in National Hysteria, 1919–1920* (Minneapolis: University of Minnesota Press, 1955), 9.

69 "An Election" and "Majority" have both been recorded in *The Complete Songs of Charles Ives*, vol. 4 (New York: Albany Records, Troy 080).

Kick him!" Prejudice and politics, and the stand-patters came in strong, and yelled, "Slide back! Now you're safe, that's the easy way!" Then the timid smiled and looked relieved, "We've got enough to eat, to hell with ideals!" All the old women, male and female, had their birthday today, and the hog heart came out of his hole; But he won't stay out long, God always drives him back! Oh Captain, my Captain! a heritage we've thrown away; But we'll find it again, my Captain, Captain, oh my Captain!

Ives writes this soliloquy in prose rather than rhyme to re-create the dynamic of political talk. Familiar villains (yellow newspapers, yellow readers) lurk in the background as the subvoices behind a text that switches narrative perspective constantly. He creates a persona for the first part, a man from the masses who lost a son in the war, and is "sitting by the road-side, looking down the valley towards the station." The words of this universal figure of loss are "half spoken," Ives writes in the score, and include word-painted recitations, sliding, shouting a "weak cheer," and mourning. The old man introduces internal indirect quotation as another kind of talk. This time, the majority speaks in verbal ostinati ("Kick him out!"), most often ridiculed by a banal ostinato accompaniment. The action breaks at the end for a lament that quotes music and text from Ives's setting of Edwin Markham's poem "Lincoln, the great commoner."[70] Only Ives's postscript to the song, reiterating material that appears in "The Majority" and in the Twentieth Amendment proposal, tempers the bleak despair in this work, reconverting the mob into the people:

The assumption, in the text, that the result of our national election in 1920, was a definite indication, that the country, (at least, the majority-mind) turned its back on high purpose is not conclusive. Unfortunately election returns coming through the present party system prove nothing conclusively. The voice of the people sounding through the mouth of the parties, becomes somewhat emasculated. It is not inconceivable that practical ways may be found for more accurately registering and expressing popular thought. . . . A suggestion to this end . . . in the form of a constitutional amendment together with an article discussing the plan in some detail and from various aspects, will be gladly sent, by the writer, to any one who is interested enough to write for it. (*114 Songs*, 55)

---

[70] I am grateful to David Nicholls for bringing this self-quotation to my attention.

Yet Ives had not lost hope for his country or for the masses gone astray. As Swafford writes, "Nor had he lost faith that the masses would someday embrace the music he had written to exalt them. He never lost that faith."[71]

If that faith speaks to us today it is because of the mutability and dual nature of political language – its sense of vitality that comes from an ability to change, its impact on emotion as well as intellect. In his music as well as in his writings, Ives used transcendental majoritarianism to fill both his private and public political language with enormous power. Was his "splendid vision of humanity," as Swafford writes, a "hopeless one"?[72] Perhaps yes, perhaps no. Today, in a time of infomercials, party conventions scripted for television, and vacuous political advertisements, Ives the citizen-composer reaches out to us still. His great political songs grab us, shake us out of denial, make us listen, and perhaps even get us to talk.

[71] Swafford, *Charles Ives*, 314–15.
[72] Ibid.

Appendix

Summary of three proposals for national direct democracy.

I   Charles Ives's proposal for a Twentieth Amendment (Essays, 204–09).

a   Nine months before presidential election, public opinions and suggestions are submitted to Congress by the electorate.

b   In four months, Congress computes the results, determining the top twenty questions raised by the people, debates them, and formulates legislation dealing with the top ten issues, as they see them. They do not create law at this time, but rather formulate ten workable legislative propositions.

c   In the remaining five months before the presidential election, Congress gathers and processes data to present to the electorate. Congress provides information summaries and digests on the issues.

d   The electorate (mandatory voting) provides responses to the top ten issues on the ballot as potential legislation, and those receiving a direct majority vote become law.

II   National Initiative sponsored by US Senator James Abourezk (D.–SD) and Congressman James Jones (D.-OK) in the late 1970s

a   A measure would be placed on the national presidential electoral ballot if the following requirements were met: the number of signatures on petitions gathered within eighteen months equaled three percent of the ballots cast in the preceding presidential election, including three percent in each of at least ten states (about three million signatures).

b   Majority approval would turn the measure into binding law thirty days later or as mandated in the law itself.

c   The NI could not be used to amend the Constitution, call up troops, or declare war.

161

d   All such laws would be subject to review by the federal courts.

e   Congress could repeal or amend such a law by a two-thirds vote in both houses within two years of its adoption.

III   *Richard Gephardt's proposal for a National Advisory (non-binding) Referendum (1980)*

a   Every two years Congress would hold public hearings around the country to determine the most pressing current issues and debate them with the electorate.

b   Congress would select up to three issues to be placed on the ballot during national elections held every two years.

c   The issues would be placed on the ballot as propositions for legislation.

d   A voter's guide would be published giving arguments for and against each position related to the three issues.

e   The voting results would be non-binding, but issues not acted on by Congress within a reasonable amount of time would be re-submitted to the electorate.

7 Charles Ives and Henry David Thoreau: "A transcendental tune of Concord"

STUART FEDER

Charles Ives's life-long fascination with Henry David Thoreau reached its creative apogee in the final movement of his Second Piano Sonata, subtitled "Concord, Mass., 1840–60." The associated prose of the Thoreau section of the *Essays Before a Sonata* was a part of this creative effort, a portion of which precedes the musical score as verbal introduction and program note.[1] Ives's knowledge of Thoreau, as person and writer, as well as his idealization of the man, began in childhood, gained impetus during his student years at Yale, and persisted well beyond his own creative period.

In this study I will explore the historical and psychological sources of Ives's inner relationship with Thoreau and trace its vicissitudes over the course of time. Its result, from a personal point of view, may be found in features of Ives's character and style – psychologically, an identification with Thoreau. From the creative standpoint, several of Ives's works reveal his profound respect for Thoreau – even his love for the man – and, reciprocally, the influence of Thoreau's life, work, and ideas. Among Ives's *114 Songs*, for example, in addition to the excerpt from the *Concord Sonata* entitled "Thoreau" (no. 48), evidence of Thoreau's influence may be found in "Walking" (no. 67), and in "Remembrance" (no. 12), the latter from a piece originally called *The Pond*.[2] Related to "Walking" is *From the Steeples and the Mountains*, an early work for bells, trumpet, and trombone. Ives's own text for what is often considered to be his last song, "Sunrise," is a Thoreauvian

---

[1] See *Essays*, 67–69.
[2] Others of the *114 Songs* containing texts that have a Thoreauvian ring include "Nature's Way" (no. 61) and "Berceuse" (no. 93). These would fall under a category Ives describes at the end of *114 Songs*: "Where no author is indicated the words are by Harmony Twichell Ives or her husband." Harmony Ives's "Mists" ("Low lie the mists," reflecting Thoreau's "Low anchored cloud") may also be in this category.

163

pastiche *sans* literal quotation. Finally, in a recently published but little known late-life letter, penned for him by Harmony Ives, Ives spoke of Thoreau being "definitely there" in "Tone Roads," which I take to be *Tone Roads No. 3*.[3]

1 Thoreau and the Iveses, father and son

The source of Ives's sentimental, intellectual, and artistic attachment to Thoreau was his father, George Edward Ives, who introduced Charles to Thoreau in family readings of the New England transcendentalists. But more than this, Ives construed much in his father's own character and style to be similar to Thoreau, an impression that engendered a degree of emotional closeness he did not have for the other transcendentalists, however much he admired them.

Following George Ives's death in 1894, the younger Ives sought solace in the writings of Thoreau. Later, in a feisty confrontation with Thoreau's critics Charles wrote, "you know your Thoreau – but not my Thoreau – that reassuring and true friend, who stood by me one 'low' day, when the sun had gone down, long, long before sunset" (*Essays*, 67). The actual "day" has long since suggested by Howard Boatwright to have been the day of George Ives's death, 4 November 1894 (ibid.). The story of the unique father-son relationship is recounted in detail in the biography *Charles Ives: "My Father's Song."*[4] What is central here is Ives's strivings throughout his creative lifetime to regain and to re-experience his father not only in the persons he encountered in actual life (such as New Haven choirmaster John Cornelius Griggs and his father-in-law, the Reverend Joseph Hopkins Twichell), but in the figures of imaginative life as well. As time went on, in his choice of heroes and ideals, Ives sought grander and purer though increasingly distorted representations of the father he needed to idealize. Eventually, human beings alone – living or dead, actual or virtual – failed to fill the void, and he turned to the mystical eschatology of the Fourth Symphony, and, in

---

[3] Stuart Feder, "Thoreau was somewhere near: the Ives-Thoreau connection," in *Thoreau's World and Ours*, ed. Edmund A. Schofield and Robert C. Baron (Golden CO: North American Press, 1993), 93–98.

[4] Stuart Feder, *Charles Ives: "My Father's Song": A Psychoanalytic Biography* (New Haven: Yale University Press, 1992).

the never-to-be-completed *Universe Symphony*, to nothing short of the cosmos itself!

Henry David Thoreau represents a distillate of these sentimental wishes and idealistic strivings, a figure whose feet were firmly planted on the banks of Walden Pond but whose spirit soared. That he was musician, experimenter, and social maverick fixed further the association between Thoreau and George Ives in the mind of Charles: "Thoreau was a great musician," the essay begins, as Ives focuses attention on the Thoreau of Walden's "Sounds." There can be little question from Ives's *Memos* but that the "great musician" of childhood, indeed the first and only one, was his father.[5] Thus did Henry David Thoreau become a powerful presence in Ives's mental life and fantasy, differently and more profoundly associated with his father than were the others of his personal musical pantheon of the "Concord": Emerson, Hawthorne, and Bronson Alcott.

The special role of Thoreau may perhaps be best perceived through a metaphor of mental life. If one imagines the *Concord* (sonata and essays together) metaphorically, as if a musical microscope through which Charles Ives endeavored to re-create and re-experience his father, one may bring to focus a differently constituted George Ives at four varying focal distances, cloaked as it were in the spiritual garb of his four subjects. Ives's Emerson is prophet, guide, and explorer; the protean teacher; the first and greatest teacher writ large: the father, seen as if through the eyes of a child. His Hawthorne is not the Hawthorne of sin and evil but rather the Hawthorne of mystery, imagination, and adventure – an American Grimm or Aesop.[6] In Alcott, the very voice of the father is invoked – "Concord's greatest talker" (*Essays*, 45) – indeed more the voice of his own father who, as Ives wrote, "didn't write text books ... and he didn't write many letters. He left little behind except memories of him in others" (*Memos*, 45). This, incidentally, is certainly not true in Alcott's case, but like George, as Ives ruefully observed, "his idealism had some substantial virtues, even if he couldn't make a living" (*Essays*, 46).

---

[5] "Father had a kind of natural interest in sounds of every kind" (*Memos*, 45).

[6] See also Robert DiYanni, "In the American grain: Charles Ives and the Transcendentalists," *Journal of American Culture* 4/4 (1981): 139–51.

2 *Concord Sonata*

In Thoreau, Ives perceived a worthy and lovable maverick through whom he could idealize his father. The elements that bind the four movements of the *Concord* are not exclusively philosophical and musical – they are human as well. And a thread that is latent in each of the three preceding movements of the *Concord* becomes increasingly clear in "Thoreau," music and essay alike: the emotions expressed become more concentrated, intense, and intimate. The elegiac mood, apotheosis of Thoreau as a great musician, and in its final section, Ives's "program for our music," with its concentrated quotations from the best of Thoreau (which in fact is the section reprinted with the music), set the Thoreau essay apart from the others. A mood for this "day" is created, that "low" day cited above that is specified in the *Essays* but only alluded to in the notes accompanying the score.[7] The time for the elegiac final set-piece of the essay – a poem in some respects, with Thoreauvian quotations incorporated as if "found objects," and thus in some respects not unlike Ives's musical style – is "an autumn day of Indian summer" (*Essays*, 67). It is at once a memorial and an artifact of mourning. And, as I have observed elsewhere about the remarkably specific mood created in word as well as reflected in tone in the sonata, it is a mood that combines the traditional blend of commemoration and eulogy with the touching sadness that characterizes the elegy. It is past lamentation and redolent of comfort.[8]

Thus is pride of place given Thoreau in the *Essays* and in the Sonata. The essay also includes an *apologia* for such "cranks" as Thoreau and the elder Ives. In fact, Ives undertakes to deal with what some may consider to be Thoreau's least attractive traits – his withdrawal, isolation, cynicism, feistiness, and downright "contrary cussedness."

George Ives was born in 1845, the very year of Thoreau's Walden Pond adventure, and a year when all four of the Concordians of the Sonata were actually residing in Concord at the same time. The spirit of Walden Pond hovers over Ives's "Thoreau" pieces as palpably as mist and haze over the pond – in Ives's words, "the last Mist at Pell's" [Pell Jones's camp in the Adirondacks],[9] or the "Low anchored cloud" quoted from Thoreau's *A*

---

[7]   Charles Ives, Piano Sonata No. 2, 2nd edn (New York: Associated Music
      Publishers, [1947]), 58.   [8] Feder, *Charles Ives*, 269.

[9]   As inscribed on a sketch page for "Mists" (*JKCat*, 194).

Week on the Concord and Merrimack Rivers.[10] The significance of "the pond" was enduring in the life of Charles Ives. Its spiritual "mists," displaced to the "last mist at Pells," were associated with the inspirational experience of the "idea of a *Concord Sonata*" (*Memos*, 202, n. 23). In fact, there were eventually three ponds in Ives's life: the spiritual Walden of Thoreau, the actual pond Ives himself constructed on his property in West Redding, and the pond of ever-present memory in Wooster Cemetery, Danbury. Only a few miles from Redding, the Ives family plot where George Ives is buried overlooks this pond. Ives knew that in time this would be the final resting place of Harmony and himself.

At the close of the Thoreau essay, the "day" is evoked a final time in the silence after the evening train has rumbled by: "It is darker—the poet's flute is heard out over the pond and Walden hears the swan song of that 'Day'— and faintly echoes.... Is it a transcendental tune of Concord?" (*Essays*, 69). The flute that Ives evokes in this passage is that of both Thoreau and George Ives, for whom (according to family legend) the flute was the first instrument.

In the final measures of the "Thoreau" movement, an optional part for flute is written in the score, the occasion rationalized by the fact that Thoreau had one with him at Walden. It is thus that in the last pages of *Concord* Thoreau is virtually brought to life, the "great musician" made audible. The "Alcotts" theme is heard,[11] and presently the "Beethoven's Fifth" motive. Elsewhere in the "Thoreau" movement Ives quotes Stephen Foster's "Massa's in the Cold, Cold Ground" – specifically, fragments from the chorus, "Down in de cornfield..." Later, when Ives adapted themes from the "Thoreau" movement for the song in his *114 Songs* (no. 48), he introduced into the score the verbal "cornfield" quotation from the Walden chapter, "Sounds," as if it were a spoken meditation: "He grew in those seasons like corn in the night, rapt in revery, on the Walden shore, amidst the sumach, pines and hickories, in undisturbed solitude." Thus the

---

10 Henry David Thoreau, *A Week on the Concord and Merrimack Rivers* (New York: Library of America, 1985), 155. Quoted in *Essays*, 67.

11 Burkholder notes: "The theme is not heard earlier in the movement; its musical function here is as a unifying element, and its programmatic role is to suggest the 'common sentiment' shared by the Concord writer." J. Peter Burkholder, *All Made of Tunes: Charles Ives and the Uses of Musical Borrowing* (New Haven: Yale University Press, 1995), 356.

cornfield motif serves as both tone painting and serious musical pun in this most programmatic movement of the sonata.

The optional flute part at the end of the sonata provides a unique and curious musical moment. For it would seem strange to expect the flutist to sit onstage through a lengthy and massive solo composition only to join in in the last few seconds; stranger still, perhaps eerie, to have the unantici-pated flute waft in from offstage. Ives here uses the mystery of music toward both an aesthetic and a memorial end. But in any case, the actual rendering is of only partial consequence, since it was the *idea* of the flute song that was paramount in Ives's musical thinking. Indeed, this musical concept may well have been a part of the initial inspiration for the *Concord* in the autumn of 1911. It was at Elk Lake in the Adirondacks, meditating in the "last mist" over the lake, that Ives said he first had the "idea of a *Concord Sonata*." If so, the germinal idea that spawned the work may have been actualized at the end of "Thoreau" in both music and prose. Through it, and through Thoreau, Ives also actualized the spirit of his father.

3 The *114 Songs*

Earlier, in *The Pond*, a brief work for small orchestra (called "Remembrance" in *114 Songs*), the sound of Ives's father was embodied in the muted trumpet as if wafting over the pond. The subvocal words of the orchestral version become audible, serving as the song's text: "A sound of a distant horn, O'er shadowed lake is borne, my father's song." Detailed dis-cussions of this song may be found in writings of Burkholder and of Feder.[12] Relevant here is the very mode of the music, the sense to which "the great musician" Thoreau was most attuned, the sense of sound. Indeed it is from the chapter "Sounds" in *Walden* that Ives drew so many of his Thoreau quotations. On his original sketch for *The Pond* he had noted "Echo Piece!!" (*JKCat*, 44), and in fact the brief nine-measure piece consists of two phrases of a canon. A Thoreauvian auditory moment is evoked reminiscent of a passage in "Sounds":

> There came to me in this case a melody which the air had strained, and
> which had conversed with every leaf and needle of the wood, that portion

12 Burkholder, *All Made of Tunes*, 360–63; Feder, *Charles Ives*, 2–4.

CHARLES IVES AND HENRY DAVID THOREAU

of the sound which the elements had taken up and modulated and echoed from vale to vale. The echo is, to some extent, an original sound, and therein is the magic and charm of it . . . partly the voice of the wood; the same trivial words and notes sung by a wood-nymph.[13]

"Walking" is another one of the *114 Songs* (no. 67) that is Thoreau-inspired though not explicitly attributed or acknowledged. Dated by Kirkpatrick to 1902, the text was Ives's own, and indeed the unembellished serial evocations of times, places, and objects are characteristic of several of his song texts: "A big October morning, the village church-bells, the road along the ridge, the chestnut burr and sumach, the hills above the bridge with autumn colors glow." In the second half of the song ("Now hark! Something bids us pause . . .") specific events are cited: "down the valley, – a church, – a funeral going on . . . up the valley, –a roadhouse, a dance going on." And in the end, a resolution is reached, not only one in the artistic sense but in the literal sense of resolve: "But we keep on a-walking . . . today we do not choose to die or to dance, but to live and walk."

Even when Thoreau was at Walden he customarily walked eight miles a day. But this is the Thoreau of the mountains – the Thoreau of *A Walk to Wachusett* and of Greylock, Katahdin, Monadnock, and Mount Washington. Although the text hardly matches Thoreau's prose, the idea of "excursion" is realized in both the words and the form of the song, a "story pattern" as William Howarth has pointed out, "that shapes most of [Thoreau's] later works: a traveler leaves home, seeking the novelty of a new land. There he encounters something – a lake, a mountain, the ocean shore – that gives him a fresh view of nature and his place in its order. With this insight he returns home, ready to resume his ties with society."[14] This is the form inherent in Ives's imitation of Thoreau and realized in the brief song.

An instrumental parallel to "Walking" may be found in Ives's *From the Steeples and the Mountains* for strings, brass, and bells. In this brief piece, dating a year earlier to 1901, Ives creates a sense of space in an auditory image of resounding bells from four separate steeples, with fanfare-like brass figures calling and answering from the distance. The town-and-mountain landscape thus evoked is similar to that of "Walking" and as dis-

13 Henry David Thoreau, *Walden* (New York: Library of America, 1985), 420.
14 William Howarth, *Thoreau in the Mountains: Writings by Henry David Thoreau* (New York: Farrar-Straus-Giroux, 1982), 24.

169

tinctly Thoreauvian, but again without specific reference. *Steeples* strives for a headier effect on the listener, with an expansion of boundaries as sound emanates both serially and simultaneously from all directions, in contrast to the exclusively serial events of "Walking" and its grounding in specific detail. The technical aspects of how this is accomplished are described by Nicholls and by Burkholder.[15] Ives wrote on the score, "From the Steeples—the Bells!—then the Rocks on the Mountains begin to shout!" Interestingly, the funereal element of the song is cited musically by the bugle-like quotation of "Taps" incorporated in the brass calls, reflecting the mourning association to Thoreau.

The song "Thoreau" (*114 Songs*, no.48) has been discussed above in the context of *Concord*. The "meditation," which the singer may speak over a sustained chord, is drawn from the same portion of Walden's "Sounds" that inspired *The Pond*, as suggested above, and that achieves its fullest musical representation in *Tone Roads No. 3*.

4 Tone Roads No. 3: "Thoreau is definitely there"

In 1943 the eminent Thoreau scholar Walter Harding wrote Charles Ives to invite him to become a member of the fledgling Thoreau Society and to attend its third meeting in Concord that July. Shortly before the meeting, Harding received a reply dated 11 July from Ives's adopted daughter, Edith Ives Tyler, who along with Ives's wife Harmony Twichell Ives now served as amanuensis for the ailing sixty-eight-year-old composer. A euphemism used habitually by both was that Ives was "not at all well" and therefore, in this instance, would not be able to attend. But, Edith went on, "Father says—'The grand old se'er of Walden will rejoice to be with you all—and his great old friend Emerson will not be far away that afternoon."[16]

Harding wrote again later that year after hearing John Kirkpatrick's performance of Ives's *Concord Sonata*. This time it was Mrs. Ives who responded. The letter is reprinted in its entirety.[17]

15 David Nicholls, *American Experimental Music 1890–1940* (Cambridge: Cambridge University Press, 1990), 21–25; Burkholder, *All Made of Tunes*, 274.
16 Edith Ives Tyler (Mrs. George G. Tyler) to Walter Harding, 11 July 1943. Private papers, Walter Harding, State University College, Geneseo, New York.
17 Harmony Twichell Ives to Walter Harding, 5 December 1943. Private papers, Walter Harding.

Mrs. Charles E. Ives
West Redding
Conn
Dec. 5, 1943

Dear Mr. Harding,

I am writing for Mr. Ives who as you know is not well and it is difficult for him to do so.

He deeply appreciated your kind letter and most interesting notes about the Kirkpatrick concert. He says "your insight into the hearts and minds of those great Concord people – olympians as you rightly say – is a great tribute and sincerely deserved." He sends his sincere thanks for your wonderfully expressed interest in the Sonata and says "There are a few passages in the Thoreau movement which intended to give in a way something of a glimpse of Thoreau's rugged side and perhaps a strain of his occasional perverseness – however these are not prominent in the movement which has more to do with the stronger inner life of Thoreau, as we say, into his calm inner soul."

As to any other Thoreau music which you kindly ask about in some of Mr. Ives's chamber music he had a feeling that Thoreau was *somewhere near* – [sic] in one of these movements called "Tone Roads" Thoreau is definitely there. There are no copies of this here but Mr. Ives will have a copy made later and sent to you.

Do you know the book by Harry Lee "More Day to Dawn" about Thoreau? It was published by Duell Sloane & Pearce about two years ago – we liked it very much.

With our kindest wishes,
I am,
Sincerely yours,
Harmony T. Ives

P.S. Mr. Ives doesn't remember receiving a report of the recent Thoreau meeting in New York but a paper came recently from Chapel Hill which says his name will be taken from the list unless his correct address is given – "West Redding Conn" is the address and he hopes you will see that he is kept on the list.

In *Memos* (114) Ives wrote: "One thing I am certain of is that, if I have done anything good in music, it was, first, because of my father, and second, because of my wife." This letter provides a vivid portrait of the second most important person in Ives's life. During their courtship in 1908 they elaborated in their correspondence a homegrown romantic aesthetic which included ideas about the kinds of things that might be represented in music. Harmony encouraged the putting of things into music "in concrete form," including those emotional experiences that foster inspiration; as she put it, "one's happiest moments."[18] In doing so she exerted considerable influence on Ives's great Civil War pieces, which are memorializations of his father, and eventually the *Concord Sonata*, with its representations of the four "olympians" of Ives's personal pantheon. Thus Harmony's contributions to the Thoreau *œuvres* are considerable. Additionally, she had generally widened Ives's literary vistas by fostering a program of home reading that served as tranquilizer for the sometimes agitated younger Ives and, at the same time, helped separate him from the circle of young men who had been his pre-nuptial companions. One result of this was Ives's plan to write a never completed overture series, "Men of Literature," which ultimately proved to be a creative way-station to the *Concord Sonata*. Finally, with regard to Harmony and the *Concord*, she may well have been a participant in another aspect of its conception: the couple visited the village of Concord during their honeymoon. There, in Sleepy Hollow Cemetery, is the only physical location – outside of the score to Ives's Second Piano Sonata – where Emerson, Hawthorne, Alcott, and Thoreau are associated in such close proximity.

Beyond commonplace romantic notions of program music, Ives himself always retained a magical sense of what music was. Stemming from the earliest musical experiences of childhood, it was this quality that informed adult thinking about a philosophy of music.[19] There are many passages in his prose writings that reveal a belief in the potential for concrete personification, and even animism, in music. In the postface to his *114 Songs*, where Ives wrote, "a song has a *few* rights the same as other ordinary citizens," he concludes with the couplet, " – In short, must a song / always be a song!" Similar notions relating to the extramusical may be found in more refined though highly abstract form in portions of the *Essays*.[20] He was thus

---

[18]   Harmony Twichell to Charles Ives, some Tuesday before 12 March 1908. Charles Ives Archive, Yale University.
[19]   See chapter 5, "Vox humana: a composer's childhood," in Feder, *Charles Ives*, 65–84.
[20]   For example: "Maybe it is better to hope that music may always be a transcendental language in the most extravagant sense. Possibly the power of

unusually receptive to a concept of music that was metaphysical – "'natural' music in its transcendental sense."[21]

However, beyond this, by the end of Ives's sixth decade a degree of mental deterioration had set in that was itself of some complexity. This circumstance was in part responsible for his need for his family's assistance in conducting correspondence, as described above. (A separate reason was a neurological disorder that led to the shaky handwriting Ives called "snake tracks.") The mental condition only served to intensify beliefs about music that had earlier been conventionally romantic, that later became colorfully idiosyncratic, and that finally became mystical, intellectualized, or philosophical. In short, it seems likely that at times Ives might have believed quite concretely that the individual could be more than represented in the music or evoked by it; that, quite literally, the person could be *there*![22] As Harmony wrote, "he had a feeling that Thoreau was *somewhere near*" (her emphasis) in the *Tone Roads*, adding, as if on further reflection, Ives's belief that "Thoreau is definitely there."

Where then, in *Tone Roads*, can Thoreau so definitely be identified? There were three pieces collectively called *Tone Roads Et Al* that Ives assembled around 1915 (see *JKCat*, 50). Each was scored for a small chamber orchestra of different instrumentation. The manuscript of the second has been lost; of the other two, it seems likely that Mrs. Ives was referring to the third of the series.[23] There, in a remarkable opening statement (marked *Andante con moto*), the chimes perform the "tone road" that is more than a foreshadowing of the "tone row" of serial music. As Henry Cowell wrote in an early account of this little-performed work, the piece "opens with a long solo in slow half-note and whole-note triplets, an atonal melody played by the chimes, which provide the tone quality that is to lie back of the whole

---

literally distinguishing these 'shades of abstraction' – these attributes paralleled by 'artistic intuitions' (call them what you will) – is ever to be denied man for the same reason that the beginning and end of a circle are to be denied" (*Essays*, 71).

21 See Charles W. Ward, "Charles Ives's concept of music," *Current Musicology* 18 (1974): 114–17.

22 This notion puts the Ives song "He is There!" (*114 Songs*, no. 50) in an interesting perspective; equally, the later version "They Are There!"

23 *Tone Roads No. 3* is scored for flute, clarinet, trumpet, trombone, chimes, piano, violins, viola, cellos, and bass.

piece. The 'tone road' is the tone of the chime, and the whole is a fantasy on the mood of the chime tone."[24]

The style of the "fantasy" connects Ives with Thoreau. It is aural in mode, philosophical in idea, and poetic in imagery, while rooted in the local detail of everyday life. At the same time, a distinctive mood is created. Yet all is integrated into a cogent music that is, in effect, a musical analogue of a characteristic passage in Thoreau. Earlier we considered Thoreau's "meditation" quoted by Ives in both the essay and song, the meditations, as he put it, "interrupted only by the faint sound of the Concord bell—'tis prayer-meeting night in the village" (*Essays*, 68). Omitted among Ives's elisions is the very passage from "Sounds" that informs *Tone Roads* and very likely conveys the Thoreau who was "somewhere near," perhaps the Thoreau who in Ives's vision "was definitely there": "Sometimes, on Sundays, I heard the bells, the Lincoln, Acton, Bedford, or Concord bell, when the wind was favorable, a faint sweet, and, as it were, natural melody, worth importing into the wilderness."[25]

Characteristic of the irony inherent in Ives's life and music are two observations, namely that in the context of strong affect and sentiment (here related to Thoreau) Ives essays some of his most venturesome musical ideas; and similarly, in the context of apparent simplicity ("Sometimes, on Sundays...") a complexity prevails approaching chaos. Nicholls has called this kind of layered, dissonant, polyphonic texture "organized chaos."[26] Cowell calls our attention to that moment toward the end of the short work when the chimes pause briefly and "the other parts go wildly every which way, until at the end the chimes reappear as a catalyst to crystallize the sound of the other instruments into sense."[27]

---

[24] Henry Cowell and Sidney Cowell, *Charles Ives and His Music* (New York: Oxford University Press, 1955), 171.

[25] This is from the same passage partially quoted (and misquoted) by Ives elsewhere that contains the metaphor of the "universal lyre" evoked by "sound heard at the greatest possible distance." Thoreau continues, "At a sufficient distance over the woods this sound acquires a certain vibratory hum, as if the pine needles in the horizon were the strings of a harp which it swept. All sound heard at the greatest possible distance produces one and the same effect, a vibration of the universal lyre." Thoreau, *Walden*, 420.

[26] Nicholls, *American Experimental Music*, 67 (referring to *Tone Roads No. 1*).

[27] Cowell, *Charles Ives*, 172.

5 "Sunrise": "... more day to dawn"

The Harding–Ives correspondence contains two more letters, one each from 1946 and 1948. The first is a reply to a request by Harding to reprint some of the Thoreau music and essay in a publication of the Thoreau Society. In Mrs. Ives's otherwise positive and cordial response, she commented that Ives was not well enough to send the "new comments which you asked for."[28] The final letter, over a year later (11 January 1948), containing at this point a warm personal greeting, notes the publication of the second edition of the *Concord Sonata*, a complimentary copy of which Ives was sending for the Thoreau Society.

The seventy-three-year-old Ives was by now incapacitated, his composing days long since over. What was probably his last creative effort, the song "Sunrise," had been written some twenty years earlier, dated August 1926 (*JKCat*, 212). Its composition would have coincided, then, with that time when Ives reportedly "came downstairs . . . with tears in his eyes and said he couldn't seem to compose anymore."[29] In a sense this final statement in music had been a collaboration with his beloved Thoreau. For the words Ives selected have a distinctly Thoreauvian ring, as if paraphrased or stitched together from such sources as "The pond in winter" or the final passages of *Walden*. More than an example of the kind of creative mimicry in which Ives was gifted, it is a reverential gesture of impersonation of Thoreau himself.

> A light low in the east,—as I lie there!—it shows but does not move—,a light—,a light—as a thought forgotten comes again. Later on as I rise it shows through the trees and lights the dark gray rock and something in the mind, and brings the quiet day. And tomorrow a light as a thought forgotten comes again, and with it ever the hope of a new day.[30]

One may speculate that at that point Harmony Ives might have been co-author, ever responsive to Ives's relationship with Thoreau. If so, the

---

28 Harmony Twichell Ives to Walter Harding, 7 December 1946. Private papers, Walter Harding.

29 John Kirkpatrick, "Ives, Charles," in *The New Grove Dictionary of Music and Musicians*.

30 Handwritten text. On the autograph sketch Ives wrote: "Taken from chords & parts of an II S.Q. & put into this song Aug. 1926—but not a good job—the words are NG. but better than the music" (*JKCat*, 212).

effort would have represented a final collaboration with both of the most important people in Ives's life: his wife, and – in fantasy, and through the good offices of Henry David Thoreau – his father. Three years later, in a discursive "footnote" to his Fourth Symphony, Ives connected Thoreau and George Ives a final time, writing of the "symphonies of the Concord Church bell when its sounds were rarified through the distant air." The footnote closes with the quotation of "an unknown philosopher of a half century ago," otherwise unidentified but with that distinctive voice reminiscent of *Memos* and the postface of *114 Songs*, the voice of Ives and his father, informed by Thoreau: "How can there be any bad music? All music is from heaven. If there is anything bad in it, I put it there—by my implications and limitations. Nature builds the mountains and meadows and man puts in the fences and labels."[31]

Harmony would in the course of time select their shared epitaph, a biblical passage, "Awake psaltery and harp: I myself will awake quite early" (Psalm 108). It strikingly mirrors Thoreau's final words of *Walden*: "Only that day dawns to which we are awake. There is more day to dawn. The sun is but a morning star."[32]

---

[31] Conductor's Note to the Fourth Symphony (New York: Associated Music Publishers, 1929, 1965), 13–14.

[32] Thoreau, *Walden*, 587.

PART THREE

The *Universe Symphony*

8 The realization and first complete performances of Ives's *Universe Symphony*

LARRY AUSTIN

Composer Larry Austin completed his realization of Charles Ives's
Universe Symphony *(1911–51) on 30 January 1993.[1] On 28 January
1994, Austin's realization was premiered by Gerhard Samuel conducting
the Cincinnati Philharmonia, combined with the Percussion Ensemble
of the Cincinnati College-Conservatory of Music, in Corbett
Auditorium at the University of Cincinnati, Cincinnati, Ohio. The
next day, these ensembles recorded the work for an internationally
distributed compact disc recording, which was released in August 1994.[2]
On 23 September 1995, Austin's realization received its European
premiere in Warsaw, in the final concert of the 38th International
Festival of Contemporary Music, "Warsaw Autumn," with Jacek
Kasprzyk conducting the National Philharmonic Orchestra of Warsaw.
This essay presents a discussion of the nature of Ives's sketches for his*
Universe Symphony *and the author's approach to what have become
the first complete performances and compact disc recording of the work.*

In 1974, the centennial year of Ives's birth, I began to study Ives's music and
descriptions for his unfinished *Universe Symphony* (*US*) from the extant
unpublished manuscripts preserved in the Charles Ives Archive at Yale
University. As a composer, I was inspired by the rich musical material and
ideas found in the manuscripts and intrigued by Ives's open invitation to
"somebody" to carry out his aspirations for the work: "in case I don't get to
finishing this, somebody might like to try to work out the idea" (*Memos*,
108). Ives described the prelude and three main sections of his *US* as
follows:

---

[1] New York: Peer International, Inc., 1994.
[2] Baton Rouge LA: Centaur Records (CRC 2205), 1994.

179

Prelude 1

I   (Past)   Formation of the waters and mountains
II (Present) Earth, evolution in nature and humanity
III (Future)   Heaven, the rise of all to the spiritual

He usually referred to the main sections simply as A, B, and C, respectively (*Memos*, 106). "Prelude #1" is the percussion orchestra music that precedes section A.

Since 1974, I have completed four compositions based on the formal continuity and distinct instrumental strata detailed in Ives's sketches. These are the *First Fantasy on Ives's Universe Symphony: the Earth* (1975), for two brass quintets, narrator, and tape; *Second Fantasy: the Heavens* (1976), for chamber ensemble and tape; *Phantasmagoria: Fantasies on Ives's Universe Symphony* (1977, rev. 1981), for orchestra, narrator, digital synthesizer and tape; and *Life Pulse Prelude* (1974–84), for twenty-member percussion orchestra.[3] I incorporated the materials and performance techniques developed for these pieces into my realization of the entire *US* (1993), certainly Ives's largest in orchestral forces and formal scale and, I believe, his most compelling and visionary work. The duration of my realization is thirty-seven minutes.

This essay explains my analysis and interpretation of the extant sketch pages, with the manuscripts central to my realization reproduced at the end of the chapter.[4] Four types of compositional material are found in Ives's sketches for the *US*: 1) virtually complete scoring, except for details of dynamics, articulation, and phrasing; 2) incomplete scoring; 3) virtually complete formal, structural, and aesthetic descriptions of the work's nature and technical specifications; and 4) brief and often fragmentary musical and textual sketches exemplifying particular aspects or techniques that Ives was developing for the symphony. My intent in transcribing and interpreting Ives's sketches was to realize and complete both Ives's explicit and what I maintain was his implicit compositional, formal, and aesthetic plan

[3] I recently completed a version of the *Life Pulse Prelude* for three percussionists, sound diffusionist, and recorded percussion on tape (1996).

[4] I have incorporated, updated, and extrapolated major portions of my article "Charles Ives's *Life Pulse Prelude for Percussion Orchestra*: a realization for modern performance from sketches for his *Universe Symphony*," *Percussive Notes* 23/6 (1985): 58–84.

and materials for the symphony. I have meant my realization and completion of Ives's US ideally to be experienced and appreciated in performance as Charles Ives's musical creation "composed out" by Larry Austin.[5]

I believe and will show that the following conclusions may be drawn from Ives's evolving plan for the US and can be well supported in my realization: 1) the formal continuity for the work is sustained in three uninterrupted sections, "Past," "Present," and "Future," preceded by the sustained "Earth chord" and the percussion orchestra cycles of "Prelude 1"; 2) the tempo for the entire work is uniformly set at $\downarrow$ =60; and 3) the instrumentation for the US is divided into seven "orchestras" (also called "groups" by Ives), primarily made up of related instruments. The seven orchestras are constituted as follows: a) the twenty-member percussion orchestra, each player performing in a different meter and at a different tempo, coming into metric phase every eight seconds; b) the four "Heavens" orchestras, each conducted in different meters and tempos by assistant conductors and scored variously for violins, violas, high winds, and solo percussion; and c) the two "Earth" orchestras, comprising the "Rock formation" orchestra, scored for brass and low winds, and the "Earth chord," scored for cellos and contrabasses.

1. The sketches

The US was Ives's last, most ambitious, but ultimately unfinished composition. Sketches for this, his fifth symphony, were begun in 1911, continued until 1915, resumed in 1927, 1928, and 1932; further, according to Henry and Sidney Cowell, "a few notes were added from time to time" up to 1951.[6] Of the forty-nine total manuscript pages designated by John Kirkpatrick as part of the US sketches, there are thirty-four that I believe form definitive sketches for the composed music and descriptions of the materials for the work.[7] These include completed music, musical sketches and fragments, narrative marginalia, and graphic outlines concerning

---

[5]   As characterized by Richard Taruskin, "Away with the Ives myth: the 'Universe' is here at last," *New York Times*, 23 October 1994, H42.

[6]   Henry and Sidney Cowell, *Charles Ives and His Music* (London: Oxford University Press, 1955), 233.

[7]   *JKCat*, 26–28. The US manuscripts primarily reside in folio 1A9.

form, continuity, and the work's transcendental aesthetic. The thirty-four pages may be categorized as follows:[8]

1   six pages primarily concerning the nature of the entire work (f1819, f1828, f1829, f1843, f1852, f3770);
2   eight pages concerning the percussion orchestra music (f1820–f1827);
3   ten pages concerning section A (f1830–f1839);
4   three pages concerning section B (f1840–f1842); and
5   seven pages concerning section C (f1845–f1848, f1850, f1851, f1853).

What follows is a discussion of each of these categories and how they relate to and were used in my realization.

2. Sketch pages concerning the entire *Universe Symphony*

Ives's folio cover page plus five manuscript sketch pages comprise what I believe are Ives's initial modeling of the overall structure, aesthetic approach, continuity, and instrumentation of the entire *US*. What follows is a discussion of each of what I call the "all-*US*" sketch pages, especially as they pertain to Ives's overall concepts of form, tempo, and instrumentation.

Cover page (f1819).

The cover page for the *US* collection of sketch manuscripts was created by Ives as part of an effort to gather together and order his manuscripts. It gives us important information. One inscription on this page, "Pages of drafts or Scetches [*sic*] or parts," suggests that Ives considered these pages to be in different states of completion: "draft" (emerging ideas expressed in music or annotations); "Scetch" (the testing of an idea in music notation, often with different shadings and effects); or "part" (completed music). Elsewhere on the page he wrote "not sure of sec[tions]"; this is puzzling, unless he is simply referring to the missing "pages of drafts or Scetch[es] or parts." The other inscriptions on the cover page list the number of pages collated for each section, showing that Ives had, at one point at least, brought together all of the materials into a single manuscript collection.

---

[8]   Ibid.

First all-US page (Plate 8.1, f1828).[9]

At what point did Ives cross out this entire sketch page? Subsequent sketches or emendations of sketches evidently superseded this wide-ranging, formative draft. Helpful clues do appear, however, about the tempo and scope of orchestration.

Tempo. Several numerical inscriptions on the page seem to refer to durations of the basic rhythmic subdivisions notated in whole notes on staves 2, 4, 6, 9, 13, and 15, and in the bottom margin. For example, the notation "1.6+" underneath stave 2 apparently indicates that the eleven notes on that line occur at intervals of approximately 1.6 seconds. The other intervals of "2.5+" (stave 4, seven notes), "3.6" (stave 6, five notes), "4 1/2" (stave 9, four notes), "6" (stave 13, three notes), and "8 or 9" (stave 15, two notes) are also subdivisions of the single note, or "basic unit" (B.U.) in the bottom margin, which is "16 or 18" seconds in duration. Mathematically, Ives's calculations are close, but not always precise: the eleven notes of stave 2 occurring at the rate of 1.6 seconds would take up 17.6 seconds (thus the "+"), and the seven notes of stave 4 at 2.5 seconds each equal 17.5 seconds (again, the "+" attempts to compensate). The other staves are exact subdivisions of 18.

Instrumentation. Ives calls for extremely large forces for the *US* in the left margin of this page. If every number given is assumed to represent a group of separate performers, the musicians needed could number as many as 4,520! This draft page may have been the outer limits of the *US* concept at some point, in the all-encompassing spirit of Ives's intentions as reported by Cowell: "Several different orchestras, with huge conclaves of singing men and women, are to be placed about in valleys, on hillsides, and on mountain tops"; and, "from 6 to 10 different orchestras placed on separate mountain tops, each moving in its own independent time orbit, and only meeting one another when their time cycles eclipsed."[10] These grand projections about the work must indeed have kept many composers from ever seriously considering Ives's invitation that "somebody might like to try to work out the idea" (*Memos*, 107).

Except for this page and a reference in *Memos* (108) to "5 to 14

---

[9] The pages identified as Plates are given in facsimile reproduction on pp. 217–232 [ed.].   [10] Cowell, *Charles Ives and His Music*, 201–03.

groups," Ives nowhere indicates anything approaching the grand plan Cowell claims for the *US*. Nothing on subsequent pages suggests the need for such large forces. I have calculated, based on a compilation of the different parts Ives refers to in all the *US* sketch pages, that about 214 instrumentalists are needed (note Ives's inscription "full orch 200 play" in the lower left), and perhaps 500 in the chorus. That would total 714 musicians, not so far from Ives's note at upper left "about 750." The problem with this conclusion is, however, that no sketches for choral music are extant; nor did Ives refer to such choral music in his *Memos*; nor was such music described specifically by the Cowells. Such was part of Ives's initial modeling for the work, but it was never musically realized.

Ives's concept of "orchestra" clearly refers to orchestras of like instruments, rather than fully instrumented symphonic orchestras. On this page Ives calls for nine such groups: 1) percussion orchestra; 2) string orchestra A; 3) string orchestra B; 4) the low strings or "Earth-chord orchestra"; 5) the brass band-like "Rock formation" orchestra of brass and low winds; and 6–9) the four similar high winds/high strings/keyboard/percussion "Heavens" orchestras. Conceivably such forces could very well be assembled in a large concert hall or cathedral, where an organ and pianos, referred to in the sketches, could be found. Indeed, they have been in my realization and in its subsequent performances.

Second all-US page (Plate 8.2, f1829).

Like the first all-*US* page, this page was, at some point, considered by Ives to have no relevance to the *US*. The "A B C D E F G H I" series – forward, reversed, segmented in sets, sequenced, and layered – serves as the basis for the primary bass lines and upper voice of Ives's song "On the Antipodes." Five references to a "chorus" appear on this page, interestingly in close proximity to Ives's serial musings.

Other notations on this page present important pitch material of the symphony. The second half of staves 6 and 7 gives the first "Earth theme" and accompanying counterpoint. Staves 11 and 12 show Ives working with three transpositions (starting on C♯, F, and F♯) of octatonic scales, presenting ideas that run throughout the sketches, especially in section B. The notation "P 10 Uni Sy" (stave 10) refers to specific chords notated here and used on page 10 of section A (f1839).

Third all-US page (f1843).

There are two systems on this twelve-stave page, the upper seven staves assigned to basses, cellos, brass, and flutes, the lower five to basses, cellos, and probably violins, all *divisi*. Entitled "2nd prelude," could this, in fact, have been one of the earliest sketches, written, along with the percussion orchestra sketches of "Prelude #1"? A reference here, "Birth of the Waters... Oceans," corresponds with the subtitle given section A in *Memos* (106), where no reference to a second prelude is found. The page also contains the following prose description:

> The "Universe in Tones" or a Universe Symphony. A striving to present and to contemplate in tones rather than in music as such, that is—not exactly within the general term or meaning as it is understood—to paint the creation, the mysterious beginnings of all things, known through God to man, to trace with tonal imprints the vastness, the evolution of all life, in nature of humanity from the great roots of life to the spiritual eternities from the great inknown to the great unknown. We know but little here below and of that little.

These words suggest that this page was an early sketch for the work. Further, could this evocation have been an early form of what Ives was composing as a possible text for choral music for the *US*? It certainly has the appropriate tone for a choral setting, especially as a choral addition to the orchestral music of the coda in section C, its majestic fullness and force not unlike the effect of the final movement of Beethoven's great choral symphony, also his last.

Tempo. Two tempo markings appear: "□ = 12 seconds" and "□ = 6 secs." If the rectangular shape is a breve, equal to two whole notes, and the square is a kind of "half-breve" or whole note, the metronome marking would be $\quarternote = 40$. This is another indication that this page was early and formative, produced before Ives had settled on a tempo for section A.

Form. Though there is a textural resemblance between material on this page and the first page of section B (f1842), I do not believe that the inscription "Prelude #2" signifies that this page represents a prelude to the B section. Ives calls this page "Birth of the Waters ... Oceans," and the writing seems to suggest the scored, graphic form of the swell of an ocean wave, but nowhere in the notes or *Memos* does he declare that the creation of the

185

"Waters" is treated separately from the "formation of the Earth and Heavens." Also, there is a reference to "sec A" (between staves 4 and 5), and a chord resembling a notation on page 4 of section A (Plate 8.8, f1834).

Fourth all-US page (f1852).

The music notated on this page does not appear to relate, metrically and thematically, to previous or subsequent *US* music; indeed, Ives indicated in the bottom margin that this "belongs to *US*," but then later crossed out the annotation. What does belong to the *US* on this page, however, is Ives's moving description of his work as "a universe of Tones," a vision of music more of the late than the early twentieth century:

> The Universe symphony is an attempt in tones, every form and position known or unknown (to me) as the eternities are unmeasured, as the source of universal substances are unknown, the earth, the waters, the stars, the ether, yet these elements as man can touch them with hand and microscope and labelled as chemicals and atoms, as the eternal motion, life of things and man, their bulk, their destiny. They are not single and exclusive strains, but incessant myriads, for ages ever and always changing, growing, but in ages ever always a permanence—in humans of the earth for a man's lifetime, of life and death and future life—the only known is the unknown, the only hope of humanity is the unseen spirit—what can't be done but what reaching out to do (as we feel like trying it) is to cast eternal history, the physical universe of all humanity past, present and future, physical and spiritual, to cast, then, a "universe of Tones."

Could this, too, have been text to set for choral music in the *US*?

Fifth all-US page (f3770).

I cannot determine at what point this page of music and important marginalia was written in the decades-long development of the *US*. Through the years, Ives went through many of the sketch pages over and over, adding comments and music, crossing out music and erasing other notations. He seemed unconcerned with the chronology of his changing ideas. This page contains descriptions of the piece that are essentially the same as those of other sketch pages. One note confirms that the "Pulse of the earth and universe" established in the prelude continues at least through the "middle movement" (i.e., section B). However, a suggestion here that "The EARTH (al[one]) may be played first, alone then the Percussion or then the Heavens etc then all together," seems to contradict a carefully worked out plan on the fifth page of the prelude sketches (Plate 8.5, f1824). I do not know whether Ives's inscriptions are final and definitive, neither final nor definitive, final but not definitive, or not final but definitive. But such apparent contradictions may not be so significant, especially given Ives's use of the equivocal terms "may" and "or" in his commentary. In my own realization, I have followed the formal continuity suggested here, as will be shown in the concluding part of this essay.

Instrumentation. Ives mentions on this page "up to 32 lines together" and "as many as 21 different groups going simultaneously." It is possible to count thirty-two lines on the first and second sketch pages of section B (f1840, f1842), assuming a broad understanding of the notion of "line" that encompasses both sonorities sounding together and separate melodies. But it is difficult to locate "21 different groups." The Heavens orchestras never contain more than six groups (f1842), the Earth orchestras four groups (f1840); then there is the percussion orchestra. At most, the total number of groups found in the sketches is eleven. Perhaps Ives was referring here to twenty-one different pulses, which, with the cross meters of the life-pulse percussion and the other orchestras, is essentially correct. But, perhaps also, Ives is laughing somewhere at our seeming confusion about such formative ideas. Ultimately, we are left with one aspect that is not confusing: that the music itself – so uplifting, so grand – is the most important aspect to contemplate. One must hear this symphony and "rise to the spiritual."

3. Sketches for "Prelude #1"

"The pulse of the universe's life beat was by the percussion orchestra" (*Memos*, 107). This "life pulse" percussion music stratum of the *US* was very important for Ives, likely the first material he sketched. Of the thirty-four extant manuscript pages that I find are definitely part of the *US*, eight were devoted to material for "Prelude #1." I have named my realization of these "rhythmic cycle[s]" (as described on page 1 of section A, Plate 8.6, f1830) the *Life Pulse Prelude* (*LPP*). The *LPP* percussion orchestra is scored for nineteen percussion parts and a piccolo, all in different meters and tempi, coming into phase every eight seconds. At those points, a "low, deep, hanging bell" is struck, establishing Ives's "B.U." (basic unit). The players enter one at a time, ultimately creating the complex meter/tempo ratio of 1:2:3:4:5:6:7:8:9:10:11:12:13:14:17:19:22:23:29:31. Then the players withdraw one at a time, in reverse order of entrance, until only the B.U. remains. Ives described the creation of one such palindrome as a "cycle," specifying that the cycle would have ten iterations. He clearly notated the first half of one cycle, then described the nine remaining cycles more in functional than in notational detail. What follows is an explication of my interpretation of the *LPP* sketches, the method of their realization for modern performance, and observations about what I term "the *Life Pulse Prelude* effect."

First LPP *page* (f1820).

The first percussion sketch page contains extensive verbal descriptions of the *LPP*, yielding valuable initial information about instrumentation and musical events. Ives writes, for example, "II only I.F.s [indivisible factors] The earth, heavens orchestra do not start until after 3rd or 4th percussion cycle." This is an important reference to the order of the music to be played, substantiated on the fourth *LPP* page (Plate 8.4, f1823), and, as a kind of poetic contradiction, curiously disputed on the fifth all- *US* page (f3770). Another inscription reads, "21 in the 2nd or 3rd Day." This could refer to the second or third section, in turn invoking the creation metaphor that is so central to the work.

Instrumentation. The curious inclusion by Ives of the piccolo in the percussion orchestra has puzzled me through the years – until, that is, just before the first performance of my realization of the *US* in 1994. It came to me then that Ives's life-long fervent patriotism, especially during the period just before the United States entered World War I (e.g., his joyously patriotic orchestral work, "The Fourth of July," or his choral memorial to the victims of the sinking of the *Lusitania* in his *Second Orchestral Set*), was symbolically invoking the military, patriotic, and revolutionary symbolism of the fife and drum corps.

Improvisation. One comment on this page speaks to the issue of improvisation:"All these can vary in later cycles will be at players' discretion (keeping to his own beats)." I interpret this to mean that Ives intended portions of the *LPP* to be "free," improvised, in this case elaborating the assigned meters with syncopations and varied rhythmic figurations. In all, six references to "free" playing are found on this page.

Second *LPP page* (f1821).

The second *LPP* page is a sketch of the highest five, prime-number meters with music figuration and comments.

Tempo. The first definitive clue to the mystery of the precise tempo of the *LPP* and the *US* is found on this sketch page. Ives felt that the "definitive single pulses" could be "heard as such" only up to 11, assuming a B.U. of 8 to 10 seconds. Above this limit, Ives declared that the pulses would sound more like rhythmic/melodic patternings than individually perceived metric pulses. I would theorize that at a tempo much slower than $\downarrow$=60, or one beat per second, one could indeed hear 13, 17, and 19 as fast metric pulses. Hence, a metronome marking of about 40 to 80 to the quarter note seems the plausible tempo range, with 60 as the median.

Instrumentation. A notation on this page reads, "(piano, piccolo, Bell-piano, celest, 3rd system, Lights. electric buttons on—see page 8." Here, "Lights" must, as it clearly does on the upcoming fourth *LPP* page (Plate 8.4, f1823) and the first all-*US* page (Plate 8.1, f1828), refer to delicate, "distant," "brittle," "high," "light" percussion instruments such as triangles, orchestra bells, piano, wood and clay pipe sounds, celeste, and so forth. The next words, "electric buttons on," certainly, at first, give us pause to think that Ives's vision of the *US* might have included some kind of signal lights to keep the percussion parts in proper phase with one another and the B.U. This, along with Cowell's observation that "the complex rhythms and timbral combinations in Ives's *US* are certainly much closer to possible realization on electrical instruments," suggests that this sketch page could have been amended later in Ives's life, when technology such as metronomic lights was feasible.[11] Is it only coincidence that Ives apparently

---

[11] Ibid., 181.

helped fund the development of Leon Theremin's Rhythmicon in the late 1920s and reportedly heard a demonstration of an accurate performance of such complex cross-rhythms? [12]

Third LPP *page* (Plate 8.3, f1822).

Here Ives lays out, in graphic analog, the cross-metric patterning of the *LPP*. Elapsed time equals spatial extensity. The sketch includes both prime number ("I.F.") meters and their related multiples.

Fourth LPP *page* (Plate 8.4, f1823).

This page represents a sample realization of one half-cycle (eleven measures – an "11 unit"), probably a later cycle (IV, V, or VI), where instruments may "exchange" meters.

Tempo. There is a wide range of information about tempo on this page. The notations here plus inscriptions on other pages offer a number of different tempo possibilities, including ♩=30, 36, 40, 46, 48, 50, 53.3, 80, and even 120. On this page, the tempo clues are "𝅝=30, 𝅗𝅥=60, ♩=120," and "better all slower about 𝅝=20, 𝅗𝅥=40, ♩=80." Here ♩=80 seems to be what Ives settled on, while still seeming equivocal.

Instrumentation. Ives is definitive about certain percussion instruments he intends to use, calling for special instruments at the right of the page, again terming six of them "light."

Improvisation. More references to improvisation appear: "when all orchestra . . . are rising high and free"; and "but the phrasing even or uneven may vary with themselves."

Fifth LPP *page* (Plate 8.5, f1824)

This page specifies the definitive structural format of the *LPP*. We learn that a "cycle" is forty measures of 4/4 or twenty of 4/2. At lower right Ives notes, "The numbers in red are . . . the order they take part," suggesting that this and the two succeeding pages were considered the final form, so noted by Ives in red ink on the pencil manuscript.

---

[12] Rita Mead, *Henry Cowell's New Music 1925–1936* (Ann Arbor MI: UMI Research Press, 1978), 188–90.

Figuration. Did the syncopated rhythms emerging in m. 5 suggest that Ives wanted, "as indicated," the "varied beats rhythmic accents" in the first cycle as well as succeeding cycles; or that he was realizing this half-cycle to suggest the style of the "changing rhythms" in later cycles? I think the second conclusion is correct.

Tempo. At lower left Ives writes, "B.U. = 10 seconds 40 met 6 beats about." As a tempo clue, however, this is somehow misleading. If Ives means that the double whole note should last ten seconds, the metronome setting would actually be ♩=48, not 40. What does "6 beats about" mean, when eight beats comprise the B.U.? Here, the apparent reference is to the staves headed 3, 6, and 9, where Ives is indicating clearly that he wants ♩=40, with six half-notes per full measure. If the six halves are to be performed at ♩=40, and the twelve quarters in ten seconds at ♩=80, as clearly indicated, then the actual time taken is not ten seconds but nine![13]

Improvisation. When Ives writes "VII (free cadenza 10 meas, all changing except 1 2 & 3 all others shift)" in the center of the page, he clearly refers to the fourth *LPP* page (Plate 8.4, f1823), where a sample format of "shift" among the meters is shown. "Changing" and "shift" here have the same meaning, a strengthening of the concept of free improvisation Ives wants to achieve in the percussion orchestra. For example, the periodic pulse in 8/4 of one quarter-note per beat can "shift" or "change" to quarter-note triplets, yielding not eight but twelve pulses per measure. Whether the players work out shifts individually or coordinate them according to the fourth *LPP* page is not revealed.

Form. Figure 8.1 shows the structural plan, drawn from the information on *LPP* cycles found on this page, with the B.U. metered in 4/2, where ♩=30. In this format, the total duration for the *LPP* is twenty-four minutes. If the tempo were ♩=53.33, as would be the case for a nine-second measure, the length would be twenty-seven minutes. I have adopted the twenty-four minute length in my realization for two reasons: nowhere in the sketches

---

[13] Let MM=metronome setting, BPM=beats per measure, and TU=number of seconds assigned each measure. MM=BPM×(60/TU). Then 80 MM=12×(60 sec/10 sec) is not correct! In fact, 72 MM=12×(60/10), while 80 MM=12×(60/9), which is much closer to 60 MM or 53.33 MM for the basic 4/2 meter (MM=8 BPM×[60/9]; MM=8×6.66; MM=53.33).

Figure 8.1 Structural plan of the *Life Pulse Prelude*

Cycle Number		Successive, Iterative Measures of Music	Total Measures
I		1,2,3,4,5,6,7,8,9,10,11,10,9,8,7,6,5,4,3,2	20
II		1,2,3,4,5,6,7,8,9,10,11,10,9,8,7,6,5,4,3,2	20
III		1,2,3,4,5,6,7,8,9,10,11,10,9,8,7,6,5,4,3,2	20
IV		1,2,3,4,5,6,7,8,9,10,11,10,9,8,7,6,5,4,3,2	20
V		1,2,3,4,5,6,7,8,9,10,11 (with no retrograde)	11
VI		"Varied rhythms" for 19 measures	19
VII		"Free cadenza," improvisation for 10 measures	10
VIII		"Continue varied rhythms for 19 measures"	19
IX		1,2,3,4,5,6,7,8,9,10,11,10,9,8,7,6,5,4,3,2	20
X	Coda	1,2,3,4,5,6,7,8,9,10,11,10,9,8,7,6,5,4,3,2,1	21
Total measures			180
Total seconds at eight seconds per measure			1440

does Ives refer specifically to $\quarternote=53.33$; and the metaphorical significance of the symbolic pulsation of a twenty-four hour day seems, in such a transcendental work, especially significant.

Sixth **LPP** *page* (f1825).

This page contains an alignment of different metric subdivisions accompanied by the note "(each part to be measured in right position in ink copy)." Thus Ives is not only leaving a reminder to himself and to a future copyist, but is also expressing a desire to see just how such complex rhythms appear to the eye.

Seventh **LPP** *page* (f1826).

A brief note on this mostly empty page expresses Ives's feeling that "the upper rhythms from 13 to 31" are rhythmic figurations too fast to be perceived as single pulses. This further substantiates $\quarternote=60$ or 53.33 as the nominal tempo.

Eighth **LPP** *page* (f1827).

This page outlines the metrical relationship of the B.U. to the percussion orchestra and the orchestral unit ("O.U.") to the Earth and Heavens orchestras. Ives associates OU1 with BU2, making the Earth and Heavens orchestras of section A twice the speed of the life pulse. Thus, it could be deduced that the anomalous metronome setting of "30=♪" found on section A page 1 (Plate 8.6, f1830) could actually refer, correctly, to the *LPP* percussion orchestra tempo, making the music of the Earth and Heavens orchestras actually ♩=60. I will show, however, that such is not the case.

Improvisation. Ives writes, "The OUs from 3 up are the varying pulse" and, elsewhere on the page, "from then on they each expand grow & create in their own way." These clear references to improvisation do not, however, refer to every part, since only prime number meters to thirteen, not their multiples, are designated as the "varying pulse." By contrast, on the fifth *LPP* page (Plate 8.5, f1824) a subdivision by a non-prime number, twelve, structures a line of syncopated rhythmic variation.

4. The realization of the *LPP*

My full realization in live performance of the *LPP* grew from experience gained in two earlier, shorter, computer-controlled and, later, computer-generated realizations for tape playback performance. The first, recorded in Florida in 1975, was accomplished by coordinating five performers with computer-generated click tracks in four recording passes, each pass a different combination of five meters/tempos/parts.[14] Two of the ten cycles were realized. My plan then was to integrate the *LPP* percussion music with my first two fantasies on the *US*. A second two-cycle realization was completed in 1981 at the University of North Texas, this time using a Synclavier II digital synthesizer to create a very precise synthetic percussion version for tape playback. That version was used in the premiere performance of my *Phantasmagoria: Fantasies on Ives's Universe Symphony* (1976, rev. 1981), for orchestra, narrator, tape, and digital synthesizer.[15]

---

[14] See Larry Austin, with Larry Bryant, "A computer-synchronized, multi-track recording system," *Proceedings of the Second Annual Music Computation Conference* (1975, Part 4): 1–12.

[15] See Larry Austin, "Phantasmagoria: chronicle of computer-assisted composition/performance," *Proceedings of the 1982 International Computer Music Conference* (Venice), 278–79.

In 1974, early in the process of transcribing the *US* sketches, I sensed how important it was to realize and complete "Prelude #1." I saw that such a project would yield valuable insights into the nature of the entire symphony. But after I had written five of the ten cycles I realized just how enormous the task had become. With no apparent performance possibilities for a completed *LPP*, I set aside further work on the *LPP* realization, promising myself that I would take up the task again someday and finish all ten cycles. That opportunity came in April 1983, when, as a guest composer at the first North American Festival of New Music in Buffalo, New York, I lectured on the *US* and discussed my work on the *LPP*. Percussionist Jan Williams, festival co-director, was intrigued with the possibility that the legendary piece could actually be realized and performed. We made a pact: I would complete the *LPP* realization and create a multi-track cue-tape for the twenty performers; Jan would provide performers and present the premiere at the second North American Festival of New Music in April 1984. In making the realization I followed Ives's instructions to create "varied rhythms," a "free cadenza," and to "exchange" metric rhythms among parts, all the while preserving the integrity of each part's tempo and rhythmic design. Seventy-three years after Ives conceived the *LPP* it was heard with its full complement of performers and in its entirety for the first time.[16]

Instrumentation of the LPP *realization.*

Figure 8.2 shows the instrumentation I selected from the instruments indicated by Ives in the *LPP* sketches, with their individual tempo and meter in my realization. The instrumentation I have designated is subject to substitution and elaboration, as future performances and experience with the *LPP* and the *US* may dictate. For instance, in the first performance Jan Williams and I agreed that the ceramic bells called for by Ives were much too "light" in an ensemble with so many louder instruments. We chose temple cup gongs as optional instruments, still "light" but more penetrating than ceramic bells. And my inclusion of a marimba allowed an enhancement of

---

[16] Ives did organize a reading of a portion of "Prelude #1," later recalling that "it sounded (with 8 players) better than I thought [it would]" (*Memos*, 125).

Figure 8.2 Instrumentation of the *LPP* realization

Instrument(s)	*LPP* Sketch Page(s)	Meter	Tempo
piano	2	31/8	♪ = 232.5
orchestra bells	2	29/8	♪ = 217.5
piccolo	2	23/8	♪ = 172.5
triangle/tambourine	2,5	19/8	♪ = 142.5
2nd xylophone	2	17/8	♪ = 127.5
4 ceramic bells (or cup gongs)	2,5	13/4	♩ = 97.5
5 woodblocks (high to low)	5	22/8	♪ = 165.0
3rd snare drum/tom-tom	4,5	11/4	♩ = 82.5
1st xylophone	5	14/4	♩ = 105.0
suspended cymbal/2nd tenor drum	4,5	7/2	♩ = 52.5
2nd snare drum	4,5	10/4	♩ = 75.0
bass drum, cymbal attached	4,5	5/2	♩ = 37.5
1st snare drum (snares off)	4,5	12/4	♩ = 90.0
marimba (for "piccolo tympanum")	4	9/4	♩ = 67.5
tympanum (32")	4,5	6/2	♩ = 45.0
tam-tam (or large gong)	4	3/1	o = 20.0
1st tenor drum (for Indian drum)	4	8/4	♩ = 60.0
low bell	4	4/2	♩ = 30.0
large bass drum	4	2/1	o = 15.0
large, low, deep hanging bell	1,4,5	2/1	o = 15.0

the instrumental color spectrum, as well as an orchestrational balance to the large number of membranophones listed by Ives. I am convinced that Ives had not settled on a definitive instrumentation for the *LPP* and was keeping his options open, knowing he would probably want to experiment with various combinations in different performance situations. I recommend and continue to follow that same rule.

Instrumental roles in the progress of the **LPP.**

It is one thing to assign the instrumentation, another to determine the form, but to decide Ives's intent about the moment-to-moment progress of the *LPP* must be left to a composer's instincts. There are, as I have pointed out, clues and models to help: the palindromic form of the twenty-measure cycle Ives actually sketched on various *LPP* pages; the clear pyramidic order of entrances, progressing from the slowest to the fastest pulses; the unchanging iterations of melodic/rhythmic sequences in the instruments playing meters of thirteen to thirty-one pulses, as well as the constancy of those playing one, two, and three pulses per measure; and the varying rhythms of other instruments, exchanging meters and improvising syncopated rhythms. Nevertheless, the most important model for my work with the *LPP* has always been Ives's evolutionary metaphor: humanity, the "life pulse" of the Universe, progressing from birth to transcendence beyond death. Through the first five cycles, the *LPP* is born and slowly grows in intensity and complexity. Through cycles VI, VII, and VIII, the "varied rhythms," the "free cadenza," and the return of "varied rhythms" create a dense, complex world of rhythmic/melodic/timbral interaction. And in the final two cycles the simpler iterations of the first cycles return, gradually attenuating until the low, deep, final toll of the hanging bell, alone, dies away. Figure 8.3 depicts the overall progress of the *LPP* through the ten cycles with respect to instrumental roles and activity.

As mentioned, I have relied on my instincts as a composer to carry me through each of the thirteen "varying" parts. The complexity of each part grows through the first half of the *LPP*, becoming most complex and improvisational in cycles VI, VII, and VIII and then returning to original patterns in the final two cycles. For the instruments playing in meters 9/4 and 14/4 I derived pitch successions and combinations from other *US* sketches, specifically the pitches of the "Earth chord" and a series of pitches from the second all-*US* page (Plate 8.2, f1829).

The **LPP** effect.

Composers, percussionists, and other musicians have all experimented from time to time with the musical effect of combining prime number pulses. This can be done, for example, by clapping two-against-three or three-against-five, or by coordinating several performers playing in different tempos and coming into phase at some agreed-upon time interval. Certainly, composers using computer music systems have enjoyed the ease of exploration of such rhythmic complexes. Is the notion of combining twenty different meters and tempos, coming into phase every eight seconds, an elementary, even primitive idea? Yes. Was Ives really serious about this experiment? Yes. Is the musical effect of the *LPP* special? Absolutely! The result is what I call "the *LPP* effect": "durational counterpoint" plus sound-

Figure 8.3 Graphic overview of the *LPP*

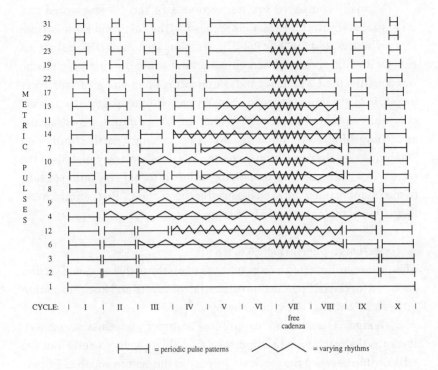

mass/pulsation-mass/event-mass/rhythm-mass/melody-mass plus the phenomenological synthesis of mesmerizing melodic/rhythmic iterations and an incessant improvisatory catharsis. In Ives's words:

> The listener, if he tries hard enough, will get the composite effect that's wanted, while each player concentrates on his particular meter, hearing the others as secondary sounds, at least while practising them . . . if the different meters are each played by groups of different sounding units, the effect is valuable, and I believe will be gradually found an important element in deepening and enriching all of the depths of music, including the emotional and spiritual. (*Memos*, 125)

It works. It does indeed enrich the depths of the music. It does indeed seem like the life pulse of the universe.

197

5. Sketches for section A

Virtually completed by Ives, section A of the *US* was scored and orchestrated for the four Heavens orchestras, the Earth and Rock Formation orchestras, and the "Life Pulse" percussion. Ives numbered the first ten pages with large, box-enclosed numerals, but could not find page 8 as he was collating the *US* sketches and commenting on them for *Memos*. Ives's page 8, in fact, has never been located. Yet even without page 8, the musical continuity sustained in section A, lasting almost five minutes, is a dramatic and compelling consummation after the opening "Earth chord" and "Prelude #1" of the percussion orchestra. What follows is my analysis of the section A sketches, and the underlying rationale for my realization of each of the extant manuscript sketch pages for this section: "Past—from chaos, formation of the Waters and Mountains."

Section A, page 1 (Plate 8.6, f1830).

This page was numbered by Ives as page 1 of his through-composed section A, scored for the *LPP* percussion orchestra, the "Earth and Rock Formation orchestras," and the "Heavens orchestras."

Tempo. The notation "Largo 30 = ♩" at upper left seems unequivocal. It means that each four-beat measure should last eight seconds! But the relationship between the music of the page at this tempo and the *LPP* percussion music preceding and accompanying it is puzzling. This page and Ives's pages 2 and 3 (Plate 8.7, f1831, and f1832) that follow do present material that is formative, slowly evolving, and seemingly in accord with the various tempi proposed for the *LPP* mentioned earlier. The situation becomes difficult, however, when one tries, at this extremely slow tempo, to perform the music of Ives's page 4 (f1834). If one keeps to ♩=30, the counter-rhythms are so slow that the recurrent counter-pulses, so necessary for musicians to execute the counter-rhythms, occur much too slowly for any degree of accuracy. At ♩=60, on the other hand, the rhythms are performable and, just as importantly, perceivable to the listener as a complex of counter-meters, Ives's "durational counterpoint." Did Ives, then, intend at some later point to double the tempo? No such point is indicated in section A. We are left, then, with several choices: to cope with a very slowly evolving section A at ♩=30; to believe instead that various tempos

suggested on the fifth *LPP* page (e.g., 𝅗𝅥=53.33) are more likely correct; to ignore the marking 𝅘𝅥=30 as incorrect; or to look for further tempo clues. I believe that the correct tempo is 𝅗𝅥=30, not 𝅘𝅥=30. I believe that Ives simply miscalculated his intention, especially since his page 2 of section A (Plate 8.7, f1831) clearly indicates "30–40=𝅗𝅥=BU." There is simply more evidence for the faster tempo.

Instrumentation. Between staves 8 and 9 in mm. 3–5, Ives writes that an "(organ starts p. 5 light strings diapason & pp mixture) ped 16–32." But, as will be seen, no organ part appears on page 5.

Form. Ives's various musings about the combination of the Earth, Rock Formation, Clouds and Life Pulse are relevant here: "The pulse of the universe's life beat was by the percussion orchestra, who play their movement first, all through, before any of the other orchestras play." The Earth and Heaven groups "come into relation harmonically only in cycles—that is, they go around their own [time] orbit, and come to meet each other only where their circles eclipse" (*Memos*, 107–08). This suggests that, while optionally separate, the percussion orchestra also served to provide the pulse and tempo for the Earth and Heaven orchestras. In the bottom margin of the page shown in Plate 8.6 Ives writes, "Through whole movement keep going in rhythmic cycle." The creation motif of the *US* is manifest throughout the page: the changing, formative, turbulent nature of the Rock Formation themes, their irregularity (staves 9–13); the elemental nature of the Earth chord, droning its cluster of fourths and tritones (staves 15–16), swelling in waves in counter-rhythms to "soil and vegetation" chords, "their roots in the Heavens" (staves 3–6); all the time with the primal "life pulse" of man resounding (added lines below stave 16).

Section A, page 2 (Plate 8.7, f1831).

Tempo. The topmost stave here, plus the extra, drawn-in stave above, indicate, as far as I am concerned, the best and latest tempo markings, where: the "basic unit" is a 4/2 bar; each half-note beat is marked "30"; each quarter-note subdivision is marked "60"; the "BU" is marked a double whole note; and Ives suggests an even faster tempo, "about 30–40=𝅗𝅥." The *US* music continues on this second page at the second system, first with two

4/4 bars, followed by an 8/4 bar, continuing with another 8/4 bar on the third system. The next measure, again in 8/4, is found on the fourth system. The remaining total of eleven measures, referred to in the line drawn in the top system, are found on page 3 (f1832) and the first measure of page 4 (Plate 8.8, f1834). The note, "or 22–4/4 meas=60" in the top margin refers to which twenty-two measures? Those that follow? 2×11? Eleven 3/2 measures do not equal twenty-two 4/4 measures in cross metering. Is this another miscalculation by Ives? Eleven is, of course, the center measure of a *complete* twenty-one measure cycle, of which there is only one: the tenth and final cycle of the *LPP*. Cycles I through IV and cycle IX all elide their last with their first measures, making each twenty measures long (see Figure 8.1).

Form. In counting every measure from Ives's page 2 (Plate 8.7, f1831) to the second measure of Ives's page 4 (Plate 8.8, f1834), where a double barline signals the beginning of cross meters for the Earth and Heavens orchestras, there are twenty-two 4/4 measures. Twenty-two measures in 4/4 is one half of a percussion cycle. The "Cloud" chords appear in the second system of page 2 and are assigned to violins, flutes, one oboe, a harp, and possibly violas. Roman numerals (I–IV) highlight separate entrances. When the chords take on their cross-metric relation to the Rock Formation themes, the "chordal cloud counterpoint gradually begins" (see lower right).

Section A, page 3 (f1832).

At some point Ives crossed out the top twelve staves of this page. These staves contain no "Cloud" chords or orchestrational directions and no musical material that is related to the music of the *US*. Only a few measures starting on the thirteenth stave seem to mark the continuation of the *US* from page 2.

Section A, page 4 (Plate 8.8, f1834).

Instrumentation. From this page forward to the end of section A (f1839) the instrumentation is generally consistent. Ives summarizes this aspect in an inscription within the third through fifth staves. Groups I, II, and IV call for *divisi* violins with some flute doublings. These are the instruments used for the Clouds or Heavens orchestras. Group III is scored for three flutes without violins. Later, in the second system, stave 6, first measure, a clarinet is added to group III as well. The reference to "1 free line" refers to the four cloud groups in free "chordal counterpoint," while the inscription "II Rigid line to Earth" assigns the Rock formation, Earth themes, and "low Earth chord" to the "Earth orchestra." The note "2 orchestras [from here]," written in the upper right margin above stave 1, apparently refers to the Heavens orchestra and the Earth/Rock formation orchestra. It is conceivable that the reference is to the two string orchestras Ives indicated for this part of section A, differentiated in section B by being tuned a quarter-tone apart.

Form. In m. 2 of stave 5, at the double bar, Ives writes "Drums gong & ch part starts here." This is a clear signal that a new cycle of the *LPP* is to begin, the B.U. stated by chimes, the 2 meter by drums, and the 3 meter by gong. In light of Ives's comment on the first *LPP* page (f1820) that "The earth, heavens orchestra[s] do not start until after 3rd or 4th Percussion cycle," we can assume that by this time in section A we have just concluded cycle V, a half-cycle of eleven 4/2 bars, and are ready to begin cycle VI.

Ives's annotation in the bottom margin, "Keep low Earth chord through here until X p. 6," is anomalous, because there is no "X" on page 6 (Plate 8.10, f1836) and because the Earth chord is scored on Ives's pages 9 and 10, held over with ties from missing page 8. Nevertheless, it seems clear that Ives did want this chord sustained all the way through section A. On the other hand, there is no specific musical or annotated reference to the chord (except in similar pitch combinations) in sketch pages for sections B and C. Is it reasonable to assume that Ives did mean for the Earth chord to sustain its elemental cluster through section A, not to be heard, at least in this form, in sections B and C? Musically and metaphorically, I believe this is the case.

Section A, page 4 patch (f1833).

This page is what Ives called a "patch" for page 4, first system, m. 3. It includes a series of notes headed "Theme II Univ Sym," a kind of pyramidic flourish, not unlike other material in this section. What is curious is that the durations of this theme, which total twenty-two beats, must apparently be played in the span of only four beats. Ives may have intended that the values are half or even a quarter of those notated. The theme, so reduced, would nicely fit the nature of the material in the preceding and subsequent measures.

Section A, page 5 (Plate 8.9, f1835).

Instrumentation. The keyboard/percussion line in stave 5 of this page, begun on the last measure of the preceding page, continues for seven measures to the note "the rest of this part is copied with drum and other bells part see sheet extra marked ⊡" at the right margin. These eight measures are quite different from the sample life pulse music for the same instruments seen on the sixth *LPP* page (f1825). This suggests that the Heavens orchestras were to have their own percussion and keyboards, distinct from the life pulse percussion. Stave 5 of the second system is headed "Bells cel" but used for "Trp 2" and the "3rd theme," part of the Earth/Rock-formation orchestra material. Ives probably affixed the heading as he was laying out the page, before notating any music.

Notation. The letters A–F in the top staves of both systems refer to a sequence of chord types (various chordal combinations of six-member, quartal/triadic harmonies) in group I to be continued with proper transpositions through this page and the two following. Ives's figurings in the bottom margin, mostly crossed out by a wavy line, probably refer to the various cross-metric ratios present in the combination of Earth and Heavens orchestras. For example, "$24 \times 2/2$" could pertain to the Earth music's twelve bars of 2/2 totaling twenty-four half notes; "$7 \times 9 = 63$" could refer to the subdivided common factor of sixty-three between Heavens groups I and III or, instead, nine measures of seven beats per measure; and the circled number 48 in the lower right corner could refer to the forty-eight quarter-note beats on the page. The sequence "6 7 8 9 10 11 12" could pertain to the variety of cross pulses present in combination, though a subdivision of eleven is present only in the underlying *LPP* percussion.

Section A, page 6 (Plate 8.10, f1836).

Instrumentation. By page 6, the relation of the Earth, Heavens, and *LPP* orchestras is distinct, and the groups are reasonably consistent in instrumentation. A "harp" chord appears in the second system, fourth stave, m.3. The only previous references to harp are on page 4 (Plate 8.8, f1834), listed on the keyboard/percussion line on stave 5 of both systems; otherwise, the rest of the music on stave 4 could not be played on a harp. The chord-type sequence A–F in the top staves continues, but with a note in the top margin indicating that unlettered chords are to repeat the last chord-type indicated, transposed in parallel motion.

Dynamics. Since beginning section A at *ppp* and *pp*, the only other dynamic markings have been on page 4 (Plate 8.8, f1834), where each cloud group's entrance is marked *pp*. On page 6 *ff* markings appear for the first time in the fifth bars of both systems in the Earth orchestra (stave 5). The almost total absence of dynamic markings, except for these, suggests that Ives simply never got to the final editing of the score for dynamics and phrasing.

The twelve non-repeating pitches lettered at the bottom margin appear to be unrelated to the spelling or sequence of pitches, chordal or melodic, on this page. Only the augmented triad subsets – D, F♯, A♯ and G♯, E, C – seem related to some of group I's chord-types. Interestingly, the interval so prevalent in the symphony to this point – the tritone – is not present in the series.

Section A, page 7 (Plate 8.11, f1837).

Instrumentation. No important changes in instrumentation occur. A note in the left margin in the second system to "see celesta piano all drums bells & percussion on sheet" reminds us that the life-pulse percussion orchestra is continuing, according to its cyclic format. In fact, cycle VII, according to the format explained on page 4 (Plate 8.8, f1834), begins at precisely this point, the first measure of the second system.

Form. In the last two measures of the second system of the Cloud group II part, new sequential sixteenth-note figurations are presented briefly with a note to "continue figure ad lib (see note bottom p 8)." This allusion to the missing page 8 and to an "ad lib" treatment of such material suggests a musical shorthand for a sequencing technique. Page 8 apparently supplied other material that was equally intriguing, as page 9 (f1838) is notably different in layout from page 7. And there are references to page 8 on five other sketch pages. Based on the *LPP* cyclic format, explained previously, and the resulting effect on the form of section A, it is probable that page 8 was exactly six 4/2 measures in length. In my realization, I have chosen not to invent material for the missing page. Rather, I have elided directly from the end of page 7 to the beginning of page 9. The elision is unnoticeable in performance.

Section A, page 9 (f1838).

Tempo. Ives mentions on this page a "red ink" percussion score, apparently referring to the fifth *LPP* page (Plate 8.5, f1824). He seems to regard the *LPP* pages as definitive score. This reinforces the validity of the tempo markings on that page (with a ten-second B.U.) and supports my subsequent arguments about tempo in the *US*.

Form. If page 8 did contain six 4/2 measures, the beginning of life-pulse cycle VIII would fall exactly at the third 4/4 measure of page 9. That is where Ives has notated a triangular symbol and a direction to "see Percussion/low cycle."

Section A, page 10 (f1839).

An admonition that this page is "sketch not score" appears in the upper margin, though this page, like the others for section A, is fully orchestrated. Most of the page is involved with the formation of a large sonority that is apparently to be played along with the Earth chord, which Ives now calls a "MASS chord." At the conclusion of the page he writes "to Sec B."

6. Sketches for section B

On the cover page of his *US* folio Ives indicated that six sketch pages comprised section B of the *US*, "II—Present—Earth and the firmament, evolution in Nature and Humanity." However, by my analysis, three of these pages contain little or no material specific to section B: f1843 is an all-*US* page; f1844 is spuriously attributed; and f1845 belongs to section C. Thus section B has the least completed scoring of the three sections and prelude. Unlike section A, it is neither complete nor fully orchestrated. Rather, each page of section B is a different collection of musical fragments and chords, scales, written plans, and lists of groups and instruments. The pages do, however, yield rich material for free and open interpretation by "somebody" wanting to "work out the idea."

First section B page (f1840).

Instrumentation. This preliminary distribution plan for instrumental forces suggests orchestral groups similar to those of section A, with an "upper orchestra" comprised of violins, flutes, and keyboard/percussion, "about 35 to 40 players," and a "lower orchestra" consisting of four similar groups of brass, bassoons, violas, cellos, and basses. One note implying a reduction in percussion forces from twenty to eleven or twelve may actually be a reference to the number of players who perform the twenty lines of life-pulse percussion music. Since each of the metric divisions except 31, 29, 23, 19, 17, and 13 can be paired with at least one multiple of the prime number involved, five percussionists of the eleven or twelve could play two or three percussion lines simultaneously. Ives did organize a reading of a portion of the life-pulse music with eight players that must have involved the same kinds of multiple percussion duplication (see *Memos*, 125). In my realization of section B – following the conclusion of the tenth and final *LPP* cycle that begins in the final measures of section A – the percussion orchestra players are, accordingly, divided into smaller groups of four to six performers, each led by an assistant conductor. These parts present free improvisations on material characteristic of their music during the *LPP*, thereby continuing their "pulse of cosmic energy."

Ives distinguishes between lines that are "Primal free," apparently a continuation of freely evolving, disjunct contrapuntal lines from section A, and "Second or Rigid," referring to particular chord complexes that evolve into themes. The latter process is illustrated on the third section B page (Plate 8.12, f1842), depicting, I believe, a musical and symbolic evolution from a chordal Earth-mass to a melodic form of "Nature and Humanity."

Second section B page (f1841).

This page contains a working out of the "rigid theme" concept and the designation of such types by numbers.[17] Circled sets of chord tones, in whole notes, have equivalent melodic versions, often alongside. Thematic

---

[17] For a transcription and discussion of this page see Philip Lambert, "Interval cycles as compositional resources in the music of Charles Ives," *Music Theory Spectrum* 12/1 (1990): 43–82 (Ex. 11, p. 64).

lines, some from section A, are here found in the lower half of the page, notated and scored for brass.

Third section B page (Plate 8.12, f1842).

Tempo. Three features of this page substantiate my theory that the tempo established in section A ($\quarternote$=60 or 53.33) continues through section B: the absence of any new tempo indication; the continuation of freely notated, non-metered lines, with the exception of the double 4/4 measures in staves 10–14; and the inscription preceding stave 6 that reads "pulse of 12 percussion universe." The latter also confirms that the percussion cycles are to continue in smaller and freer formations.

Instrumentation. Ives makes several changes in the forces described on the first section B page (f1840). He adds a "group of 12 violin[s] tuned in 1/4 tones" (stave 3); a "perfectly tuned overtone machine" (upper margin, two text lines above stave 1); "a kind of self-playing organ" (upper right side margin), sustaining the "Earth Formation chords"; and refers to some instrument (an organ?) that is "either to be mechanically held or played by 2 men" (between staves 5 and 6).

Form. Altogether, Ives's sonic universe, "now formed," includes quarter-tone, just-intoned, and equal-tempered tunings, as well as a "new scale no octaves" (staves 7 and 8), and a "perfectly tuned scale of overtones not well-tempered" (upper margin, just above stave 1), all in their "Primal" states. The symbolism is clear: from this mix of elemental tunings, Ives's musical universe is diverse and thriving. While section A was completed, scored, and notated in metered time, section B is a collection of non-metered chords, themes, and ideas for the primal growth of Ives's newly created universe. Could it be that these unrealized conceptions were intended as a kind of chaotic representation of the newly created world, musically represented by a free orchestral cadenza or improvisation based on each group's Earth formation chord or scale? Would all this chaos be "let loose," while the violins, harp, and organ sustain a twenty-four note cluster in "the Firmament and the Heavens" above, as the *LPP* percussion improvises in cross rhythms? This one page could certainly have been – and perhaps was intended to be – fully realized in through-composed form. It is intriguing to ponder that Ives's open invitation for "somebody" to try his/her hand at finishing and/or adding to this work is nowhere better expressed in the sketches than here: could it also have meant that the performers themselves could improvise their parts with guidance from the materials on this page? In my realization, I followed both paths concurrently: a through-composed "universe of Tones" with performers improvising rhythmic designs and durations on select materials created from these sketch pages in harmony with Ives's subtitle: "Present—Earth and the firmament, evolution in Nature and Humanity."

7. Sketches for section C

Ives's sketch pages for section C, subtitled "Future—Heaven, the rise of all to the Spiritual," number seven. These comprise fully composed short scores, chordal charts, and fragments of thematic and chordal materials. Thus section C is more complete in musical continuity and specific material than section B, but less so than A. The end of section C includes a fully notated but not fully orchestrated "coda"; the beginning is less clear. In my realization section C begins with chords from the first page and a slowly rising Earth-chord glissando in the low strings, moving then to the final music of section C and the coda.

First section C page (Plate 8.13, f1846).

Form. This page contains a "chord scale system" for the "3rd section" of the *US* that formalizes the "Rigid theme" concept of section B. Here, not five but twenty-four different "chordal scales" are to be "used for the themes ... thus each theme of the 24 will be its own ... varying intervals and overtone vibrations" (lower right side margin). It is an Ivesian, democratically planned dispersion of tonal worlds. His designation of this sound world as the "foreground harmonic basis" (upper margin), a surface layer of a multi-layered texture, expands the concept of layering of section A as well, especially if all twenty-four tonal realms busy themselves at once. As proposed earlier, the twenty separate percussion parts of the life pulse continue their final cycles.

The admixture of twenty-four- and twelve-tone tuning systems is a logical extension: in section A, only one tuning system – twelve-notes-per-octave equal temperament – was used; in section B, several different tunings were present, each assigned to a specific instrumental grouping; in section C, the complete synthesis of tuning systems is accomplished. I believe that such a transformation in tuning systems through the *US* is a musical metaphor for Ives's creation motif: birth, life, and the "rise to the spiritual," the final synthesis.

Second section C page (Plate 8.14, f1847).
The lower four staves of this page contain some provocative ideas: the widely separated, non-repeated pitch classes connected by lines could be imagined as a graphic analog of a mountain range or, more likely, Ives's notational experimentation with the relationship of time and spatial extensity. In the lower margin he writes "rhythm time road and space swings [graphically] as to interval continuity." Further, this may be another application of the "chordal scale system" or "Rigid theme" concept, which transforms a chord into a melodic theme.

Third section C page (f1848).
A date in the upper margin of this page, "Oct 1915," is the same date Ives mentions in his account of the origins of the *US* in *Memos* (106–08). A large "III" and reference to a "chord scale system" confirm that this is the beginning of the final sketches for section C. This page, like the first pages of sections A and B, is a scenario of the progress of the section and its "rise of all to the spiritual." An annotation, "all in layer[s] and different lines," refers to the "foreground harmonic basis" of the first section C page (Plate 8.13, f1846).

Instrumentation. Isolated references to instruments appear on this page, but, overall, the musical material is yet to be orchestrated. The plan of separate Earth and Heavens orchestras prevails throughout section C.

Tempo. Though no marking appears, the thematic figuration is not unlike sections A and B, suggesting that the tempo of the preceding sections is to be maintained. There is no mention of the percussion orchestra.

Fourth section C page (f1850).
This page of short score is marked "Largo," providing further evidence that the tempo remains unchanged from section B. There is a curious comment about a "medium orchestra" that probably refers not to the entire orchestral assemblage but rather to *one* of the orchestras. Another inscription pro-

vides a rare hint of a choral component: "1st 2 voices alternate" might refer to human voices rather than musical lines. The majestic, processional nature of the music certainly could be set for added choral forces. No text appears, however.

Fifth section C page (f1851).

Instrumentation. There is some material on this page that does not belong to the *US*, but what does belong includes notes on instrumentation and reference to an organ part. Another reference to an organ was noted on page 1 of section A (Plate 8.6, f1830). If the *US* was conceived to be performed by orchestras on mountain tops, how would an organ have been added? Nowhere in these sketch pages is there any reference, musically, to Henry Cowell's claim that Ives really meant the piece to be performed outdoors.[18] It is my belief that Ives's conceptual modeling for the piece may indeed have included musings about such a grand outdoor realization, which he may have discussed in conversations with Cowell; but references to such an idea in practical terms do not appear in the sketches.

Sixth section C page (Plate 8.15, f1853).

This is the conclusion of the symphony, as indicated by Ives's heading "end of Sec C / universe Sym" at the top of the page, and by the double bar at lower right. As in Ives's song "On the Antipodes," where a pedal C is sustained by an "organ ad lib" through the last seven bars, the "gradual clearing up to A min" (far right of stave 11) is supported by a pedal A (13.75 Hz!) through the last several measures. Here, finally, is music for the organ!

Instrumentation. The reference to a "piano on stage" in stave 15 demonstrates further that Ives meant the *US* to be presented in a theater or concert hall. (Though, of course, stages can be outdoors as well.) The Heavens and Earth orchestras continue to the end, as the life-pulse percussion orchestra ends its final cycle.

Seventh section C page (Plate 8.16, f1845).

Form. This thicket of themes, chords, and written references seems mainly concerned with material for the *US* "Coda." Since Ives conceived the

---

[18]   See p. 183 above.

work in three continuous sections, a coda for the entire piece, rather than separate codas for each successive section, seems likely. The "Main E[ar]th" theme from section A is found on staves 7, 8, and 15; material from section C and two references to the coda are found on staves 4–7, in the annotation at the top of the page, and on staves 11 and 12. There is music from page 6 of section A (Plate 8.10, f1836) on stave 13, a transposed version for trumpets, all appearing as back references that a composer might use for a coda. There is no music similar to the section B material here.

8. The *US* realization

Form. In his *US* sketches through four decades, Ives remained ambivalent about the continuity of the work's component parts. Was the percussion orchestra of "Prelude #1" to be heard once all the way through before the subsequent sections were heard? Ives had, after all, indicated that it could be played alone. Was the prelude then to be repeated, *in toto*, while sections A, B, and C were performed? Or, as Ives suggested another time, was the Earth chord to sound first, followed by "Prelude #1" eliding with section A, the Prelude ending sometime after section B began, never to be heard again? Sections A, B, C – Past, Present, Future – are unequivocally ordered, of course, with a finale leading to a Coda to end the piece. I "composed out" the formal continuity for my realization of the *US* based on creative extrapolation, both from what Ives "argued" with himself about *US* continuity and from what I, as a self-commissioned composer-arbiter-collaborator, thought would work musically and – for this great transcendental work – dramatically.

Figure 8.4 is a diagram of my realization. The Earth chord orchestra is heard first, continuing alone and quietly for the first two minutes. Then, gradually, the first of the ten percussion orchestra cycles of the *Life-Pulse Prelude* joins the Earth chord orchestra. The *LPP* builds in volume, density, and rhythmic complexity through the next sixteen minutes, culminating with the "varied rhythms" of cycle VI. The percussion orchestra reaches its peak *ff*, as the improvised "free cadenza" of cycle VII begins and as the Heavens and Rock Formation orchestras enter with introductory material in a discontinuous montage of scattered sonorities, masked at first by the

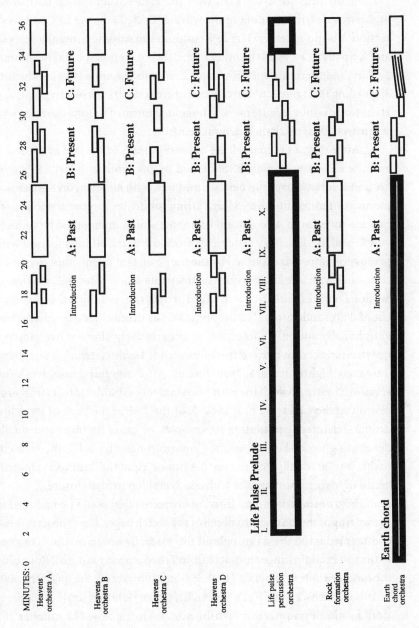

Figure 8.4 Formal continuity chart of the realization

overpowering *LPP* orchestra. The *LPP* begins to subside through the "varied rhythms" of cycle VIII, with the Heavens and Rock Formation orchestras clearly emerging in the texture. Cycle IX of the *LPP* and Ives's section A begin together. The *LPP* continues to subside through cycles IX and X finally to *pp*, as all the other orchestras of section A build in volume, density, and rhythmic-metric complexity. At that point all five conductors are leading their respective orchestras in cross-metrical counterpoint, and at the twenty-four minute mark – the golden mean of its total duration – all seven orchestras reach their denouements.

After that, a gradual release of tension leads to the end of section A and the elision to section B, underlaid by the tenth and last *LPP* cycle. Section B follows over the next six minutes, with all seven orchestras in a montage of different tunings, high string sonorities in a twenty-four note quarter-tone chord, and natural harmonic scales, interrupted by sudden, antiphonal, declamatory statements from the brass, all interspersed with percussion improvisations led by the four assistant conductors. Section B concludes with a solo viola quietly cadencing to a few seconds of silence. Section C ensues, with the Earth chord orchestra beginning a three-minute chordal glissando ascent "to the Spiritual," as the four Heavens orchestras antiphonally sound a succession of progressively shorter, overlapping, quarter-tone chords derived from Ives's "chord scale system," all dissolving into their highest textural "firmament." After a grand pause, Ives's full seven-orchestra finale of the entire *US* suddenly explodes into its final procession to the Coda. We hear cycle X of the *LPP* at the peak of its palindrome, relentlessly pounding its complex of cross rhythms and finally descending to the last toll of the "low, deep hanging bell"; the Heavens orchestras "gradually clearing up to A minor"; and the "trumpets (muted) gradually dying," bringing the *Universe Symphony* to final closure.

Instrumentation. Ives listed instruments that could be included in the scoring of the *US* on virtually all of the sketch pages. I have observed and commented upon these throughout this essay. By my calculations the size of the forces could range anywhere from 714 to as many as 4,520! Rounding the more feasible number of 714 to 700 and subtracting the unscored 500-member chorus, I chose Ives's "full orch[estra of] 200 play[ers]" as the practical, maximum number of instrumentalists to employ. The number 200 includes at least thirty-six wind, brass, and keyboard instrumentalists, twenty-three percussionists, and the equivalent of two expanded string orchestras with up to seventy players each. The number of percussionists and wind, brass, and keyboards cannot be reduced; the number of string doublings is reducible, as long as the number of violins does not fall below twenty-four and the number of violas below eight. As I have calculated, except for the nineteen extra percussionists needed, most modern symphony orchestras have, then, the requisite, minimum number of instrumentalists to perform the *US*. An ideal performance would call for twice the normal complement of strings, better to balance the formidable wind, brass, percussion, and keyboard forces. Figure 8.5 shows the instrumentation of my realization of the *US*, both overall and specific to each of the seven "orchestras."

9. A collaboration accepted, the concept realized, the symphony completed

Ives's open invitation for a collaborator to complete his *Universe Symphony* stands in vivid contrast to Henry Cowell's account of Ives's intentions:

> This is the last large work that Charles Ives has worked on: he added a few notes as late as 1951. It is unfinished, and intentionally so, as it is the culminating expression of Ives's "music of the Idea"—so gigantic, so inclusive and so exalted that he feels its complete realization is beyond any single man, and so has invited collaboration from various composers, the writer among them. Although a fuller expression of the universe in sound will surely come about as growth and freedom create men able to encompass it, Ives has never intended the *Universe Symphony* to be brought to an end, for it represents aspects of life about which there is always something more to be said.[19]

Elaborating on Henry's description twenty years later, Sidney Cowell remembered her and Henry's visits with the Iveses up to 1951 and Charles and Henry's lively sessions on the *US*:

---

[19] Cowell, *Charles Ives and His Music*, 203.

Figure 8.5 The instrumentation of the realization

Overall instrumentation of the US
Principal conductor plus 4 assistant conductors A, B, C, D

piccolo	4 horns
2 flutes	4 trumpets
alto flute (picc.)	2 tenor trombones
2 oboes	2 bass trombones
English horn	tuba
3 B♭ clarinets	23 percussionists
bass clarinet	2 pianos
2 bassoons	celesta
contrabassoon	harp
organ (optional)	

strings (52 players minimum, 60 nominal, 140 ideal)

Instrumentation by orchestras of the US
Orchestra A, The Heavens, prin. & asst. conductor A
Solo B♭ clarinet, solo viola, piano/celesta, percussion (1 player with vibraphone, 5 temple cup gongs, 4 roto-toms, 2 log drums, flexatone, wooden wind chimes, metal wind chimes), violins 1–5 (10 players minimum), viola (2 players minimum)

Orchestra B, The Heavens, prin. & asst. conductor B
2 oboes, English horn, percussion (1 player with marimba, 4 temple blocks, claves, small gong, triangle, large suspended cymbal, wooden wind chimes, woodblock, bass drum), violins 1–4 (8 players minimum), violas (2 players minimum)

Orchestra C, The Heavens, prin. & asst. conductor C
2 flutes, alto flute (piccolo), 2 B♭ clarinets, bass clarinet (B♭ clarinet), percussion (1 player with vibraphone, 4 ceramic cup gongs, 1 crotale [pitched on A], large tam-tam, large triangle, small cymbal, metal wind chimes)

Orchestra D, The Heavens, prin. & asst. conductor D
Harp, percussion (1 player with marimba, 4 woodblocks, crotale [pitched on E], large gong, castanets, medium large cymbal, wooden wind chimes, bass drum with cymbal attached) violins 1–3 (6 players minimum), violas (2 players minimum)

Orchestra E, The Life Pulse, prin. & asst. conductors A, B, C, D
Percussion orchestra of 20 players, individually performing piano, orchestra bells, piccolo, 2 triangles/tambourine, xylophone 1, xylophone 2, ceramic bells/small pipes, 5 woodblocks, snare drum 1, snare drum 2, snare drum 3 and tom-tom, tenor drum 1, small Chinese gong/piccolo tympanum, bass drum with cymbal attached, marimba, 1 tympanum (32″), tam-tam, low bell, large bass drum, and deep hanging bell

Orchestra F, The Earth and Rock Formations, prin. conductor
4 B♭ trumpets (2 doubling on B♭ piccolo and 1 on D trumpets), 4 horns, 2 tenor trombones, 2 bass trombones, tuba, 2 bassoons, contrabassoon

Orchestra G, The Earth Chord, prin. conductor
Celli (5 players minimum), basses (5 players minimum), organ (optional)

At one time the chief subject of conversation was the *Universe Symphony*, which Ives hoped my husband would collaborate on. They held energetic discussions about the advisability of adding this note or that and about the consequences each note might have as the music developed its meaning. Mr. Cowell appreciated the concept of the *Universe Symphony*, which Ives hoped would express aspects of the Idea so various and so lofty that no single man could ever complete it, but as for himself Henry found he simply could not compose in tandem. So he began what was to be a complete movement, as his contribution to the piece. But he was dissatisfied with it and left it unfinished. The two composers were never able to decide just how their respective contributions were to be combined, though they found it stimulating to ponder the possibilities.[20]

In 1971 Christine Loring (then Mrs. Rodman S. Valentinc), a neighbor who had done secretarial work for the Iveses in the 1940s, recounted to Vivian Perlis her own memories of Ives and his intentions for the *US*:

> Mr. Ives mentioned his *Universe Symphony* to me more than once. . . . It was to be religious (a paean of praise, I believe he said), and it was a real and continuing interest for years. Once, after he stood looking out the picture window toward the mountains, he restlessly paced about, not conversing but as if he were thinking aloud with gestures and humming and singing bits of music. He said, "If only I could have done it. It's all there—the mountains and the fields." When I asked him what he wanted to do, he answered, "the *Universe Symphony*. If only I could have done it."[21]

It is done. I believe that Ives always intended to complete the *US*.[22] I have realized the musical material of the sketches and finished the *US* in

---

[20] Sidney Cowell, "Ivesiana: more than something just unusual," *High Fidelity/Musical America* 24/10 (October 1974): MA16.

[21] Vivian Perlis, *Charles Ives Remembered: An Oral History* (New Haven: Yale University Press, 1974), 117.

[22] Yet after Henry Cowell found he could not "compose in tandem" with Ives, he and his wife perpetuated a view that the *US* was not meant to be completed. Nowhere did Ives write, nor is there any record that he ever said, that this was the case. But with the Cowells' published declaration, the myth was created: the *US* was "music of the Idea," never intended to be finished. I say that only Henry Cowell decided not to realize and complete the piece, and that he and his wife invented and held to the myth that, in any event, it could not be done.

what I have felt is a genuine musical and even spiritual collaboration with Ives's music of the *US*, his words about the music, and with the conductors, performers, scholars, and sponsors of my two-decade-long personal commission to finish the *Universe Symphony*. Envision. Listen.

Plate 8.1 First all-*US* page (f1828)

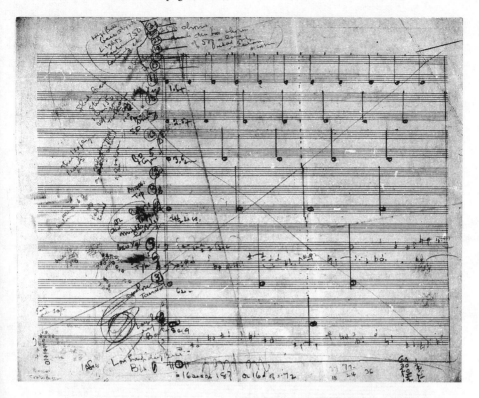

Plate 8.2 Second all-*US* page (f1829)

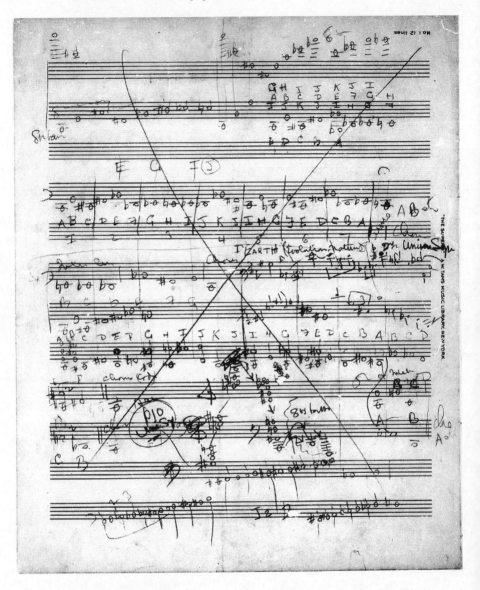

Plate 8.3 Third *LPP* page (f1822)

Plate 8.4 Fourth *LPP* page (f1823)

Plate 8.5 Fifth *LPP* page (f1824)

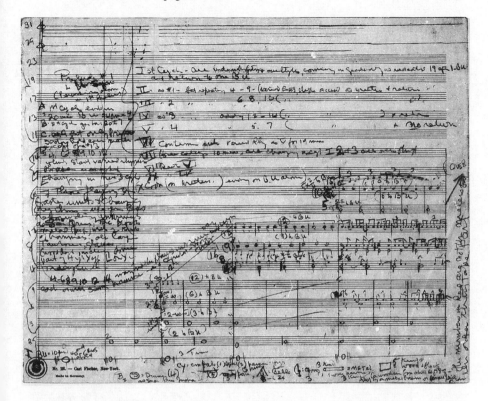

Plate 8.6 Section A, page "1" (f1830)

Plate 8.7 Section A, page "2" (f1831)

Plate 8.8 Section A, page "4" (f1834)

Plate 8.9 Section A, page "5" (f1835)

225

Plate 8.10 Section A, page "6" (f1836)

Plate 8.11 Section A, page "7" (f1837)

Plate 8.12 Third section B page (f1842)

Plate 8.13 First section C page (f1846)

229

Plate 8.14 Second section C page (f1847)

Plate 8.15 Sixth section C page (f1853)

Plate 8.16 Seventh section C page (f1845)

9 Ives's *Universe*

PHILIP LAMBERT

> *The whole universe is comprised of nine circles, or rather spheres. The outermost of these is the celestial sphere, embracing all the rest, itself the supreme god, confining and containing all the other spheres. In it are fixed the eternally revolving movements of the stars. Beneath it are the seven underlying spheres, which revolve in an opposite direction to that of the celestial sphere. . . . I stood dumbfounded at these sights, and when I recovered my senses I inquired: "What is this great and pleasing sound that fills my ears?" "That," replied my grandfather, "is a concord of tones separated by unequal but nevertheless carefully proportioned intervals, caused by the rapid motion of the spheres themselves. The high and low tones blended together produce different harmonies. . . . Gifted men, imitating this harmony on stringed instruments and in singing, have gained for themselves a return to this region, as have those who have devoted their exceptional abilities to a search for divine truths."*
> —Cicero, *De Re Publica*[1] (first century BC)

When Ives set out, in his *Universe Symphony*, to depict "the evolution of all life, in nature of humanity from the great roots of life to the spiritual eternities" (*JKCat*, 27, f1843), he joined a timeless tradition of universal contemplation and cosmological speculation. In a sense every philosopher, theologian, scientist, and artist addresses some aspect of the cosmic mystery, whether isolating a particular subatomic particle of special interest or individual achievement, or theorizing about the forces that bind such particles together and energize their movements. But only a select few assume a perspective of such scope and grandeur that nothing is excluded,

[1] From *Somnium Scipionis* ("The Dream of Scipio") in Macrobius, *Commentary on the Dream of Scipio*, transl. with an introduction and notes by William Harris Stahl (New York: Columbia University Press, 1952), 73–74.

233

"from the great inknown to the great unknown" (ibid.). Humanity reserves its highest ambitions for these visionaries, and Ives felt able and ennobled to accept such an exalted role. He had already asked the unanswered question; with the *Universe Symphony* he aspired to answer it.

The nature of his answer reveals much about the world-view he held and the philosophical-literary tradition he revered. His debts to some aspects of this tradition are now well documented,[2] but the sources for his understanding of the physical and spiritual universe and the broad sweep of history – his cosmology – extend more broadly to those pillars of western culture upon which values-systems have been based for centuries. In particular, it is not so much the tradition of scientific cosmological inquiry – Plato of the *Timaeus* – that represents Ives's most direct ancestry, as it is the pursuit of cosmic answers in artistic form – Plato of the "myth of Er" at the end of *Republic*. Taking advantage of the artist's palette and opportunities for analogy, metaphor, and syntactic drama, creators of artistic cosmologies pursue their lofty goals both in the subject matter of the works themselves and in the manner in which such ideas are communicated.

An interest in artistic cosmological reflection flourished as well among Ives's predecessors in the American intellectual tradition. A. D. Van Nostrand characterizes treatments of universal themes by Emerson, Thoreau, Whitman, and others as "romantic gospels" attempting through their individuality to "proclaim a new world."[3] James Vincent Kavanaugh describes Thoreau's and Hawthorne's reliance on ancient notions of universal harmony as a "transcendental Pythagoreanism."[4] American

---

[2] See, for example, Audrey Davidson, "Transcendental unity in the works of Charles Ives," *American Quarterly* 22/1 (1970): 35–44; Frank R. Rossiter, *Charles Ives and His America* (New York: Liveright, 1975); James Vincent Kavanaugh, "Music and American Transcendentalism: a study of transcendental Pythagoreanism in the works of Henry David Thoreau, Nathaniel Hawthorne, and Charles Ives" (Ph.D. dissertation, Yale University, 1978); and J. Peter Burkholder, *Charles Ives: The Ideas Behind the Music* (New Haven: Yale University Press, 1985).

[3] A. D. Van Nostrand, *Everyman His Own Poet: Romantic Gospels in American Literature* (New York: McGraw-Hill, 1968), 20.

[4] Kavanaugh, "Music and American Transcendentalism." For more information on the influence of nineteenth-century American writers on Ives, and on the *Universe Symphony* in particular, see Wolfgang Rathert, "Paysage imaginaire et perception totale: l'idée et la forme de la symphonie *Universe*," *Contrechamps* 7 (1986): 129–54.

Transcendentalism became for Ives the sieve through which conventional cosmological notions were filtered, leaving him with the musico-literary vision that found voice in his greatest works.

> *My soul would sing of metamorphoses.*
> *But since, o gods, you were the source of these*
> *bodies becoming other bodies, breathe*
> *your breath into my book of changes: may*
> *the song I sing be seamless as its way*
> *weaves from the world's beginning to our day.*
> —Ovid, *Metamorphoses*[5] (first century CE)

A work of art – any work of art – reflects cosmic themes by defining its own self-contained world, by exhibiting a structure that borrows and analogizes "universal" ideas. Any creator can come to identify with some larger image of "Creator," whether or not the creation itself has an explicit cosmic theme. "The art of the novelist," wrote Joseph Conrad, "is the creation of a world. This world cannot be made otherwise than in his own image."[6] Works that have been deemed "great" lend special insight into their cosmic subtexts, presenting what might be called the author's "cosmology" even while the literal text may be more earthbound.[7] The creator of a "great" work achieves special insight, as if communicating directly with some higher power. In the words of S. K. Heninger, Jr.,

> The poet is the creator of his metaphor in the same sense that the deity is creator of the universe; he is immanent in it, so that the poem is a dynamic

---

[5] *The Metamorphoses of Ovid*, transl. Allen Mandelbaum (New York: Harcourt Brace & Company, 1993), 3.

[6] From "Books" (1905), in *Joseph Conrad on Fiction*, ed. Walter F. Wright (Lincoln: University of Nebraska Press, 1964), 79.

[7] Cf. Leonard Meyer's discussion of "greatness" in music:
> For when we talk of greatness, we are dealing with a quality of experience which transcends the syntactical. We are considering another order of value in which self-awareness and individualization arise out of the cosmic uncertainties that pervade human existence: man's sense of the inadequacy of reason in a capricious and inscrutable universe; his feeling of terrible isolation in a callous and indifferent, if not hostile, nature; and his awareness of his own insignificance and impotence in the face of the magnitude and power of creation.

Leonard B. Meyer, "Some remarks on value and greatness in music," in *Music, The Arts, and Ideas: Patterns and Predictions in Twentieth-Century Culture* (Chicago: University of Chicago Press, 1967), 38.

expression of the poet's being. By correspondence, then, the poet himself is a metaphor for the creating deity, occupying a place in the hierarchy of existence just a bit lower than God.[8]

Jung describes the creative individual as an archetype that serves society's primordial need for a physician/healer. When we have grasped artistic meaning by allowing an artwork to shape us as it shaped its creator, he says,

> we also understand the nature of the primordial experience. [The artist] has plunged into the healing and redeeming depths of the collective psyche, where man is not lost in the isolation of the consciousness and its errors and sufferings, but where all men are caught in a common rhythm which allows the individual to communicate his feelings and strivings to mankind as a whole.[9]

As explained by Joseph Conrad,

> To arrest, for the space of a breath, the hands busy about the work of the earth, and compel men entranced by the sight of distant goals to glance for a moment at the surrounding vision of form and colour, of sunshine and shadows; to make them pause for a look, for a sigh, for a smile – such is the aim, difficult and evanescent, and reserved only for a very few to achieve. But sometimes, by the deserving and the fortunate, even that task is accomplished. And when it is accomplished – behold! – all the truth of life is there: a moment of vision, a sigh, a smile – and the return to an eternal rest.[10]

Creators of artistic cosmologies reflect self-consciously on their roles and obligations and overtly celebrate their self-ascribed power and fated vision. They give special emphasis to the conflation of creator with Creator, just as their artistic results bring into emphatic relief the conflation of one act of creation with the other. The works themselves typically represent pinnacles of personal artistic achievement, revealing a full depth and range

---

[8] S. K. Heninger, Jr., *Touches of Sweet Harmony: Pythagorean Cosmology and Renaissance Poetics* (San Marino CA: The Huntington Library, 1974), 364.

[9] C. G. Jung, *The Spirit in Man, Art, and Literature*, transl. R. F. C. Hull, vol. 15 of *The Collected Works of C. G. Jung* (Princeton: Princeton University Press, 1966), 105.

[10] From the preface to *The Nigger of the "Narcissus,"* reprinted in *Conrad on Fiction*, 164.

of thought and ability. They are inevitably an artist's *magnum opus*, produced over years, perhaps a lifetime, of planning, drafting, and revising.
Indeed in many cases the process never stops, as the artist cannot consider
the work "complete," usually because it defies completion as conceived and
must exist in a perpetual state of evolution along with the ever-maturing
vision of its creator.

> *From the intellectual universe the sensible universe was born, perfect from
> perfect. The creative model exists in fullness, and this fullness imparted itself to
> the creation. For just as the sensible universe participates in the flawlessness of
> its flawless model, and waxes beautiful by its beauty, so by its eternal exemplar
> it is made to endure eternally.*
> —Bernardus Silvestris, *Cosmographia*[11] (twelfth century)

Historically there have been several periods of heightened interest in cosmology by leading artists and thinkers. The theme appears with regularity
in writings of Jewish, Pagan, and Christian authors of the early Christian
era.[12] During the later Platonic revival, Pythagorean cosmology "had a
special hold upon renaissance poets."[13] In the nineteenth and early twentieth centuries these ideas were in the air not only among Ives's American
predecessors and contemporaries but also throughout Europe. The sense of
optimism and rapid progress around the turn of the century, fostering a
belief that humanity "was finally in a position to solve all its material problems, perhaps even its social ones as well," coupled with the Darwinian
belief that the world is a "complex organism steadily moving toward its own
perfection, controlled through the mechanism of a universal law," naturally
found artistic expression in works of grandiose vision.[14] At the same time,
challenges by Einstein and Freud to long-held scientific notions, plus the
end of the realist tradition in art and literature and, ultimately, the First

---

11 *The* Cosmographia *of Bernardus Silvestris*, transl., with introduction and notes,
    by Winthrop Wetherbee (New York: Columbia University Press, 1973), 89.
12 See Kathi Meyer-Baer, *Music of the Spheres and the Dance of Death* (New York:
    Da Capo Press, 1984), 29–41.
13 Heninger, *Touches of Sweet Harmony*, 341.
14 Robert P. Morgan, *Twentieth-Century Music: A History of Musical Style in
    Modern Europe and America* (New York: Norton, 1991), 12. Important ideas in
    the next sentence are also taken from Morgan (12–17). See also Carl Schorske,
    Fin-de-Siècle Vienna: Politics and Culture (New York: Knopf, 1980).

237

World War, brought about a sense of upheaval that gave rise to a whole other strain of monumental artistic expressions. In pre-revolution Russia, the sense of a looming apocalypse pervaded symbolist literature and played a role in the full blossoming of an already vibrant mystical tradition.[15]

The musical apocalypse of that period in Vienna and Paris had a spiritual sympathizer across the Atlantic. Ives responded to the societal transformation and pre-war mood with a musical progressivism that he traced to the influence of his free-thinking father but that owes as much to the direct impact of the same forces that were shaping and revolutionizing musical Europe.[16] Ives's absorption of western practices, plus his conscious molding of New-World musical and literary traditions into a distinctive language perfectly suited for his aesthetic aims, are now fully recognized. What is less well understood, however, is the consequential role played by his most progressive musical ideas, those compositional techniques that have often been termed "experimental."[17] Ives's systematic processes of compositional calculation are not tangential to his overall musical ambitions – as the word "experiment" can suggest they are – but rather are active and important participants in an evolving musical vision that reaches an idealized state with the *Universe Symphony*. If Ives's response to his times was fully consistent with the prevailing mood and fully sensitive to the forces that shaped it, it is the *Universe Symphony* that best thus illustrates.[18]

[15] See Samuel D. Cioran, *The Apocalyptic Symbolism of Andrej Belyj* (The Hague: Mouton, 1973), 9–25; Malcolm Brown, "Skriabin and Russian 'Mystic' Symbolism," *19th-Century Music* 3/1 (1979): 42–51; Louis W. Marvick, "Two versions of the Symbolist apocalypse: Mallarmé's *Livre* and Scriabin's *Mysterium*," *Criticism* 28/3 (1986): 237–306; and Maria Carlson, "*No Religion Higher Than the Truth*": *A History of the Theosophical Movement in Russia, 1875–1922* (Princeton: Princeton University Press, 1993).

[16] See J. Peter Burkholder, "The evolution of Charles Ives's music: aesthetics, quotation, technique" (Ph.D. dissertation, University of Chicago, 1983); and Geoffrey Block and J. Peter Burkholder, eds., *Charles Ives and the Classical Tradition* (New Haven: Yale University Press, 1996).

[17] For a discussion of the inadequacy of this term and the nature of the musical ideas that have been so characterized, see Philip Lambert, *The Music of Charles Ives* (New Haven: Yale University Press, 1997), 1–22.

[18] For discussion of the *Universe Symphony* as part of a "New World vision" see Raymond H. Geselbracht, "Evolution and the New World vision in the music of Charles Ives," *Journal of American Studies* 8/2 (1974): 211–27 [221].

For surely not by planning did prime bodies
find rank and place, nor by intelligence,
nor did they regulate movement by sworn pact,
but myriad atoms sped such myriad ways
from the All forever, pounded, pushed, propelled,
by weight of their own launched and speeding along,
joining all possible ways, trying all forms,
whatever their meeting in congress could create;
and thus it happens that, widespread down the ages,
attempting junctures and movements of all kinds,
they at last formed patterns which, when joined together,
became at once the origin of great things,
earth, sea, and sky, and life in all its forms.

—Lucretius, *De Rerum Natura*[19] (first century BC)

Philosophers have always used music to explain their cosmologies, following Pythagorean doctrine as transmitted by Plato and others.[20] It is only natural, then, that musicians wishing to express cosmological ideas have drawn from philosophy, in particular the notion of a "harmony of the spheres." One of the earliest examples is an anonymous inscription on an eleventh- or twelfth-century manuscript of Boethius's *De Institutione musica* that includes a diagram of the celestial scale and a musical setting of a poem on the subject of celestial harmony.[21] The early history also includes an expected intensified interest in the theme during the Renaissance, evident for example in *fêtes* in certain fifteenth-century court festivals, the best known being the *Festa del Paradiso of Ludovico Sforza* (1490), and in late sixteenth-century *intermedi*, such as those used in a performance of

[19] *The Nature of Things*, transl. Frank O. Copley (New York: Norton, 1977), 122.
[20] Valuable summaries of this tradition include James Haar, "'Musica mundana': variations on a Pythagorean theme" (Ph.D. dissertation, Harvard University, 1961); Joscelyn Godwin, *Harmonies of Heaven and Earth: The Spiritual Dimension of Music from Antiquity to the Avant-Garde* (London: Thames & Hudson, 1987); Joscelyn Godwin, ed., *The Harmony of the Spheres: A Sourcebook of the Pythagorean Tradition* (Rochester VT: Inner Traditions, 1993); and Jamie James, *The Music of the Spheres: Music, Science, and the Natural Order of the Universe* (New York: Grove Press, 1993).
[21] See Jacques Handschin, "Ein mittelalterlicher Beitrag zur Lehre von der Sphärenharmonie," *Zeitschrift für Musikwissenschaft* 9/4 (1927): 193–208; Haar, "'Musica mundana,'" 277–87; and Godwin, *Harmony of the Spheres*, 123–25.

Girolamo Bargagli's *La Pellegrina* in Florence in 1589.[22] Interest in celestial music among later composers is evident in the treatments of the "Ode to St. Cecilia's Day" by Purcell and Handel, and in Mozart's dramatic serenade based on Cicero's "Dream of Scipio."[23] One might even say the tradition has continued in modern times, quirkily, in John Rodgers and Willie Ruff's literal (electronic) realization of the sounds of planetary orbits as postulated in Johannes Kepler's *Harmonices Mundi* (1619).[24]

But there is a difference between works such as these that celebrate or imitate a literal "harmony of the spheres," and other works that attempt to present a more comprehensive view of the world, while invoking celestial harmony as an essential metaphor. When such music additionally attempts a broad historical-evolutionary sweep, the result is a "musical cosmology" mindful of literary analogues in Ovid or Dante. And what has been most appealing to musical cosmologists is not only the connotations of celestial harmony, but also the singular ability of music to evoke transcendental experience. Once a scenario and context have been established through a text, title, program, or other extra-musical source – in Lawrence Kramer's terminology, through "designators"[25] – musical cosmologists may make this ineffability a central feature of their artistic visions. Music is a "language of gestures," in the words of Edward T. Cone, uniquely capable of simulating and symbolizing the "gestural aspect of utterance."[26] In Schopenhauer's doctrine, "Music is by no means like the other arts, namely a copy of the Ideas, but a copy of the will itself, the objectivity of which are the Ideas."[27] Schoenberg follows this same reasoning in describing music's

---

22 The *fête* is described by Haar, "'Musica mundana,'" 447–50, the intermedi by James, *Music of the Spheres*, 101–06.

23 James discusses the Mozart work in *Music of the Spheres*, 173–75.

24 John Rodgers and Willie Ruff, "The Harmony of the World: a realization for the ear of Johannes Kepler's astronomical data from *Harmonices Mundi* 1619" (The Kepler Label, 1971), and "Kepler's Harmony of the World: a realization for the ear," *American Scientist* 67/3 (1979): 286–92.

25 Lawrence Kramer, "Music and representation: the instance of Haydn's *Creation*," in *Music and Text: Critical Inquiries*, ed. Steven Paul Scher (Cambridge: Cambridge University Press, 1992), 140.

26 Edward T. Cone, *The Composer's Voice* (Berkeley: University of California Press, 1974), 164–65.

27 Arthur Schopenhauer, *The World as Will and Representation*, transl. E. F. J. Payne (New York: Dover, 1966), 257.

ability to express the ultimate irrationality of the cosmos: since music is the language best suited for this purpose, he says, "The musical genius perceives the innermost essence of the cosmos."[28]

The composer is like the poet in that the primary channel of communication is beneath the surface of the text. As Cone says, "in music both the verbal gestures of poetry and the bodily gestures of the dance are symbolized in the medium of sound."[29] The composer's "mode of discourse," like that of the poet, is metaphorical – "metaphorical in a literal sense, because it translates meaning from one level to another, from the conceptual to the physical."[30] And yet the composer's literal text can never be as concrete as the poet's. While music's metaphorical meaning can be made clear by designators, and in fact could be identical to that of a poem, its literal meaning can only be understood in the framework of its own language – a language that is itself purely gestural.

> The comly order and proportion faire
> On every side did please his wandring eye,
> Till glauncing through the thin transparent aire
> A rude disordered rout he did espie
> Of men and women, that most spightfullie
>   Did one another throng, and crowd so sore,
>   That his kind eye in pitty wept therefore.
>
> And swifter then the Lightning downe he came,
> Another shapelesse Chaos to digest,
> He will begin another world to frame,
> (For Love till all be well will never rest)
> Then with such words as cannot be exprest
>   He cutts the troups, that all a sunder fling,
>   And ere they wist, he casts them in a ring.
>   —Sir John Davies, *Orchestra*[31] (1594)

---

[28] See Charlotte M. Cross, "Three levels of 'Idea' in Schoenberg's thought and writings," *Current Musicology* 30 (1980): 24–36 [33].

[29] Cone, *The Composer's Voice*, 164.

[30] Heninger, *Touches of Sweet Harmony*, 325.

[31] *The Poems of Sir John Davies*, ed. Robert Krueger, with introduction and commentary by the editor and Ruby Nemser (Oxford: Clarendon Press, 1975), 97–98.

Ives's predecessors in musical cosmic contemplation form part of a tradition Richard Taruskin has called "European symphonic transcendentalism," a tradition that begins with Haydn's *Creation* and continues through Beethoven's Ninth, Wagner's *Ring*, and Mahler's *Das Lied von der Erde*.[32] We might also include Mahler's Eighth Symphony and Strauss's *Also sprach Zarathustra*. According to Taruskin, "All of these works strove to give through musical tones an intimation of the sublime – which is to say, the superhuman." As artistic cosmologies, these works display universal themes strongly in their subtexts but in varying degrees as text. Haydn's cosmology is clearly displayed, especially in the "Vorstellung des Chaos" with which the *Creation* opens. Beethoven does not intend to create a cosmology with the specificity of Haydn's, but nevertheless projects various levels of cosmic themes, from the implicit metaphor for creation in the opening primeval motives to the explicit appeal to universal brotherhood in the "Ode to Joy."[33] Wagner amplifies and embellishes the cosmic subtexts of his mythological texts in his establishment and perpetuation of a rich musical cosmos.[34] The enormity of his conception – the notion that the representation of cosmic events can only succeed in an artistic structure of analogous size and weight – brings it quite close to a modern type of musical cosmology. The sources of Mahler's universal themes in the Eighth Symphony are religious symbols of salvation and communion with God; the sense of grandiosity and transcendental human experience arise as well from the sheer magnitude of its musical dimensions. In describing his intentions Mahler wrote, "Think of the whole universe beginning to ring and resound. These are no longer human voices, but planets and suns revolving."[35] Strauss's goals in *Also sprach Zarathustra* are more focused on Nietzsche than on any particular cosmology, but there is an unmistakable sense of cosmic beginning in the work's initial "sunrise." As the opening simple

---

[32] Richard Taruskin, "Away with the Ives myth: the 'Universe' is here at last," *New York Times*, 23 October 1994, H42.

[33] Maynard Solomon discusses this aspect of the Ninth and its treatment in Beethoven commentary in "Beethoven's Ninth Symphony: a search for order," *19th-Century Music* 10/1 (1986): 3–23.

[34] See, for example, Sally Kester, "The archetypal motives of cosmogony and apocalypse in the *Ring*," *Miscellanea Musicologica* 14 (1985): 99–116; and Warren J. Darcy, "The metaphysics of annihilation: Wagner, Schopenhauer, and the ending of the *Ring*," *Music Theory Spectrum* 16/1 (1994): 1–40.

[35] From a letter to Willem Mangelberg, 18 August 1906, in *Gustav Mahler Briefe*, ed. Herta Blaukopf (Vienna: Paul Zsolnay, 1982), 312.

intervals unfold, it is hard not to think of Haydn's primordial octaves, Beethoven's open fifths, and the emergent tonal cosmos at the beginning of the Prelude to *Das Rheingold*.

Ives's goals were more ambitious than those of his predecessors: "to contemplate in tones rather than in music as such, that is – not exactly within the general term or meaning as it is so understood – to paint the creation the mysterious beginnings of all things, known through God to man, to trace with tonal imprints the vastness, the evolution of all life, in nature of humanity from the great roots of life to the spiritual eternities."[36] Thus he shared every cosmologist's interest in the depth and breadth of evolution and history, but he aspired to imbue his rendering with an unprecedented specificity and monumentalism. He also expanded upon the Wagnerian sense of the artistic experience itself as a metaphor for cosmic forces and events. Ives was said to have envisioned a performance of the *Universe Symphony* by "several different orchestras, with huge conclaves of singing men and women . . . placed about in valleys, on hillsides, and on mountain tops."[37] In such a setting, not just the tones and rhythms but the experience itself assumes epic-cosmic proportions. Indeed, the experience becomes a subtext: if Ives's text is his "universe in tones," one subtext is the intensified cosmic perspective gained by each participant. As the composer contemplates the universe, the listeners do the same, allowing his musical representations of cosmic forces and events to shape and reflect their own sentiments about the landscape around them. They come to feel more a part of the surrounding universe and more understanding of its mysteries.

It is a vivid demonstration of a composer overtly and ambitiously ascending to that role society reserves for its artists and visionaries. In making the Creator's work an integral part of his own creation, Ives further encourages the perception of his own divinity.[38] In facilitating the participants' enlightenment, he relishes and embraces the obligation he feels to

[36] From an inscription on sketch page f1843, transcribed in *JKCat*, 27.

[37] Henry and Sidney Cowell, *Charles Ives and His Music* (reprint, with revisions, New York: Da Capo Press, 1973), 201. Cowell's description is corroborated by two of Ives's close associates: see Vivian Perlis, *Charles Ives Remembered: An Oral History* (New Haven: Yale University Press, 1974), 117, 188. There is, however, no surviving description of this scenario by Ives himself.

[38] Stuart Feder discusses this phenomenon from a psychological point of view in *Charles Ives: "My Father's Song": A Psychoanalytic Biography* (New Haven: Yale University Press, 1992), 292–97.

bring the experience of the sublime to those with feet more firmly planted on the ground. And while saturating the participants' senses with natural wonder, his means of transporting them to unknown and incomprehensible realms is musical sound, the ideal language of ineffability.

> Among these remarkable spectacles, and the movements of the Fortunes, even when the wind was the merest whisper, a tuneful modulation sounded with a kind of musical vibration. For the topmost layers of the tall trees, being correspondingly stretched tight, resonated with a high-pitched note; but whatever was near the earth and close with its down-bending branches vibrated with a low note. But the rest of the trees sang together, because their middle portions were joined, in harmonies of octave, fifth, not to mention fourth. . . . Thus it happened that the grove sounded a full gamut and the song of the gods with matching modulations. When Cyllenius explained this, Virtus learned that even in heaven the spheres similarly yield harmony in octaves or match the lower voices. Nor was it surprising that the grove of Apollo should accord with such carefully planned modulation, since Delius harmonizes the spheres of heaven too in the sun.
> —Martianus Capella, De Nuptiis Philologiae et Mercurii[39] (c. 500)

Much can be learned about a musical representation from its designators. In many cases the designators are the work – to study the composer's intended images is to study the work's text and any accompanying commentary. When performed outdoors as Ives had apparently envisioned, the *Universe Symphony* might need no textual designators; in effect the setting would be the designator. A hypothetical participant who brings to that experience no awareness of the customary clues – the piece's title, the composer's commentary, and the like – might fully comprehend Ives's intent simply by inference. But that blissfully ignorant perceiver might also realize that the same inference could be drawn from a wide variety of musical experiences. The process of presenting simple initial musical ideas, using their features to create and develop primary themes, depicting an evolution in intensity of musical association, and ultimately arriving at some kind of

---

[39] Transl. in Danuta Shanzer, *A Philosophical and Literary Commentary on Martianus Capella's* De Nuptiis Philologiae et Mercurii *Book I* (Berkeley: University of California Press, 1986), 206–07.

goal that places previous ideas in perspective, is a process used in countless ways in diverse music that has obvious roots in the universal model of creation and evolution, whether or not the work has any explicit cosmic pretensions. The perceiver of any musical work might rightfully infer a cosmic subtext. Similarly, the goal of many musical analyses – regardless of musical subject – is to describe just such a process: how musical details are formed and developed, how musical ideas create a drama of evolutionary progression, how the musical structure anticipates and builds to its point of ultimate arrival.

To describe such procedures in a musical cosmology, then, is to reveal much about its success as a work of art, but is to say little about its distinctiveness in communicating its specific subject matter. Any work – cosmological or otherwise – that follows the evolutionary model uses musical events as metaphors for cosmic ones. Rather than focusing on such universal metaphors that have little relevance to a particular representation, what is most interesting in cosmological terms is a musical metaphor whose meaning is more confined to a particular cosmic image or theme. If a work is its own cosmos, fashioned by its own Creator, and if its individual musical details are the substance and nature of this cosmos, then the construction and development of such details afford the composer with the particular opportunity to draw concrete analogies between the structure of the music and the structure of the universe. By using structural metaphors that are easily, perhaps exclusively, associated with universal themes, the musical cosmologist can transcend the ordinary need for designators and extend and enrich the identification between creator and Creator.

What the composer-cosmologist must do, in other words, is employ a musical idea or device whose essence depends upon some of the same structural forces that control the universe. Ives found such a thing in musical processes that invoke periodic repetition until returning to a point of origin, or "cycles," drawing analogies with cyclic aspects of nature, such as the passage of time as defined by planetary orbits. That does not, of course, mean that such a metaphor is limited to a cosmic application; it means simply that in the context Ives establishes, given the intentions spelled out by his designators, a process of musical circularity invites comparisons with more universal cyclic phenomena. Indeed, Ives explores musical cycles throughout his music, often without an explicit cosmic connection. His cycles are usually best described as patterns of transposition, achieved by repeatedly transposing, by the same amount, some musical entity such as a note, motive, or chord. He usually continues the pattern until reaching cyclic completion, although even when he does otherwise – even when he sets a pattern in motion but abandons it before it returns to its starting point – he seems to value and recognize an underlying cyclic model.[40] Generally speaking, then, cycles would simply seem to represent one of the more productive fruits of Ives's search for what George Perle calls (after James Gleick) "windows of order" in post-tonal music.[41] At the same time, however, one could also argue that Ives's interest in musical cycles stems from a general cosmic orientation that somehow affects musical decisions in a variety of his works. In this respect, and in others, the *Universe Symphony* represents an ultimate usage of such ideas, drawing upon the experience gained from exploring and developing them elsewhere. The work looms as a coalescence and culmination of a life's work – a true *magnum opus*.

Cycles pervade the symphony from the beginning of the *Life-Pulse Prelude*, with its repeated, cumulative subdivisions of a basic pulse that Ives describes as "the eternal pulse & planetary motion & of the earth & universe. . . ."[42] The cycles operate in two respects: each layer is a different repeated subdivision given cyclic organization by periodic returns to the basic pulse, and the cumulative process itself controls the gradual statement and then withdrawal of these layers in a cyclic fashion. The simple yet imposing result has an elemental quality that effectively portrays an underlying cosmic energy; as Larry Austin has observed, "It does, indeed, seem like the life pulse of the Universe."[43] Cyclic pitch structures are immediately apparent in section A ("Formation of the waters and mountains") in what

---

40 For extensive technical discussion of Ives's uses of cycles see Philip Lambert, "Interval cycles as compositional resources in the music of Charles Ives," *Music Theory Spectrum* 12/1 (1990): 43–82; and Part III of Lambert, *Music of Charles Ives*.

41 George Perle, *The Listening Composer* (Berkeley: University of California Press, 1990), 63–64.

42 Inscribed on sketch page f1820 (*JKCat*, 26).

43 Larry Austin, "Charles Ives's *Life Pulse Prelude for Percussion Orchestra*: a realization for modern performance from sketches for his *Universe Symphony*," *Percussive Notes* 23/6 (1985): 58–84. See also pp. 196–97 above.

Ives calls the "Earth Chord," a cyclic alternation of two intervals (tritone-perfect fourth). This chord comes to represent the raw material of the universe – cyclic, of course – that subsequently becomes linearized as a melodic line representing some aspect of the evolving earth.[44] The surviving sketches for section B ("Earth, evolution in nature and humanity") include a single page with numerous cyclic structures written out, without a musical context.[45] Presumably these would have represented additional fundamental cosmic materials that would have been linearized and developed as aspects of the progress of evolution. Finally, a sketch page for section C ("Heaven, the rise of all to the spiritual") contains a series of cyclically generated chords, some with quarter-tone intervals, which at first progresses through gradated reductions in interval size similar to the chord sequence in the song "On the Antipodes."[46] It is not clear how the series would have been used, but what is clear is that Ives's idea of "heaven" was to receive musical representation with a structure of extraordinary organization and logic. The cyclic basis of the chord series, plus the principle by which it is ordered and the thoroughness with which cyclic possibilities are summarized, lend a sense of cosmic overview and completion that bursts forth even in the absence of a musical realization.

> He durst not enter into th'open greene,
>> For dread of them vnwares to be descryde,
>> For breaking of their daunce, if he were seene;
>> But in the couert of the wood did byde,
>> Beholding all, yet of them vnespyde.
>> There he did see, that pleased much his sight,
>> That euen he him selfe his eyes enuyde,
>> An hundred naked maidens lilly white,
> All raunged in a ring, and dauncing in delight.

[44] Despite the sketchy nature of the surviving materials, Ives makes his intentions clear both in the music and commentary on the manuscript pages and in his remarks in *Memos*.

[45] That is page f1841 (*JKCat*, 27). It is transcribed and discussed in Lambert, *Music of Charles Ives*, 194–195.

[46] On the song, see Domenick Argento, "A digest analysis of Ives' 'On the Antipodes,'" *Student Musicologists at Minnesota* 6 (1975): 192–200; and Lambert, *Music of Charles Ives*, 178–185. The sketch page from the symphony is transcribed and discussed in Lambert, *Music of Charles Ives*, 200–205.

All they without were raunged in a ring,
  And daunced round; but in the midst of them
  Three other Ladies did both daunce and sing,
  The whilest the rest them round about did hemme,
  And like a girlond did in compasse stemme:
  And in the middest of those same three, was placed
  Another Damzell, as a precious gemme,
  Amidst a ring most richly well enchaced,
That with her goodly presence all the rest much graced.
          —Edmund Spenser, *The Faerie Queene*[47] (1596)

There is another pervasive structural metaphor in Ives's symphony: pitch structures with maximal pitch-class variety, often all twelve notes of the chromatic scale, used to convey notions of totality and universality. The Earth Chord, for example, is such a structure; that is one reason Ives chose the particular intervals with which it is constructed. Considerable pitch-class variety is evident in virtually all of the cyclic formations on the various sketch pages, suggesting that an important purpose in sketching some of the materials was to explore the capability of various cycles to state as many pitch classes as possible without repetition. And as is the case with cycles, the deployment of maximal variety in the *Universe Symphony* brings together ideas that Ives had explored and developed in a number of other works.[48]

It is the interest in pitch-class saturation that plays a central role, according to Richard Taruskin, in the "birth of modernism out of the spirit of Romantic transcendentalism," not only in the *Universe Symphony* but also in two of its close contemporaries: Scriabin's *Mysterium* and Schoenberg's *Die Jakobsleiter*.[49] "The prospect of representing the universe," according to Taruskin, "drew the same maximal response from all three composers.... It marked a musical limit; and to Schoenberg it gave the first intimation of twelve-tone composition." In Ives's case, the symphony

---

[47] Edmund Spenser, *The Faerie Queene*, ed. Thomas P. Roche, Jr., with the assistance of C. Patrick O'Donnell, Jr. (New Haven: Yale University Press, 1978), 990–91 [VI.x.11–12].

[48] See Philip Lambert, "Aggregate structures in music of Charles Ives," *Journal of Music Theory* 34/1 (1990): 29–55, and *Music of Charles Ives*.

[49] Taruskin, "Away with the Ives myth." See also Rathert, "Paysage imaginaire."

brings together romantic and modernist tendencies that elsewhere assert themselves separately, as one would expect of a *magnum opus*. The context of Scriabin's evolution toward post-tonality is the theosophical and symbolist movements in late nineteenth-century Russia, which drove the composer's interest in sensory saturation and universality.[50] For Schoenberg it was Swedenborg and Balzac who set the universalist tone within which the composer took his first steps "to replace the structural functions of harmony."[51]

The similarities do not end there. Scriabin imagined a setting in the Himalayas for his vast ritual celebration for orchestra, voices, and dancers.[52] He viewed the *Mysterium* as the culmination of his life's work toward which all his previous efforts had been directed. His identification with the Creator is particularly strong, even pathological, manifested throughout his writings in poetic proclamations of self-deification.[53] Though the work as conceived, with its epic, impossible dimensions, has no peer before or since, Scriabin planned a more realistic "Prefatory Action"

---

[50] See Boris De Schloezer, *Scriabin: Artist and Mystic*, transl. Nicolas Slonimsky, with introductory essays by Marina Scriabine (Berkeley: University of California Press, [1923] 1987); and Brown, "Skriabin and Russian 'Mystic' Symbolism."

[51] Arnold Schoenberg, "Composition with twelve tones (c. 1948)," in *Style and Idea*, ed. Leonard Stein, with transl. by Leo Black (Berkeley: University of California Press, 1975), 247–48. Schoenberg also mentions the role of *Die Jakobsleiter* in the development of the twelve-tone method in a 1937 letter to Nicolas Slonimsky: see Nicolas Slonimsky, *Music Since 1900* (New York: Norton, 1937; 4th edn 1971), 574. On the influence of Swedenborg and Balzac, see John C. Crawford, "The relationship between text and music in the vocal works of Arnold Schoenberg, 1908–1924" (Ph.D. dissertation, Harvard University, 1963), 322–25; Karl Wörner, "Schönberg's Oratorium *Die Jakobsleiter*: Musik zwischen Theologie und Weltanschauung," *Schweizerische Musikzeitung* 105 (1965): 250–57, 333–40; Jean Marie Christensen, "Arnold Schoenberg's oratorio *Die Jakobsleiter*," 2 vols. (Ph.D. dissertation, University of California at Los Angeles, 1979), vol. 1, 9–15; Alan Philip Lessem, *Music and Text in the Works of Arnold Schoenberg: The Critical Years, 1908–1922* (Ann Arbor MI: UMI Research Press, 1979), 180–85; and John R. Covach, "Schoenberg and the occult: some reflections on the *Musical Idea*," *Theory & Practice* 17 (1992): 103–18.

[52] Faubion Bowers, *The New Scriabin: Enigma and Answers* (New York: St. Martin's, 1973), 97; Schloezer, *Scriabin*, 264.

[53] For example: "I am God! / I am nothing, I am play, I am freedom, I am life. / I am the boundary, I am the peak." Faubion Bowers, *Scriabin: A Biography of the Russian Composer 1871–1915* (Tokyo: Kodansha International Ltd., 1969), vol. 2, 61.

that would be a "practical version of the *Mysterium*, reduced to terrestrial dimensions and subject to rational planning."[54] It was to be an account of "the development of the cosmos, the emergence of all mankind, and the individual growth of individual personalities: from Oneness to Duality, into Multiplicity and finally to return to the initial Oneness."[55]

Schoenberg's most grandiose ambitions are evident in his plans during 1911–12 for a huge choral symphony, no doubt modeled on Mahler's recently premiered Eighth Symphony.[56] *Die Jakobsleiter* grew out of the abandoned symphony and was to be a representation of how "the man of today, who has passed through materialism, socialism, and anarchy, who was an atheist but has still preserved a remnant of ancient beliefs (in the form of superstition) – how this modern man struggles with God (see also *Jakob ringt* by Strindberg) and finally arrives at the point of finding God and becoming religious."[57] As the archangel Gabriel leads us up the ladder, past various individual souls who have misconceived their societal roles, we encounter Schoenberg's alter ego in the "Chosen One"; he is "the type of the true, inspired artist . . . [who] finds himself rejected and humiliated by his fellow men because of the originality of his vision, yet . . . feels his own humanity and kinship with them, inescapably."[58] At one point the Chosen One asks, "Am I the one who shows them the hour and the course of time, who is at the same time the scourge and mirror, lyre and sword, both their master and servant, their wise man and fool?"[59]

Ives's "rise of all to the spiritual" is Scriabin's "return to the initial Oneness" is Schoenberg's "point of finding God and becoming religious." Aside from any attempts to offer musical representations of cosmic events, what each work depicts above all is a spiritual journey ultimately reaching

---

54 Schloezer, *Scriabin*, 179; see also 291–306.
55 Bowers, *The New Scriabin*, 124.
56 See Crawford, "Relationship between text and music," 322–25.
57 From a 1912 letter to Richard Dehmel, as translated by Dika Newlin in "Self-revelation and the law: Arnold Schoenberg in his religious works," *Yuval* 1 (1968): 204–20 [205].
58 Malcolm MacDonald, *Schoenberg* (London: J. M. Dent and Sons, 1976), 204.
59 Transl. in Christensen, "Schoenberg's *Die Jakobsleiter*," vol. 2, 37. This text is set in mm. 374–81.

its destination in communion with God. Each composer sees it as his role to lead us on such a journey, and each attempts to do so by offering a cosmic perspective that other humans are presumed incapable of comprehending. The evolution of nature and humanity becomes a metaphor for the process of spiritual maturation and self-discovery experienced by each artist and, by extension, every pilgrim that joins in.

> *Idealism sees the world in God. It beholds the whole circle of persons and things, of actions and events, of country and religion, not as painfully accumulated, atom after atom, act after act, in an aged creeping Past, but as one vast picture which God paints on the instant eternity for the contemplation of the soul.* —Ralph Waldo Emerson, *Nature*[60] (1836)

Yet the best ambitions of many guides to the cosmos are ultimately derailed by their inability to complete their work, or at least to consider it "complete." Ives expressed a desire to finish his symphony, but in virtually the same breath also seemed to doubt that he would.[61] Scriabin died before he could complete even the scaled-down "Prefatory Action"; the surviving fragments are even sketchier than those for the *Universe Symphony*. Schoenberg returned to his sketches in 1944, some thirty years after his initial work, but eventually abandoned the project altogether.[62] Even artistic cosmologies that reach some state of completion often undergo a lifetime of subsequent revisions, maturing along with the world-view of the author. Such is the case in the "romantic gospels" of Whitman, Thomas Wolfe, and others as described by Van Nostrand.[63] To adapt Cowell's description of Ives's *Universe*, a true artistic cosmology is "so gigantic, so inclusive and so exalted" that the creator feels its complete realization is

---

[60] *Selected Essays, Lectures, and Poems of Ralph Waldo Emerson*, ed. and with an introduction by R. E. Spiller (New York: Simon and Schuster, 1965), 209.

[61] *Memos*, 108. Some have quoted Ives as expressing an intent not to finish the work; see the remarks by Dr. Charles Kauffman and by George F. Roberts in Perlis, *Charles Ives Remembered*, 112, 188. The Cowells also state that "Ives has never intended the *Universe Symphony* to be brought to an end." See Cowell, *Charles Ives and His Music*, 203.

[62] See Willi Reich, *Schoenberg: A Critical Biography*, transl. Leo Black (New York: Da Capo, 1981), 94–106.

[63] Van Nostrand, *Everyman His Own Poet*, 1–2.

beyond any single person; "it represents aspects of life about which there is always something more to be said."[64]

That is the irony: the composer who has ordained himself surrogate Creator and spiritual emissary is ultimately humbled by his own mortality. He realizes finally that his ambitious goals are in fact beyond his own comprehension. While it may be true, as Feder observes, that the *Universe Symphony* "was meant to be imagined, not performed," the fact is that it could never be fully imagined by a creature of earth.[65] Perhaps Schoenberg, in conceiving *Die Jakobsleiter*, felt perilously close to hearing cosmic secrets not intended for human ears. He may have felt an uncomfortable kinship with the composers of Ninth symphonies he discusses in his essay on Mahler: "It seems that the Ninth is the limit. He who wants to go beyond it must pass away. It seems as if something might be imparted to us in the Tenth which we ought not yet to know, for which we are not yet ready. Those who have written a Ninth stood too near to the hereafter."[66] And in the years just before his untimely death, Scriabin was approaching a psychological-metaphysical crisis, set to arrive with the realization that in fact his powers stopped short of his self-described divinity. He planned that the conclusion of *Mysterium* would bring about the actual destruction of the world, but he soon would have been forced to recognize that he could no more destroy the world than could he have created it.[67]

The most cosmologists can ultimately expect is to see themselves as collaborators in some larger exploration of great mysteries, an ever-evolving response to the human condition to which each artist makes a new contribution. For that reason it seems appropriate that Ives, Schoenberg, and Scriabin have themselves inspired later attempts to "complete" their works. Ives actually invited such a collaboration and discussed the matter in specific terms with Henry Cowell. The two composers made plans to work together on such a project, then in 1943 Cowell started a separate movement representing his contribution to a collaborative effort; only fragmen-

---

[64] Cowell, *Charles Ives and His Music*, 203.

[65] Feder, *Charles Ives*, 296.

[66] *Style and Idea*, 470. See also the discussion of Schoenberg's views on such matters in Newlin, "Self-revelation and the law," 216; and Cross, "Three levels of 'Idea,'" 31.

[67] See Marvick, "Two versions of the Symbolist apocalypse," 289.

tary sketches of that movement survive.[68] More recently, in addition to Larry Austin's "realization/completion," separate, purportedly more literal, versions of the *Universe Symphony* have been made by David Porter and Johnny Reinhard.[69] The portion of *Die Jakobsleiter* that Schoenberg had sketched was completed by Schoenberg's pupil Winfried Zillig, who had to make many decisions about orchestration but did not presume to add any newly composed material to fill out the work as Schoenberg had originally planned it. Alexander Nemtin, by contrast, used Scriabin's sketches for part one of the "Prefatory Action" along with ideas from various late Scriabin piano pieces to create a new composition, entitled *Universe*.[70] It is a "magnificent work of pastiche"[71] but is surely far removed from the *Mysterium* that Scriabin originally conceived; one wonders whether he would have welcomed the collaboration.

The Glass Bead Game
We re-enact with reverent attention
The universal chord, the masters' harmony,
Evoking in unsullied communion
Minds and times of highest sanctity.

We draw upon the iconography
Whose mystery is able to contain
The boundlessness, the storm of all existence,
Give chaos form, and hold our lives in rein.

---

[68] See Sidney Cowell's new preface to the Da Capo reprint of *Charles Ives and His Music* (New York: Da Capo Press, 1973), VII; and William Lichtenwanger, *The Music of Henry Cowell: A Descriptive Catalogue* (Brooklyn: Institute for Studies in American Music, 1986), 200. Ives's open invitation for collaborators is in *Memos*, 108.

[69] Porter's version of the symphony's first section was premiered on 29 October 1993 at the University of Northern Colorado, conducted by Kenneth Singleton. It is mentioned in H. Wiley Hitchcock, "Ivesiana on disk," *Newsletter of the Institute for Studies in American Music* 24/2 (1995): 7. Reinhard, who finds in the sketches a "fully formed symphony," conducted the premiere of his version of the complete work on 6 June 1996 in New York City. See Alex Ross, "Bringing Ives's notes to life with Ives's voice," *New York Times*, 22 March 1995, C15; and Richard Taruskin, "Out of hibernation, Ives's mythical beast," *New York Times*, 2 June 1996, H26, 33.

[70] A recording of the work was released by Melodiya (SR 40260).

[71] Hugh Macdonald, *Skryabin* (London: Oxford University Press, 1978), 66.

The pattern sings like crystal constellations,
And when we tell our beads, we serve the whole,
And cannot be dislodged or misdirected,
Held in the orbit of the Cosmic Soul.

—Hermann Hesse, *Das Glasperlenspiel*[72] (1943)

Around the same time that Ives and Schoenberg were devising radical and original methods of communicating cosmic themes, the spirit of progressivism also touched Ivan Wyschnegradsky (1893–1979), whose oratorio *La journée de l'existence* (1916–17) opened a pathway toward a system of microtonal harmony that he then spent a lifetime exploring.[73] Scriabin's *Mysterium* was an obvious and acknowledged model;[74] among Wyschnegradsky's other works is *Cosmos* (1945) for four pianos tuned in quarter tones. Scriabin also profoundly influenced Nicolas Obouhov (1892–1954), who spent his entire creative life composing a reflection on religious, mystical, and cosmological themes entitled *Le livre de vie* that employs a system of "absolute harmony" based on combinations of all twelve pitch classes. He explained his compositional practices in *Traité d'harmonie tonale, atonale et totale* (1946). Obouhov followed the familiar path of the artistic cosmologist: he saw himself as a divinely ordained religious mystic creating a ritual celebration to be held in a special circular temple; he produced some two thousand manuscript pages, but could not consider the work complete.[75]

---

72 Hermann Hesse, *The Glass Bead Game* ["posthumous poem of Joseph Knecht"], transl. Richard and Clara Winston, with foreword by Theodore Ziolkowski (New York: Henry Holt, 1969), 445.

73 *Baker's Biographical Dictionary of Musicians*, 8th edn (New York: Schirmer Books, 1992), 2080. See also Ivan Wyschnegradsky, "Ultrachromatisme et espaces non octaviants," *La Revue Musicale* 290–91 (1972–73): 73–130; and Gail Dixon, "The harmony of the spheres revisited: cosmic and mystical thought in early twentieth-century theory," *Studies in Music from the University of Western Ontario* 8 (1983): 93–106.

74 See Gottfried Eberle, "'Absolute Harmonie' und 'Ultrachromatik': Nikolaj Obuchov und Ivan Wyschnegradsky – zwei radikale Fälle von Skrjabin-Nachfolge," in *Alexander Skrjabin*, ed. Otto Kolleritsch (Graz: Universal, 1980), 95–111 [107–10].

75 See *Baker's Biographical Dictionary*, 1326; Dixon, "The harmony of the spheres revisited"; Eberle, "'Absolute Harmonie' und 'Ultrachromatik'"; Carlos Larronde, *Le livre de vie de Nicolas Obouhow* (Paris: Jacques Haumont, 1932); and Boris De Schloezer, "Nicolas Obouhow," *La Revue Musicale* 290–91 (1972–73): 41–54.

Varèse first began conceiving a cosmic musical experience in the late 1920s with *L'astronome*, "a work to be set in AD 2000 with a plot involving interstellar communication and the visitation of universal disaster upon the earth."[76] His ideas evolved into plans for a "symphony of tomorrow" based on themes of universal brotherhood and cosmic oneness called *Espace*. The goal of *Espace* was, in the composer's words, "to encompass everything that is human from the most primitive to the farthest reaches of science."[77] The project attracted a lot of attention in the 1930s, including that of Antonin Artaud (whom Varèse had approached) and André Malraux, but ultimately his ideas lay unrealized. Amidst the threat of imminent war, his interests shifted from "*Espace*, a work celebrating brotherhood, to *Déserts*, a work that is like a cry against all that is barbarous, savage, and absurd."[78]

The maximal efforts drawn by musical cosmologies out of post-war composers have yielded a predictable plurality of styles, techniques, and technological innovations, not to mention goals and pretensions. Krzysztof Penderecki's *Kosmogonia* (1970), written for the twenty-fifth anniversary of the founding of the United Nations, effectively evokes universal themes employing texts taken from Sophocles and Ovid to early Soviet and American space explorers, but does so in a single movement taking us from the beginning of time to the modern era in under twenty minutes. The four books of George Crumb's *Makrokosmos* (1972–79) and other works such as *Vox Balaenae* (1971) offer similarly concise, finite reflections on cosmic events. These works fall outside the tradition of cosmology-as-ritual: they are more detached artistic commentaries on the cosmos than they are musical universes of their own attempting to draw disciples into their spiritual orbits.[79] Two late-century composers stand out as keepers of the *Universe Symphony-Mysterium* tradition. R. Murray Schafer (b. 1933), who

76 Jonathan W. Bernard, *The Music of Edgard Varèse* (New Haven: Yale University Press, 1987), 238–39.

77 Dorothy Norman, "Edgard Varèse: Ionization – Espace," *Twice A Year* 7 (1941): 259–60.

78 Fernand Ouellette, *Edgard Varèse*, transl. Derek Coltman (New York: Orion Press, 1968), 132.

79 Other works that could be similarly described include Akira Nishimura's tetralogy *The Navel of the Sun* (1989) / *Cello Concerto* (1990) / *Into the Lights of the Eternal Chaos* (1990) / *A Ring of Lights* (1991) and Tokuhide Niimi's *Eye of the Creator* (1993).

wrote a study of sound entitled *The Tuning of the World* (1977), has been engaged since 1966 in an epic music/theater piece entitled *Patria*, a commentary on contemporary society and humanity. In the words of a biographer, "*Patria* creates a universe so saturated with information that information becomes a blur, so full of communication that communication withers."[80] Karlheinz Stockhausen (b. 1928) was in Japan in 1977 when he first envisioned a huge cosmological opera and wrote a multi-layered musical "formula" on which the whole work would be based.[81] He has labored since then on *Licht: Die sieben Tage der Woche*, a cycle of seven separate operas to be performed on successive evenings within a single week. The work, parts of which have already been completed and performed, will use music, dance, drama, and ritual to present a mythical life cycle steeped in mystic symbolism.[82] Nowhere is the identification of creator with Creator more apparent than in Stockhausen's autobiographical dramatic characterizations, his creation and pervasive usage on multiple structural layers of a musical formula purported to encapsulate elemental cosmic energies, and in the perpetual, dynamic nature of his creative agenda.

> How incomplete is speech, how weak, when set
> against my thought! And this, to what I saw
> is such—to call it little is too much.
> Eternal Light, You only dwell within
> Yourself, and only You know You; self-knowing,
> Self-known, You love and smile upon Yourself!
> That circle—which, begotten so, appeared
> in you as light reflected—when my eyes
> had watched it with attention for some time,
> within itself and colored like itself,
> to me seemed painted with our effigy,
> so that my sight was set on it completely.
> As the geometer intently seeks

80 Stephen Adams, *R. Murray Schafer* (Toronto: University of Toronto Press, 1983), 171.
81 See Michael Kurtz, *Stockhausen: A Biography*, transl. Richard Toop (London: Faber and Faber, 1992), 1–2.
82 For a discussion of the work as it existed up until the late 1980s, see Robin Maconie, *The Works of Karlheinz Stockhausen*, 2nd edn, foreword by Karlheinz Stockhausen (Oxford: Clarendon Press, 1990), 261–94.

> to square the circle, but he cannot reach,
> through thought on thought, the principle he needs,
>   so I searched that strange sight: I wished to see
> the way in which our human effigy
> suited the circle and found place in it—
>   and my own wings were far too weak for that.
> But then my mind was struck by light that flashed
> and, with this light, received what it had asked.
>   Here force failed my high fantasy; but my
> desire and will were moved already—like
> a wheel revolving uniformly—by
>   the Love that moves the sun and the other stars.
>
> —Dante, *Paradiso* (c. 1307)[83]

In his study of American "romantic gospels" A. D. Van Nostrand writes,

> If I could diagram my subject I would draw a series of concentric circles
> and call the center of them "the drama of the author's consciousness." Let
> each circle mark the relative distance of a work of fiction from this center,
> and let the radius of each represent the extent to which the author had
> removed himself from the drama. This would be a descriptive figure
> measuring what is known in literary criticism as "aesthetic distance," that is,
> the author's apparent objectivity. The circles of shorter radius in this
> diagram would mark the romantic cosmologies that emphasize the drama
> of the author in his own person. Successively wider circles would mark
> those fictions that transfer to a persona and then to characters the attempt
> to build a cosmology.[84]

To adapt this model to musical cosmologies, the "drama of the composer's consciousness" resides in the literal depiction of cosmic events, where no personae or characters intervene between the creator and his cosmological vision. In the outer circles of the musical model would be works with mythological texts such as the *Ring*. A slightly smaller circle would represent Schoenberg's search for spiritual enlightenment via "Jacob's ladder."

---

83 *The Divine Comedy of Dante Alighieri* (Paradiso XXXIII), transl. with
    introductions and commentary by Allen Mandelbaum (Berkeley: University of
    California Press, 1982), 296.
84 Van Nostrand, *Everyman His Own Poet*, 141.

Another circle of about the same size would stand for Stockhausen's *Licht*, with its personae of "spiritual absolutes in human guise" and drama of thinly veiled symbols and allegories. Working our way inward, the circles of moderate size would show more direct expressions of universal themes, yet still have rich cosmological subtexts swirling beneath the surface, as in Schafer's *Patria*, Mahler's Eighth Symphony, and Beethoven's Ninth. The circles nearest the center would depict a search for enlightenment in which the composer is both guide and pilgrim. In terms of the composer's vision of himself, these circles depict the most explicit identifications of creator with Creator. Scriabin's *Mysterium* is close to the center. So is the *Universe Symphony*.

But there is also a whole other dimension to a musical work that gives the composer opportunities for cosmic representation that the poet, for example, does not have. What is constant among the circles of all sizes is the potential of a musical cosmology – of any piece of music – to represent the cosmos in a pure form. Whereas words can never be more than symbols, however literal or metaphorical, and musical sounds can also stand for things, music can also stand for nothing but itself. The musical microcosm plays out its drama within the context it creates, using musical gestures that need relate only to one another. Designators are not required to recognize this property that all musical works share. That is one reason literary cosmologists have been so drawn to music as a metaphor for their most fundamental themes.

To examine a particular circle in the diagram, to explore its texts, designators, subtexts, and the structure of its musical microcosm, is ultimately to learn more not about what is in the circle but about what is in the center. The drama of a cosmologist's depiction of creation, evolution, humanity, and an ultimate transcendence is really the drama of that artist's own quest for knowledge, understanding, enlightenment, and immortality. What each visionary finally learns is that the rewards come not in discovering the answers, but in asking the questions.

> And so, Glaucon, the tale was saved from perishing; and if we will listen, it
> may save us, and all will be well when we cross the river of Lethe. Also we shall
> not defile our souls; but, if you will believe with me that the soul is immortal
> and able to endure all good and ill, we shall keep always to the upward way
> and in all things pursue justice with the help of wisdom. Then we shall be at

peace with Heaven and with ourselves, both during our sojourn here and when, like victors in the Games collecting gifts from their friends, we receive the prize of justice; and so, not here only, but in the journey of a thousand years of which I have told you, we shall fare well.

—Plato, *Res Publica*[85] (fourth century BC)

[85] *The Republic of Plato* ("The myth of Er"), transl., with introduction by Francis MacDonald Cornford (Oxford: Oxford University Press, 1941), 359.

PART FOUR

Envoi

10 Ives today

J. PETER BURKHOLDER

In 1944, Charles Ives's seventieth year, the young composer Elliott Carter took stock of Ives, his music, and his reputation in an essay titled "Ives today: his vision and challenge."[1] Carter depicted Ives as "a devout believer in transcendental philosophy," a composer of "free, almost random music," for whom "difficulty of performance is the performer's problem, not his." He praised the early performers of Ives's music, Bernard Herrmann, Nicolas Slonimsky, and John Kirkpatrick, for their ability to "enter into the spirit of this music and then recreate it," sometimes by changing the notes to suit the overall vision. He traced Ives's "rather spasmodic development" through brief characterizations of his major symphonic works, including those which "depict, in rather literal fashion, by quotation of themes and in other ways, the noisy or religious or patriotic episodes of everyday life," using "naively pictorial" music over ostinatos that create a "transcendental background of faint sounds." Reminding his readers that little of Ives's music had as yet been heard and that "real consideration of his music still lies in the future," he concluded that "it is about time for a real demonstration."

Thirty years later another young composer, William Brooks, perhaps unconsciously echoed Carter's title in his own "Ives today," a talk at the 1974 Ives Centennial Festival-Conference.[2] In the intervening time, almost all of Ives's major works had been premiered, published, and recorded, providing

---

[1] Elliott Carter, "Ives today: his vision and challenge," *Modern Music* 21/4 (May–June 1944): 199–202; repr. in *Charles Ives and His World*, ed. J. Peter Burkholder (Princeton: Princeton University Press, 1996), 390–93.

[2] William Brooks, "Ives today," in *An Ives Celebration: Papers and Panels of the Charles Ives Centennial Festival-Conference*, ed. H. Wiley Hitchcock and Vivian Perlis (Urbana: University of Illinois Press, 1977), 209–21.

the "real demonstration" Carter had asked for, and several books and numerous articles, book chapters, and theses had appeared, beginning the process of "real consideration." But in other ways, Carter's view of Ives – as a transcendentalist composer of "almost random music" that was laced with literal quotations, who was unconcerned by the difficulties he created for the performer yet allowed performers unprecedented latitude to change even the notes themselves, and whose development as a composer was "spasmodic" – was still widely shared. Without questioning these received views, but far more familiar with Ives's music than Carter had been, Brooks asked, "What is there about the way we structure our world today that draws Ives's work to our attention?" In response, Brooks linked Ives's work to structuralism in its emphases on systems over objects, selection and permutation over creation, and synchronic coexistence over chronology and causality, and to Buckminster Fuller's concerns with self-reference, paradox, process, and cyclic, recursive systems that transform themselves through constant self-examination.

While offering intriguing parallels between Ives's music and intellectual currents that came to prominence in the 1960s, Brooks's approach was focused on contemporary patterns of thinking that found echoes in Ives more than on what Ives himself was trying to do. This was a common thread among considerations of Ives in the 1960s and early 1970s, in part because avant-garde composers of the time saw Ives as a model for their own work.[3] In comments prepared for the 1974 Festival-Conference, the American composer Lou Harrison credited Ives with opening up composition to an unprecedented range of possibilities: "My thought was that if

---

[3] For articles by composers and others that stress technical and philosophical links between Ives and composers working at the time, see for example Hans G. Helms, "Der Komponist Charles Ives," *Neue Zeitschrift für Musik* 125/10 (1964): 425–33; Eric Salzman, "Ives," in *Twentieth-Century Music: An Introduction* (Englewood Cliffs NJ: Prentice-Hall, 1967), 143–48; James Drew, "Information, space, and a new time-dialectic," *Journal of Music Theory* 12/1 (1968): 86–103, and "Modern music and the debt to Charles Ives," Parts I and II, *Yale Reports* (27 December 1970 and 3 January 1971); Niksa Gligo, "Prostornost i pokret u imanenciji glazbe," *Zvuk – Jugoslovenska Ruzicka Revija* 111–12 (1971): 1–20; Robert P. Morgan, "Rewriting music history: second thoughts on Ives and Varèse," *Musical Newsletter* 3/1 (January 1973): 3–12, and 3/2 (April 1973): 15–23 and 28; and comments by composers in "Five composers' views" and "Essays by foreign participants," in *An Ives Celebration*, 187–208 and 227–56.

Mr. Ives could permit himself to do these things, and of course did do them, well then, you could do *anything*."[4] And Karl Aage Rasmussen noted that, "When at long last European interest in Ives began to quicken, it was apparently due to the fact that the European avant-garde suddenly could *use* this odd American phenomenon."[5] Throughout this period, Ives and his music were viewed through the lens of contemporary music and current concerns.

Over the two decades since Ives's centennial, our vision of his music and his career has changed greatly. The Charles Ives Society has sponsored numerous critical editions of his music, and very few works remain unpublished. There are more recordings of his music available now than ever before, including performances by such major orchestras as the New York Philharmonic, Boston, Chicago, Cleveland, Detroit, and St. Louis symphonies, and the Concertgebouw Orchestra. The last decade has seen four major music festivals centered on Ives in both Europe and the United States: a year-long concert series in 1987–88 in Duisberg, Germany, and an associated symposium at the University of Cologne in February 1988; an Ives–Copland festival at the University of Northern Colorado at Greeley in October 1993; the BBC Music Festival in London in January 1996; and the Bard Music Festival at Bard College in August and in Lincoln Center in November 1996. And the pace and intensity of scholarly work on Ives is now greater than ever. Over twenty books, more than half the number that have ever been published on Ives, have appeared since the mid-1980s, including biographies by Stuart Feder and Jan Swafford; research guides by Geoffrey Block and Wolfgang Rathert; analytical surveys of Ives's music by Rathert, Larry Starr, Thomas Giebisch, and Philip Lambert; studies of the piano music by Michael Alexander, Felix Meyer, and Block; explorations by MacDonald Smith Moore of Ives's relation to American musical culture, by David Nicholls of Ives's place in the American experimental tradition, and by David Michael Hertz of his place in the Emersonian tradition; a source book by Clayton Henderson of music Ives borrowed; my own studies of Ives's aesthetic evolution and uses of musical borrowing; and four collections of essays that explore Ives's place in the

---

[4] "Five composers' views," 191.
[5] Karl Aage Rasmussen, "Thoughts on Ives," in *An Ives Celebration*, 251.

American tradition, his links to the European tradition of art music, and a range of other topics.[6]

The challenge has been to see Ives as he actually was, beyond the myth that had grown up around him, to discover his place within the musical and social culture of his time, more than his significance for the work of composers two or three generations later. Almost all the major work on Ives since 1974 has been revisionist, and newer work has revised the earlier revisers. Through it all, a new view of Ives is emerging as a composer of his time, less isolated and better informed about the music of his era than we had thought, more like his European contemporaries than had been imagined, and in far better command of his materials than had been realized.

[6] Stuart Feder, *Charles Ives: "My Father's Song": A Psychoanalytic Biography* (New Haven: Yale University Press, 1992); Jan Swafford, *Charles Ives: A Life with Music* (New York: Norton, 1996); Geoffrey Block, *Charles Ives: A Bio-Bibliography* (New York: Greenwood Press, 1988); Wolfgang Rathert, *Charles Ives*, Erträge der Forschung 267 (Darmstadt: Wissenschaftliche Buchgesellschaft, 1989 ; rev. edn, 1996), and *The Seen and Unseen: Studien zum Werk von Charles Ives* (Munich: Emil Katzbichler, 1991); Larry Starr, *A Union of Diversities: Style in the Music of Charles Ives* (New York: Schirmer Books, 1992); Thomas Giebisch, *"Take-Off" als Kompositionsprinzip bei Charles Ives*, Kölner Beiträge zur Musikforschung 181 (Regensburg: Gustav Bosse, 1993); Philip Lambert, *The Music of Charles Ives* (New Haven: Yale University Press, 1997); Michael J. Alexander, *The Evolving Keyboard Style of Charles Ives* (New York and London: Garland, 1989); Felix Meyer, *"The Art of Speaking Extravagantly": Eine vergleichende Studie der "Concord Sonata" und der "Essays before a Sonata" von Charles Ives* (Bern and Stuttgart: Paul Haupt, 1991); Geoffrey Block, *Ives: Concord Sonata* (Cambridge: Cambridge University Press, 1996); MacDonald Smith Moore, *Yankee Blues: Musical Culture and American Identity* (Bloomington: Indiana University Press, 1985); David Nicholls, *American Experimental Music, 1890–1940* (Cambridge: Cambridge University Press, 1990); David Michael Hertz, *Angels of Reality: Emersonian Unfoldings in Wright, Stevens, and Ives* (Carbondale and Edwardsville: Southern Illinois University Press, 1993); Clayton W. Henderson, *The Charles Ives Tunebook* (Warren MI: Harmonie Park Press, 1990); J. Peter Burkholder, *Charles Ives: The Ideas Behind the Music* (New Haven: Yale University Press, 1985), and *All Made of Tunes: Charles Ives and the Uses of Musical Borrowing* (New Haven: Yale University Press, 1995), *Bericht über das Internationale Symposion "Charles Ives und die amerikanische Musiktradition bis zur Gegenwart," Köln 1988*, Kölner Beiträge zur Musikforschung 164, ed. Klaus Wolfgang Niemöller (Regensburg: Bosse, 1990); *Charles Ives and the Classical Tradition*, ed. Geoffrey Block and J. Peter Burkholder (New Haven: Yale University Press, 1996); Burkholder, *Charles Ives and His World*; and the present volume. In addition, a new *catalogue raisonné* by James B. Sinclair is expected soon.

The penetration of this new view of Ives into the consciousness of musicians and of the musical public has been frustratingly slow, as the old bromides are still frequently repeated in the popular press and even in textbooks. Yet the impact is beginning to be felt; the most recent edition of *A History of Western Music* by Donald Jay Grout and Claude V. Palisca, the leading music history text in the United States, devotes three to four times as much space to Ives as did earlier editions, and emphasizes themes that have emerged in recent scholarship, including his solid training in the Western tradition and both the variety and the innately musical logic of his methods of musical borrowing.[7]

Ives's command of musical materials

In contrast to Carter's view of Ives as a composer of "free, almost random music" or William Austin's infamous assertion that "his command of musical materials is deficient,"[8] one of the most prominent themes of Ives scholarship since 1974 has been the demonstration that Ives is a skilled composer with excellent command of his materials. This can be seen particularly well in studies of Ives's approaches to form, compositional systems, and musical borrowing. As a corollary, such studies often reveal that Ives's practices are closer to those of his European predecessors and contemporaries than had been previously realized.

In a pair of articles published in 1977, Larry Starr showed that Ives's use of multiple, contrasting musical styles within a single work was not a defect, but a basic element of the musical form.[9] Through analyses of the "Alcotts" movement of the *Concord Sonata* and the song "Ann Street," Starr illustrated Ives's tendency to distinguish sections, phrases, or smaller

---

7 Compare the discussion of Ives in Donald Jay Grout, *A History of Western Music*, rev. edn (New York: Norton, 1973), 644, taken over with little change in the 1980 and 1988 editions by Claude V. Palisca, with the discussion in Grout and Palisca, *A History of Western Music*, 5th edn (New York: Norton, 1996), 772–75.

8 William W. Austin, *Music in the 20th Century: From Debussy through Stravinsky* (New York: Norton, 1966), 59.

9 Lawrence Starr, "Charles Ives: the next hundred years – towards a method of analyzing the music," *The Music Review* 38/2 (1977): 101–11; "Style and substance: 'Ann Street' by Charles Ives," *Perspectives of New Music* 15/2 (1977): 23–33.

elements of a work's form from each other by changing many parameters simultaneously, including figuration, rhythmic and melodic character, and harmonic language. These contrasts between adjacent phrases are often so strong that they are heard as changes of style, which listeners can experience as disruptive interruptions in musical continuity. It was Starr's great insight to realize that Ives made such stylistic heterogeneity a key element in the form. For example, "Ann Street" traces a stylistic arch, moving from a relatively simple, diatonic style at the entrance of the voice to dense, chromatic complexity in the middle of the song and back to simplicity at the end; each segment is marked off with a unique figuration, and the brief piano introduction matches the central peak in density and chromaticism. At the same time, as Starr points out, Ives unifies these disparate sections through pitch-centering, repeated intervallic and rhythmic motives, and other standard devices. While the specific design varies considerably from piece to piece, a great number of Ives's works are delineated formally by such contrasts of style, as Starr has subsequently shown in his book *A Union of Diversities: Style in the Music of Charles Ives* and as others who have adopted his approach have confirmed.[10]

Starr's work is important because it shows that what was thought by some to be a weakness in Ives's music, its stylistic heterogeneity, is actually a strength – that what was seen as a sign of his lack of control of compositional materials is instead evidence of a very sophisticated grasp of those materials. This is important work also because it places Ives solidly in the great tradition of classical music and of the great European music of his time, though Starr tries to emphasize Ives's uniqueness.[11]

Strong contrast of figuration, character, and idiom between sections – in Starr's terms, stylistic heterogeneity – is fundamental to many musical genres. A Gregorian chant Mass already features a variety of styles from simple recitation to melismatic responsorial chants. Eleventh-century organum contrasts note-against-note polyphony, sung by soloists, with

[10] Starr, *Union of Diversities*. Others who have applied Starr's approach include J. Peter Burkholder, "The evolution of Charles Ives's music: aesthetics, quotation, technique" (Ph.D. dissertation, University of Chicago, 1983), 551–64, and Paul Franklyn Taylor, "Stylistic heterogeneity: the analytical key to movements IIa and IIb from the First Piano Sonata by Charles Ives" (DMA dissertation, University of Wisconsin at Madison, 1986).

[11] See his comments in *Union of Diversities*, 9–15.

268

monophonic chant sung by the choir. Notre Dame polyphony adds to this the contrast between florid organum over long notes in the tenor and rhythmic discant over a more quickly-moving tenor, producing, within a single element of the liturgy, three very diverse styles that delineate the musical form. Machaut's Mass contrasts isorhythmic movements and sections with others in free conductus style and organizes both kinds of section through contrasts of slow and rapid figuration. Sixteenth-century motets and madrigals often give each phrase of text a distinctive musical treatment, alternating imitation with homophony, duets with full textures, and diatonic with chromatic passages. Seventeenth-century keyboard canzonas feature sections that contrast in meter, texture, figuration, and affect, and preludes like those of Buxtehude alternate improvisatory, toccata figuration with fugal passages. Even as such genres evolved into multi-movement works with strong contrasts between rather than within movements, the idea of contrast as an element of form was preserved in the eighteenth-century concerto and the Classic-era sonata and rondo forms. The coordination of heterogeneous styles within a unified musical discourse reached its peak in the mature music of Haydn and especially of Mozart, as Leonard Ratner demonstrates in his book *Classic Music*. Ratner characterizes the first movement of Mozart's *Prague* Symphony as "a panorama of topics [i.e., styles], old and new, in which a change of subject occurs every few measures," and identifies fourteen changes of style in the first sixty measures of the allegro.[12] This is roughly one change every four measures, almost as frequently as in Ives's "Ann Street." Strong contrasts of style continue to delineate form and create drama throughout the nineteenth century, from the symphonies of Beethoven and Mahler to the operas of Wagner and Verdi. In Ives's own era, the music of Debussy, Scriabin, and Stravinsky is marked by changes of pitch collection, figuration, motive, and orchestral timbre from one short phrase or passage to the next, in ways exactly analogous to Ives's practice.

Ives differs from these predecessors and contemporaries by the degree of contrast between adjacent passages, and by his willingness to extend these contrasts to include evocations of familiar musical styles such

[12] Leonard G. Ratner, *Classic Music: Expression, Form, and Style* (New York: Schirmer Books, 1980), 9–29 [27]; his analysis of the *Prague* Symphony movement appears on 27–28.

as ragtime, band marches, or popular songs right next to novel harmonies and blistering dissonance. But this is a difference in degree, not in kind. As astonishing as the stylistic contrasts within Ives's music may be, his approach has a long history and many parallels among his European contemporaries. And seeing his practice in the context of other music that uses similar ideas makes still clearer that the stylistic variety of his music indicates neither randomness nor lack of control of his medium, but is an extension of the tradition in an individual idiom. William Austin's notion that Ives, "disdaining purely musical articulation," wrote music "that simply had no unity short of the unity of the cosmos" and depended instead on "literary associations" to achieve a semblance of coherence, can now be seen as dead wrong. Ives's use of stylistic contrast articulates phrases and delineates the form through purely musical means, remains independent of extramusical associations (although it can certainly be useful in invoking them), and helps to create coherent works that do not rely on simple repetition and variation.[13]

A second area in which Ives's skill as a composer has been amply demonstrated is his use of alternative compositional systems. It has long been recognized that Ives experimented with novel compositional devices. Ives himself wrote about them in his *Memos*, they were discussed in profiles published during Ives's lifetime, and John Rinehart's 1970 dissertation explored them at greater length.[14] But the impression persisted that the main body of Ives's music was unsystematic, even disordered. Several studies in the last decade have made clear Ives's careful organization of his music. In his 1986 dissertation, Thomas Winters showed that Ives systemat-

---

[13] Austin, *Music in the 20th Century*, 59. Lloyd Whitesell mounts a different defense of Ives, suggesting that the concept of "unity" itself as a necessary aspect of a musical work needs to be challenged. See his "Reckless form, uncertain audiences: responding to Ives," *American Music* 12/2 (1994): 304–19.

[14] John McLain Rinehart, "Ives' compositional idioms: an investigation of selected short compositions as microcosms of his musical language" (Ph.D. dissertation, Ohio State University, 1970). For examples of early profiles that discuss some of Ives's compositional devices, see Goddard Lieberson, "An American innovator, Charles Ives," *Musical America* 59/3 (1939): 22 and 322–23, and Nicolas Slonimsky, "Charles Ives – America's musical prophet," *Musical America* 74/4 (1954): 18–19. The former is reprinted and the latter excerpted in Burkholder, *Charles Ives and His World*, 377–89 and 430–32, respectively.

270

ically used wedge-palindromes, ostinatos, and imitation in his short experimental works and in larger pieces as well to create coherent processes of
repetition and change. In his 1987 dissertation, subsequent series of articles, and recent book *The Music of Charles Ives*, Philip Lambert expanded
this list of systematic procedures to include not only wedges, palindromes,
mirrors, ostinatos, and contrapuntal devices such as canon and fugue, but
also manipulation of pitch-class sets, thematic and motivic transformation, methods of circulating all twelve tones, and interval cycles.[15] David
Nicholls's 1990 book *American Experimental Music, 1890–1940* confirmed
the systematic nature of Ives's compositions and placed Ives at the start of
an American experimental tradition that includes Cowell, Charles Seeger,
Cage, and other composers. In addition to Lambert, several other analysts
have explored Ives's use of intervallic structures or pitch-class sets and their
transformation over the course of a work. After preliminary investigations
by Gordon Cyr, Allen Forte, and Nors Josephson in the 1970s, this line of
inquiry blossomed in the 1980s in dissertations by Lora Gingerich, Carol K.
Baron, and Lambert.[16] As with Starr's work on musical form, this line of
research indicates not only how motivically coherent Ives's music is, but
also that he was much closer to his European contemporaries than had been
realized. Gingerich's work reveals how close Ives's developmental strategies

[15] Thomas Dyer Winters, "Additive and repetitive techniques in the experimental
works of Charles Ives" (Ph.D. dissertation, University of Pennsylvania, 1986);
and Philip Lambert, "Compositional procedures in the experimental works of
Charles E. Ives" (Ph.D. dissertation, Eastman School of Music, 1987); "Interval
cycles as compositional resources in the music of Charles Ives," *Music Theory
Spectrum* 12/1 (1990): 43–82; "Aggregate structures in music of Charles Ives,"
Journal of Music Theory 34/1 (1990): 31–38, 50; "Ives and counterpoint,"
American Music 9/2 (1991): 119–48; "Toward a theory of chord structure for the
music of Ives," *Journal of Music Theory* 37/1 (1993): 55–83; and *The Music of
Charles Ives*.

[16] Gordon Cyr, "Intervallic structural elements in Ives's Fourth Symphony,"
Perspectives of New Music 9/2 and 10/1 (1971): 291–303; Allen Forte, "Ives and
atonality," in *An Ives Celebration*, 159–86; Nors S. Josephson, "Charles Ives:
intervallische Permutationen im Spätwerk," *Zeitschrift für Musiktheorie* 9/2
(1978): 27–33; Lora Louise Gingerich, "Processes of motivic transformation in
the keyboard and chamber music of Charles E. Ives" (Ph.D. dissertation, Yale
University, 1983); Carol K. Baron, "Ives on his own terms: an explication, a
theory of pitch organization, and a new critical edition for the *3-Page Sonata*"
(Ph.D. dissertation, City University of New York, 1987); Lambert,
"Compositional procedures."

are to Schoenberg's concept of developing variation.[17] And Lambert has recently shown strong parallels between Ives and Berg in the methods they used to organize atonal music.[18]

The *Universe Symphony* (c. 1915–51), which Ives left unfinished but has been heard in the 1990s in three different realizations, now appears as the culmination of Ives's interest in systematic composition, as Lambert argues in his essay in this book.[19] Elsewhere in this volume, Larry Austin describes his realization of the work and the compositional materials Ives used in his sketches, including octatonic scales, twelve-tone series, and other pitch series; quarter tones and just intonation alongside equal temperament; clusters and other novel chords; palindromes, wedges, cycles, and related processes; and the simultaneous sounding of up to twenty different subdivisions of a basic metric unit.[20] All of these ideas have roots in such earlier works as *All the Way Around and Back* (c. 1906), a palindromic piece that uses repeating pitch series, chords based on semitones, and simultaneous subdivisions of 1, 2, 3, 4, 5, 7, and 11 beats per measure. Austin demonstrates in his essay and particularly through his completion of the work that the *Universe Symphony* was not a fanciful *idea* for a piece whose realization was unattainable, as Henry Cowell characterized it in the first Ives biography in a description that formed our view of it, but a real

---

[17] Gingerich, "Processes of motivic transformation," and "A technique for melodic motivic analysis in the music of Charles Ives," *Music Theory Spectrum* 8 (1986): 75–93. See also Burkholder, *All Made of Tunes*, 160–61 and 453, notes 23 and 24, and the unpublished paper cited there, Evan Rothstein, "'What its signs of promise are': Ives, the tradition of 'developing variation' and the problem of 'folkloristic' music in Ives's First Violin Sonata, third movement" (typescript, 1988).

[18] Philip Lambert, "Ives and Berg: 'normative' procedures and post-tonal alternatives," in *Charles Ives and the Classical Tradition*, 105–30.

[19] Philip Lambert, "Ives's *Universe*," in this volume. The three realizations are those by David Porter of the prelude and section A, premiered in October 1993 at the Ives-Copland Festival at the University of Northern Colorado at Greeley; by Larry Austin of the entire work, premiered in Cincinnati on 28 January 1994 by the Cincinnati Philharmonia and the Percussion Ensemble of the Cincinnati College-Conservatory of Music, conducted by Gerhard Samuel; and by Johnny Reinhard, premiered at Lincoln Center in New York on 6 June 1996 by the American Festival of Microtonal Music Orchestra, conducted by Johnny Reinhard.

[20] See also Lambert's descriptions in chapter 9 of the present volume.

piece that succeeds on its own terms, acclaimed by Richard Taruskin in a *New York Times* review of the premiere recording.[21] And as Taruskin and Lambert point out, it is part of a tradition of musical contemplations of the cosmos with a long history among European composers and close parallels with unfinished cosmic works by Scriabin (*Mysterium*) and Schoenberg (*Die Jakobsleiter*).[22] Once again, what has seemed to some observers unique, ill-made, or even bizarre in Ives has been shown to have ample precedent and to be very carefully constructed.

The same could be said for Ives's uses of musical borrowing, as my own recent work in that area has shown.[23] The quantity and prominence of Ives's borrowings has seemed unprecedented to some critics, and his frequent recourse to American popular tunes has struck Carter and others as a weakness in his music.[24] Yet, as in his use of stylistic heterogeneity, the differences between Ives and other composers are more of degree than of kind. The key lies in the recognition that Ives used more than a dozen different techniques for reworking musical material in new compositions. In relatively few pieces are the quotations strictly programmatic; in most cases, Ives used the borrowed material as the foundation for the new work, as in a Bach chorale prelude, Mozart variation set, or Dvořák overture on national themes. Indeed, more than half of the procedures Ives used were traditional, including using an existing work as a model, writing a new setting of or variations on a given melody, reshaping a national tune for use as a theme, treating an existing melody as a cantus firmus, combining several tunes in a medley or quodlibet, transcribing a piece for another medium, alluding to a familiar style in order to suggest a certain musical character, or quoting a familiar tune for programmatic purposes. Three of

---

[21] See the final section of Austin's essay; Henry Cowell and Sidney Cowell, *Charles Ives and His Music*, 2nd edn (New York: Oxford University Press, 1969), 203; and Richard Taruskin, "Away with the Ives myth: the 'Universe' is here at last," *New York Times*, 23 October 1994, H42.

[22] Ibid., and Lambert, "Ives's *Universe*."

[23] Burkholder, *All Made of Tunes*, and "The uses of existing music: musical borrowing as a field," *Music Library Association Notes* 50/3 (1994): 851–70.

[24] See for example Elliott Carter, "Shop talk by an American composer," *The Musical Quarterly* 46/2 (1960): 199–200 (repr. in *Problems of Modern Music*, ed. Paul Henry Lang [New York: Norton, 1962], 61–62); and Kurt Stone, "Ives's Fourth Symphony: a review," *The Musical Quarterly* 52/1 (1966): 1–16.

Ives's procedures are unusual in the European tradition: settings in cumulative form, in which the borrowed tune used as a theme appears near the end, preceded by its development; patchwork, in which a melodic line is assembled from fragments of familiar tunes, a technique Ives may have borrowed from Tin Pan Alley songwriters; and collage, in which a swirl of quotations superimposed on the musical framework suggests a dream or stream of consciousness. Yet these also depend upon techniques of melodic transformation and thematic development that Ives absorbed from his nineteenth-century predecessors. His cumulative settings, for instance, combined the notion of a movement built on the presentation and development of themes, drawn from sonata and variation forms, with the nationalist practice of using native melodies as themes and the nineteenth-century tendencies of invoking yet distorting sonata form, shifting the weight to the end of a movement, and minimizing exact repetition in favor of continuous development.[25] Thus in spite of their use of American hymn tunes as themes, Ives's violin sonatas, piano sonatas, and orchestral works that use cumulative form participate in the major trends of late-nineteenth-century European music in respect to form, rhetoric, and procedure and are thematically coherent even for listeners who do not recognize a single borrowed theme.

Finding Ives's uses of stylistic diversity, compositional systems, and musical borrowing to be systematic and logical has provided space to clear up other misunderstandings about Ives. When these aspects of Ives's music are understood, it becomes no longer necessary to ascribe them to transcendentalist influence, as many writers have done, nor to psychological causes. My first book showed that Ives was exploring these musical devices well before he developed the strong interest in Emerson and Thoreau that characterized his maturity and later years.[26] Frank Rossiter's argument in his biography that Ives put dissonance and quotations from vernacular styles into his music in order to protect and declare his masculinity in an art he considered effeminate has been discredited by Judith Tick, who has demonstrated that gender ideology in music at the turn of the century was

[25] See Burkholder, *All Made of Tunes*, 244–45.

[26] On Transcendentalism as an influence on Ives, see Burkholder, *Charles Ives: The Ideas Behind the Music*, 20–32, and the works cited there in notes 1–14 on pp. 121–23.

more complex than Rossiter assumed. The classical genres in which Ives was composing were all considered masculine, and it was common for the male establishment to use gendered terms to promote and defend music that aspired to a depth beyond light entertainment. Ives simply adopted this terminology and turned it on the establishment, promoting and defending his own more difficult music against "classical" music that in his view lacked depth or left its hearers unchallenged. Ives's gendered rhetoric emerged only after he had written the music, and it cannot have been the cause for Ives's use of dissonance or of vernacular tunes and sounds.[27] Understanding the musical logic behind Ives's dissonant structures and his manipulations of borrowed material helps us reserve extramusical explanations for their presence in his music for matters that are actually relevant to his artistic aims in individual works – as in Stuart Feder's essay in this volume, which notes the influence of Thoreau on particular Ives compositions – rather than seeking oversimplified, global explanations that suggest as a subtext that Ives's use of his materials was musically arbitrary.

Similarly, understanding the musical logic in Ives's works helps to provide a corrective to the long-standing views, articulated by Carter in "Ives today," that Ives paid no attention to the difficulty of his music for the performer and welcomed performers' alterations to his music. Geoffrey Block shows in his essay in this volume that Ives's many revisions to the *Concord Sonata* do not imply permission for performers to make their own versions of the piece by picking and choosing variants; rather, Ives tried out alternatives and revised repeatedly until he achieved the final text he wanted, represented by the 1947 second edition. The *Concord Sonata* is not a work of indeterminacy but a composition that underwent a process of refinement even after its initial publication, as was the typical practice of Liszt. Moreover, Ives demonstrated his concern for the performer in notes on how to execute or simplify difficult passages, in the spirit of *ossias* in nineteenth-century virtuoso pieces. John Kirkpatrick used the first edition for his 1939 premiere of the *Concord Sonata*, resisted some of Ives's revisions and restorations of earlier variants, and felt – probably wrongly – that

---

27 Frank R. Rossiter, *Charles Ives and his America* (New York: Liveright, 1975); Judith Tick, "Charles Ives and gender ideology," in *Musicology and Difference: Gender and Sexuality in Music Scholarship*, ed. Ruth A. Solie (Berkeley: University of California Press, 1993), 83–106.

Ives's toleration of alternatives gave him leave as a performer to play the variants he liked best or even to synthesize his own. Kirkpatrick has been the most significant editor of Ives's music and was for years the supervising editor for the Charles Ives Society, which sponsors critical editions of Ives's works. In his editorial work, Kirkpatrick often added barlines, changed notes to their enharmonic equivalents, and made other alterations, considering that Ives had given his editors leave to renotate his music in order to make it easier to read just as he had allowed players to alter it in performance.[28] But Ives was unhappy with editors who made such alterations to his music during his lifetime.[29] Informed by new understandings of the logic behind Ives's musical choices, the Ives Society in 1996 adopted new guidelines that preserve his notation while making necessary corrections. As H. Wiley Hitchcock points out in his essay in this collection, Ives needs an editor, to proofread, root out errors, idiosyncrasies, and inconsistencies, and provide indications of tempo, dynamics, and other expressive markings when these are lacking from the published version or final manuscript. But he does not allow his editors any more leeway than we customarily exercise in editing Chopin or Liszt. The better we understand the logic behind Ives's musical choices, from the systems that generate his pitches to the extramusical image behind the "eye music" in "The Cage" and other songs, the better able we will be to create editions that convey Ives's thought clearly without interposing our own interpretations.

The examinations of Ives's approaches to musical form, compositional systems, and musical borrowing cited above, along with other studies of his musical techniques over the last two decades, have shown that his command of musical materials was secure. We may prefer some pieces, may regard others as less successful, or may question some of Ives's aesthetic assumptions, as we might with any composer, but the old charges of incompetence do not stick when the music is examined on its own terms. After decades of doubt, we now have to agree that Ives knew exactly what he was doing. And often, what he did was a response to or extension of European common practice. Thus these studies of Ives's compositional

---

[28] This point of view was articulated in the editorial guidelines of the Charles Ives Society during the time Kirkpatrick was the editorial coordinator.

[29] See for instance his draft of a letter to Sol Babitz and Ingolf Dahl, in *Charles Ives and His World*, 249–50.

procedures overlap with another recent trend, which insists on his close ties with the European tradition.

The European connection

Writings about Ives from the 1950s through the 1970s tended to emphasize his Americanness and his independence from Europe, as in Leonard Bernstein's characterization of Ives as "our Washington, Lincoln and Jefferson of music," and Eric Salzman's description in his influential textbook on twentieth-century music of Ives as "the first important Western composer to stand essentially outside the mainstream of European culture."[30] But starting in the 1970s, and increasingly in the 1980s and 1990s, scholars have stressed his debt to the European tradition of the nineteenth century and parallels to the major European modernists of his own time.

This wave of reconsideration was perhaps begun by David Eiseman's 1972 dissertation, which showed the close ties between the nineteenth-century symphonic tradition and Ives's first two symphonies. My own more recent research found numerous links between the first two Ives symphonies and nineteenth-century symphonic works he used as models or alluded to directly, including Beethoven's Ninth, Schubert's "Unfinished," Brahms's First and Third, Dvořák's New World, Tchaikovsky's Fourth and Sixth symphonies, and Wagner's Prelude to Tristan und Isolde. My essay in the 1996 collection Charles Ives and the Classical Tradition draws attention to Ives's roots in the nineteenth-century European tradition in every aspect of his music from aesthetic to procedure, and Geoffrey Block's essay in the same book shows Ives's particularly close affinity for Beethoven. Jeffrey Gibbens's 1985 dissertation traced the dissemination of Debussy's music in the United States in the first decade of the century, suggested that Ives became familiar with it soon after 1902, and argued that Ives was strongly influenced by Debussy, adopting the French composer's characteristic textures and procedures in several works while rejecting much of his aesthetic

---

[30] Leonard Bernstein, quoted in the liner notes for his recording with the New York Philharmonic of Ives's Symphony No. 2 (New York: Columbia KL 5489, 1960); Eric Salzman, Twentieth-Century Music: An Introduction, 2nd edn (Englewood Cliffs NJ: Prentice-Hall, 1974), 128.

stance. David Hertz has further pursued this line of inquiry, comparing passages in music of these two composers that seem strikingly parallel. In a recent essay, Hertz links Ives's *Concord Sonata* to the textures and formal devices of nineteenth- and early twentieth-century piano masterworks from Beethoven's "Hammerklavier" Sonata, Liszt's B Minor Sonata, and the Chopin ballades, etudes, and scherzos to the piano works of Debussy and the sonatas of Scriabin.[31] Robert P. Morgan's essay in the present volume demonstrates, for all Ives's uniqueness, how deeply he drew on the conventions of nineteenth-century European music. Even Wolfgang Rathert's essay in this collection, which ostensibly seeks to show how different Ives's musical concept is from those of European composers, ends up demonstrating how central to his music are ideas he absorbed from European Romantic aesthetics and music, from thematic transformation to the realization at the end of a work of a potential foreshadowed at the beginning.[32] Taken together, all of these studies show that Ives's roots in nineteenth-century European Romanticism are as strong as those of any of his European contemporaries. Indeed, as I have argued elsewhere, his very

[31] David Eiseman, "Charles Ives and the European symphonic tradition: a historical reappraisal" (Ph.D. dissertation, University of Illinois at Urbana-Champaign, 1972); Burkholder, *All Made of Tunes*, 88–136; Burkholder, "Ives and the nineteenth-century European tradition," and Geoffrey Block, "Ives and the 'Sounds that Beethoven didn't have,'" in *Charles Ives and the Classical Tradition*, 11–33 and 34–50 respectively; John Jeffrey Gibbens, "Debussy's impact on Ives: an assessment" (DMA dissertation, University of Illinois at Urbana-Champaign, 1985); Hertz, *Angels of Reality*, 97–113, and "Ives's *Concord Sonata* and the texture of music," in *Charles Ives and His World*, 75–117.

[32] In trying to make a case for Ives's distinctiveness, Rathert (in chapter 5) continues to read into Ives some of the concerns of the 1960s. For example, he insists that the *Concord Sonata* was left "unfinished" and that its multiple versions and sharing of material with other works "perfectly demonstrates the intentional instability of Ives's formal conception" (see p. 121). As Block demonstrates in chapter 2, the *Concord Sonata* is no more unfinished or open in form than a Liszt Hungarian Rhapsody or other work that exists in more than one published version and includes alternatives to make certain passages easier to play. Ives's musical concept is a thoroughly Romantic one, and has little or nothing to do with mid-twentieth-century concepts of "open form." It is striking that Rathert, the most important Continental Ives scholar, continues to stress how different his music is from European music of the period, while American scholars have recently been emphasizing the opposite.

Americanism is a European Romantic trait, an expression of nationalism akin to the national focus of Dvořák, Tchaikovsky, Albéniz, or Bartók.[33]

Out of that shared tradition came striking similarities in idea, approach, and technique between Ives and his European contemporaries, even ones whose music he did not know. When *Three Places in New England* was first played in Europe in 1931, Henry Prunières asserted in the *New York Times* review that "there is no doubt that [Ives] knows his Schönberg, yet gives the impression that he has not always assimilated the lessons of the Viennese master as well as he might have." Ives objected in a letter to a friend that he had "never heard nor seen a note of Schoenberg's music."[34] Although Ives is probably correct, Prunières was right to note the audible similarities in their music while observing the overall difference in effect. As Keith Ward has recently shown, there are remarkable parallels in their aesthetic ideals and their independent attitudes, and they shared a devotion to the German heritage of Bach, Beethoven, and Brahms and to certain procedures stemming from that heritage. Their music can sound quite different, but it often reveals parallel solutions to the common problems faced by composers of their generation.[35] The similarities in method are even stronger between Ives and Berg, as shown in the Philip Lambert essay that has already been mentioned. Andrew Buchman has shown many parallels of procedure between Ives and Stravinsky, including quotation, paraphrase, stylistic allusion, polyrhythmic layering, bitonality, and juxtaposed blocks of sound. He attributes these to the similar situation of the American and the Russian as composers from nations peripheral to the central European tradition, who sought to achieve an individual voice within that tradition by writing music that reflects on the experience of music itself, including the vernacular music of their own regions. Comparisons of Ives with other composers, such as Richard Strauss, Sibelius, Satie, or Bartók, have been suggested but not fully explored.[36]

[33] Burkholder, "Ives and the nineteenth-century European tradition," 13.

[34] Henry Prunières, "American compositions in Paris: works by advance guard of native writers introduced in French capital at season's end," *New York Times*, 12 July 1931, sec. 8, p. 6. The passage on Ives is reprinted in *Charles Ives and His World*, 304. Ives's letter is published in *Memos*, 27–29.

[35] Keith C. Ward, "Ives, Schoenberg, and the musical ideal," in *Charles Ives and the Classical Tradition*, 87–104.

[36] Lambert, "Ives and Berg"; Andrew Buchman, "Ives and Stravinsky: two angles

The composer most often mentioned in tandem with Ives is Mahler. Gianfranco Vinay drew parallels with Mahler and Debussy in a 1973 article and suggested on the basis of musical similarities that Ives was influenced by their music. Wulf Konold and Donald Mitchell also explored similarities between Ives and Mahler.[37] In a 1978 article, Robert P. Morgan highlighted a number of correspondences that sprang from the composers' common goal of reflecting in music the experience of life in all its diversity, openness, and multiplicity: the use of familiar musical materials that are fragmented, distorted, and juxtaposed with different kinds of music to create extraordinary effects; the appearance of heterogeneous styles simultaneously or in rapid succession; and the sense of space achieved through contrasts of dynamic level, key, timbre, and placement of instruments. These procedures and the goal they serve are parts of Mahler and Ives's shared response to the state of European music at the turn of the century.[38] A recent essay by Leon Botstein deepens the comparison. Both composers, believing that music could serve as a moral force, sought to celebrate in their music the rural past and its common virtues as a counterweight to modern urban society, yet used radical musical devices to do so in order to avoid simply assuaging the complacency of the concert audience. Thus the music of both composers bends modernist techniques to serve antimodernist aims, producing a peculiarly affecting music.[39]

All these parallels, together with those mentioned in the previous

on 'the German stem,'" in *Charles Ives and the Classical Tradition*, 131–49. For an overview of comparisons of Ives and others, see J. Peter Burkholder, "Introduction: 'a continuing spirit,'" in *Charles Ives and the Classical Tradition*, 1–8: Strauss, Satie, and Bartók are mentioned on p. 6. A comparison with Bartók is also briefly explored in Burkholder, "Ives and the four musical traditions," in *Charles Ives and His World*, 5–6.

[37] Gianfranco Vinay, "Charles Ives e i musicisti europei: anticipazioni e dipendenze," *Nuova revista musicale italiana* 7/2 (1973): 417–29, repr. in *L'America musicale di Charles Ives* (Turin: Giulio Einaudi, 1974); Wulf Konold, "Neue Musik in der Neuen Welt: Der Komponist Charles Ives," *Musica* 26/3 (1972): 240; Donald Mitchell, *Gustav Mahler: The Wunderhorn Years* (London: Faber and Faber, 1975), 169–71.

[38] Robert P. Morgan, "Ives and Mahler: mutual responses at the end of an era," *19th-Century Music* 2/1 (1978): 72–81; repr. in *Charles Ives and the Classical Tradition*, 75–86.

[39] Leon Botstein, "Innovation and nostalgia: Ives, Mahler, and the origins of modernism," in *Charles Ives and His World*, 35–74

section in regard to Ives's use of stylistic diversity, compositional systems, musical borrowing, and formal procedures, are more than merely coincidental. They show that Ives shared with his European contemporaries a common heritage of procedures and artistic ideals, particularly from the central Austro-German tradition, and confronted similar issues of how to compose and what to compose when faced with the daunting task of writing music for inclusion in the great musical museum, the permanent repertoire of immortal musical classics, that had evolved during the nineteenth century and seemed virtually full by the time Ives's generation reached maturity.[40] That his solutions to these common problems are similar to those of his European peers, even when there is no possibility of influence, shows how deeply Ives was rooted in European Romanticism and in step with the temper of his times.

Training, development, and chronology

Ives's apparently solid knowledge of nineteenth-century European music and his acquaintance with modern composers up through Strauss, Debussy, and Scriabin raise two other issues that have been explored in the recent literature, often in tandem: his education, particularly in European art music, and his development as a composer. The traditional picture has been that Ives received thorough training from his father, George, writing accomplished band marches, church music, and experimental works while still in his teens; deepened his knowledge of the art music tradition through studies with Horatio Parker at Yale; and then retreated into isolation as a composer, writing music to please only himself while working in the insurance business. Ives's development as a composer was unclear and appeared "spasmodic" to Carter and to others because he seemed to use so many different types of music at the same time. As John Kirkpatrick wrote in *The New Grove Dictionary of Music and Musicians*,

> Any attempt to find in Ives a consistent development of musical style would have encountered his scorn for the whole idea of "manner." . . . Right

---

[40] See Burkholder, "The evolution of Charles Ives's music," 462–92, esp. 463–68, and "Museum pieces: the historical mainstream in music of the last hundred years," *Journal of Musicology* 2/2 (1983): 115–34.

through from 1893 (*Song for Harvest Season* and *There is a Certain Garden*) to 1925 (*Johnny Poe* and the harmonization of Edith's *Christmas Carol*), he used the whole spectrum of complex-to-simple, serving the statement at hand as if improvising freshly each time.[41]

In the 1980s and 1990s, by contrast, Ives's development as a composer has started to become clear. In my dissertation and two subsequent books, I showed that Ives's aesthetic philosophy, including his interest in Transcendentalism, and his uses of musical borrowing had both changed over the course of his career, although they had previously been regarded as aspects of his music that had remained consistent throughout his life.[42] In this account, Parker was a particularly significant influence, co-equal with Ives's father, for it was Parker who gave Ives the aspiration to write art music and to leave behind the utilitarian vernacular music and church music of his Danbury days. I suggested that other aspects of Ives's music also evolved in a logical manner from the musical conventions he learned in the 1880s and 1890s through gradual intensification or exaggeration to the extraordinary procedures of his mature music. Lambert's work on Ives's compositional systems confirmed his gradual, logical growth as a composer, as individual devices could be seen to develop from piece to piece.[43]

The foundation for both the traditional and the emerging new view of Ives's development was shaken profoundly in 1987, when Maynard Solomon questioned Ives's veracity about what his father taught him, about when he composed each work, and especially about when he developed the procedures that had earned him a reputation as a radical innovator. While it

---

[41] John Kirkpatrick, "Ives, Charles E(dward)," in *The New Grove Dictionary of Music and Musicians*, vol. 9, 420. Kirkpatrick's second sentence, about the range of styles Ives used in any one year, is certainly true, but this is not because his style did not develop in a logical manner. Both issues have recently been highlighted in Burkholder, "Ives and the four musical traditions," 3–34.

[42] Burkholder, "The evolution of Charles Ives's music"; *Charles Ives: The Ideas Behind the Music*; and *All Made of Tunes*. For the older view, see for example Cowell, *Charles Ives and His Music*, on Transcendentalism; and Kirkpatrick, "Ives," on Ives's use of "musical quotation, a habit that stayed with him as long as he composed."

[43] Burkholder, *Charles Ives: The Ideas Behind the Music*, 58–67, and "The evolution of Charles Ives's music," 462–83; Lambert, "Compositional procedures" and *The Music of Charles Ives*.

was seen by some as an attack on Ives and was treated as a scandal in the press, Solomon's article was a valuable corrective for Ives scholarship, in three areas.[44] First, he reminded us that we know less than we would like to know about George Ives's activities and that we should rely less on his son's idealized recollections. Second, he suggested that Ives was less isolated from current musical life than had been supposed, was more deeply influenced by other Romantic and modern composers than he admitted, and had attempted to hide the depth and even the fact of their influence behind a story that attributed everything important about his music to his father. Third, by calling into question the dates Ives assigned to works and highlighting Ives's practice (already known to John Kirkpatrick) of entering dates, addresses, and other memoranda on manuscripts long after the music itself, Solomon forced Ives scholarship to revisit the chronology of Ives's music established by Kirkpatrick in his landmark 1960 catalogue, which relied on Ives's dates and memoranda and upon which all Ives scholarship was built.[45] These three areas of inquiry have all been explored subsequently, with very fruitful results.

In the first area, Carol K. Baron has returned to George Ives's essay on music theory, publishing an edition of it and arguing that it provides the main documentation we have for his theoretical point of view and its possible influence on his son. George's essay does not include or discuss the radical experiments Ives describes from his youth, nor would we expect it to do so in the course of an explanation of basic music theory. But it does show George's very independent turn of mind in his willingness to question received theory and propose more logical alternatives. Baron concludes that George's call for changes in both theory and notation to accommodate

[44] Maynard Solomon, "Charles Ives: some questions of veracity," *Journal of the American Musicological Society* 40/3 (1987): 443–70. For press reaction, see especially Donal Henahan, "Did Ives fiddle with the truth?," *New York Times*, 21 February 1988, sect. 2, pp. 1 and 25. See also the response by Philip Lambert and Solomon's reply to it in the *Journal of the American Musicological Society* 42/1 (1989): 204–18, and Stuart Feder's response in *Charles Ives*, 351–57. Solomon's charges of deliberate falsification have not been supported by subsequent research; see for example the essays by Hitchcock and Block in the present volume, and the writings of Gayle Sherwood cited below.

[45] See *JKCat*. Kirkpatrick comments on some of the retrospective entries and other dating problems on pp. vii–ix, and he notes "how cautiously all the chronological evidence must be viewed" (*JKCat*, viii).

music that uses all twelve tones and his discussion of the contradiction between how dissonance is described in theory and perceived by the ear, along with other critical modes of thought, opened up regions of non-diatonic music that his son then explored compositionally, years before European composers.[46]

Yet some of Charles Ives's views of his father have been revealed as idealizations. Stuart Feder has shown that George's service as a bandmaster in the Civil War was marred by a series of events in which he asked to be reduced to the rank of private, destroyed his cornet, subsequently was absent without leave, and was court-martialed, receiving relatively mild punishment.[47] It appears he may have snapped psychologically. These were not the actions of a hero, and they went unmentioned in family recollections and in Charles Ives's own account of his father; he may not even have known of them. Another Feder discovery proves the reality of one of George's experiments while revealing a gap between what Ives attributed to his father and what George actually did. In his *Memos*, Ives mentions the "humanophone," "an idea of Father's" in which "songs of wide leaps were to be sung [with the] different notes by different voices—not a duet, quartet, etc.—but one voice taking a high note, a middle voice, and another man taking [a] low note, etc."[48] The melody he offers as an example is atonal and very widely spaced. Feder discovered, however, that the "humanophone" was a comic stunt staged in a performance when Charles was a teenager: a massive "organ" consisting of a dozen people costumed as organ pipes who sang while George "played" the organ. The *Danbury News* account of the event treated this as hilarious and concluded with the comment that "The kazoo and chestnut bell stops were great 'take offs'"; this is one possible source for the "take-off," an important term for Ives's experimental music. Feder observes that "Charlie was somehow able to turn the embarrassment of his father's exhibitionism into pride in his father. As apologist, he later dignified the City Hall performance by calling it one of George's 'experiments in music.'"[49] If this incident is characteristic, George's importance

---

46 Carol K. Baron, "George Ives's essay in music theory: an introduction and annotated edition," *American Music* 10/3 (1992): 239–88.

47 Feder, *Charles Ives*, 40–43.

48 *Memos*, 142; editorial emendations by John Kirkpatrick.

49 Feder, *Charles Ives*, 105–06. On the "take-off" in Ives, see Giebisch, *"Take-Off" als Kompositionsprinzip bei Charles Ives*.

for Ives may have derived less from his own experimentation than from the permission he gave his son to indulge in a little "boy's fooling," and the radical innovations, like the widely spaced atonal melody Ives cites in the *Memos*, can be credited to the son, not the father.[50]

Reducing George Ives's influence on his son opens up room for other teachers. I suggested in a response to Solomon that the greatest significance of his study may lie in leading us to re-evaluate what other music Ives knew and what he absorbed from other composers, the second area of research mentioned above.[51] Some of what Ives attributed to his father derives instead from Parker, revealing the need for further exploration of correspondences between these composers. Nicholas Tawa has recently described a wide range of similarities in music and aesthetics between Ives, Parker, and the older New England composers Chadwick and Paine.[52] The effect of Parker's teaching also bears further investigation. Ann Besser Scott has demonstrated that Ives's music adapts a number of procedures common in Medieval and Renaissance music, including stratification of layers, use of cantus firmus, stylistic heterogeneity, and parallel sonorities that resemble fauxbourdon or parallel organum, and she makes a case, through comparison with Parker's lecture notes, that it was Parker's class on music history that introduced Ives to these techniques.[53] While this is somewhat speculative, it implies that Parker's influence extends far beyond the ways in which Ives's music resembles Parker's and affects Ives's experimental music as well as his concert music.

Invoking Harold Bloom's theory of *The Anxiety of Influence*, I suggested in my response to Solomon that Ives's critical comments about other composers and his attempts to deflect our attention toward his father are both signs of anxiety about being over-influenced, and thus that the composers Ives criticized may be among his most important influences. David Hertz has followed up on this line of thinking in a very helpful way, showing

---

50 See Ives's comments in *Memos*, 46–47, and Burkholder, *Charles Ives: The Ideas Behind the Music*, 47–50.

51 J. Peter Burkholder, "Charles Ives and his fathers: a response to Maynard Solomon," *Institute for Studies in American Music Newsletter* 18/1 (1988): 8–11.

52 Ibid., 9; Nicholas E. Tawa, "Ives and the New England School," in *Charles Ives and the Classical Tradition*, 51–72.

53 Ann Besser Scott, "Medieval and Renaissance techniques in the music of Charles Ives: Horatio at the bridge?," *The Musical Quarterly* 78/3 (1994): 448–78.

how Ives, like Wallace Stevens in poetry and Frank Lloyd Wright in architecture, used Emerson as an influence in order to escape being overwhelmed by the influence of European composers, especially that of Debussy, the composer whose aims were nearest his own, and achieve originality as an American within the European tradition of art music.[54] Here is the true role of Transcendentalism for Ives; it was not a lifelong and all-encompassing influence, the very air he breathed, as Carter implied by describing Ives as "a devout believer in transcendental philosophy" and as the Cowells pictured him in their biography, but an influence he chose in his maturity that provided a path out of the dilemmas he faced as a creative artist.[55] As mentioned above, Hertz has subsequently explored the apparent influence on Ives of other composers he praised (Beethoven), mentioned (Scriabin), slammed (Chopin and Debussy), or virtually ignored (Liszt).[56] Similar studies could be done on Wagner, Tchaikovsky, Strauss, Reger, Ravel, Daniel Gregory Mason, John Alden Carpenter, and many other composers whose music Ives knew and commented on, whether they were predecessors with whom he struggled or contemporaries from whom he sought to distinguish himself and, perhaps, to learn. Ives seems to have been aware of and may have been influenced by a wide range of art music current in the years during which he was composing. Just as a recent study by Michael Broyles and Judith Tick's essay in the present volume show how much of his political thinking and writing was derived from streams of

---

[54] Harold Bloom, *The Anxiety of Influence: A Theory of Poetry* (New York: Oxford University Press, 1973); Burkholder, "Charles Ives and his fathers," 10–11; Hertz, *Angels of Reality.* On the similarity between Ives's aims and Debussy's, see the path-breaking study by Leo Schrade, "Charles E. Ives: 1874–1954," *Yale Review,* n.s., 44 (June 1955): 535–45, reprinted in *Charles Ives and His World,* 433–42.

[55] See Carter, "Ives today," 199; Cowell, *Charles Ives and His Music,* 7; and Burkholder, *Charles Ives: The Ideas Behind the Music,* where the limits of Transcendentalism in Ives's earlier life and its role as a solution to the creative problems of his maturity were first described. Michael Broyles has recently shown how many of Ives's social and political ideas also have sources independent of Transcendentalism, including ideals articulated by insurance executives in defense of the industry during the Armstrong hearings in 1905, the republican concept of personal responsibility, and the myth of the New England town meeting as the cradle of democracy, promulgated by historians associated with the colonial revival; see Michael Broyles, "Charles Ives and the American democratic tradition," in *Charles Ives and His World,* 118–60.

[56] Hertz, "Ives's *Concord Sonata* and the texture of music."

thought current in his own time, rather than stemming directly from Emerson and other nineteenth-century sources,[57] it is likely that examination of the music Ives owned and the music he heard in concert will reveal how much he drew from recent art music, an influence we now know that he tried to obscure.

The third and most fundamental area of research in response to Solomon has been the dating of Ives's manuscripts and the chronology of his music. This is work still in progress, but even the preliminary results have contributed to a fresh picture of Ives's development that is as illuminating as the new chronologies of Bach, Mozart, and Beethoven developed in recent decades. Carol K. Baron used comparisons of Ives's handwriting with securely datable manuscripts to confirm the dates of three works within five years of Ives's date. Gayle Sherwood has subsequently developed a method for dating the music paper Ives used and has refined the handwriting comparisons by using a greater number of datable manuscripts. Combining these two methods, she is able to date most of Ives's manuscripts to a range of no more than seven and often as little as one or two years.[58] In her essay in the present collection, Sherwood summarizes the results of her work on the choral music. Many works were written a few years later than previously assumed. This is significant, because a few years make a considerable difference in tracing influences on a young composer's development. In the new chronology, there is a close correlation between the genres and performing forces Ives used in his choral music and the requirements and resources of the various churches he served as an organist; this is certainly what one would expect, and provides independent confirmation of Sherwood's approach. Parker emerges as a much more important influence than has been realized, for the choral works Ives wrote

---

57 See Broyles, "Ives and the American democratic tradition," and Tick, chapter 6 above.

58 Carol K. Baron, "Dating Charles Ives's music: facts and fictions," *Perspectives of New Music* 28/1 (1990): 20–56; Gayle Sherwood, "Questions and veracities: reassessing the chronology of Ives's choral works," *The Musical Quarterly* 78/3 (1994): 429–47 and "The choral works of Charles Ives: chronology, style, and reception" (Ph.D. dissertation, Yale University, 1996), 1–82, 306–63, and 366–70. Sherwood cites the work on Bach, Mozart, Beethoven, and other composers that she used as models for her own work on Ives on pp. 25–30 of the dissertation.

before entering Yale in 1894 are considerably less sophisticated than those of his Yale years, which adopt many of Parker's methods.[59] Most surprisingly, Ives's psalms date from the period 1898–1902, *after* his studies with Parker, not from as early as 1894, where Kirkpatrick had placed them. Thus they reflect the influence of Parker's teaching and not the direct influence of George Ives. Yet the general order in which Ives composed his choral works is essentially the same in the revised chronology as in Kirkpatrick's, and Ives's radical compositional innovations still pre-date parallel developments in Europe. Sherwood has extended her work to include preliminary datings for most of Ives's other major works as well, and she plans a book on the new chronology.[60]

In the revised chronology, Ives owes less to his father, emerging from his Danbury years as still a very limited composer. He owes much more to Parker, who trained him thoroughly in European styles and may have introduced him to concepts and methods from a wider range of periods and composers than has been assumed. And perhaps he owes still more to himself, for his first major works, the First String Quartet and First Symphony, which established his command of these important genres and of the common nineteenth-century language, and his first fully developed experimental works, the choral psalms, were completed only during his early years in New York, not at Yale under Parker.[61] With the greater influence of Parker, the Romantic art music tradition, and modern composers such as Debussy and Scriabin solidly established, and with a new chronology that places Ives's development somewhat later than previously believed while confirming his reputation as an innovator, Ives can now be seen as a composer whose career very closely parallels those of such peers as Schoenberg and Stravinsky, with a slower, more gradual growth from assimilation of the Romantic tradition to what remains an extraordinary final group of compositions.

---

[59] In her dissertation Sherwood lays out three overlapping stages in Ives's development as a composer of music for Protestant church services, showing the strong influences of hymnody, Dudley Buck, and Parker in succession. See Sherwood, "The choral works of Charles Ives," 84–153.

[60] Her preliminary revised dates for the manuscripts of the works that use musical borrowings appear in Burkholder, *All Made of Tunes.*

[61] See ibid., 49 and 436–37, note 16, for the dates of the First Quartet, and 89 and 441, note 2, for the dates of the First Symphony.

If the writing on Ives fifty years ago emphasized his uniqueness, his isolation, and his Americanness, and the view of the 1960s and early 1970s emphasized his links to current compositional and social trends, Ives today appears to us as a man of his time, a composer with solid training and command of his craft, who engaged the same aesthetic and compositional problems as his great contemporaries in Europe and, like them, achieved highly individual solutions which blended the traditional and the extraordinary. Increasingly, we see him in his own context, rather than seeing in him projections of our own concerns. It is now clear how much of Ives's output was in traditional nineteenth-century styles, and clear that some of it is very compelling musically; at the Bard Music Festival, one concert paired songs of Ives in Romantic style with songs on the same texts by Brahms, Schumann, and Cornelius, and the Ives stood up well to the comparison. Yet this does not diminish the appeal of his most radical and dissonant pieces. Rather, we have come to realize that there is an Ives work, or several works, for almost every taste, and the diversity and generally high quality of his compositions are perhaps what make him most engaging as a composer and are most likely to ensure our continued interest in him.[62] We are continuing to learn, as we grow more familiar with all aspects of Ives's music, life, and career, how much deeper, fuller, and more complex they are than the picture that was presented when he first made his reputation as an isolated, innovative, somewhat amateurish one hundred percent American composer in the period between the world wars. Yannis Ioannidis's observations on the occasion of Ives's 1974 centennial now seem prophetic:

> Ives has always been presented to us [outside the United States] with words of extreme admiration; he has always been mentioned as "great" and "incredible" by those who wished to win our interest in him. However, he has been praised only for the most external of his achievements: his "experimental spirit," his "being ahead of his time" or "the first poly-, a-, or microtonalist," and so on; these are the virtues that have always been pointed out.
>
> Now we know that what has real value and importance in his output is not the fact that he was the first in the history of music who used this or that technique, but the fact that his works are products of a purely musical, artistic thinking – products of an absolute necessity to express himself with

---

[62] See also Burkholder, "Ives and the four musical traditions," 29–31.

tones – and that this necessity guided him to the use of all those new technical devices in the most normal and natural way. We are learning now to admire Ives as he really deserves to be admired: for the beauty and meaning of his works. And, there is no doubt, on this subject there is still much to be said.[63]

Yannis Ioannidis, "Thoughts on Ives," in *An Ives Celebration*, 250.

Index

291